The Fife Coast

The Fife Coast

From the Forth Bridges to Leuchars by
the Castles Coast and the East Neuk

HAMISH BROWN

MAINSTREAM
PUBLISHING
EDINBURGH AND LONDON

First published in Great Britain in 1994 by
MAINSTREAM PUBLISHING COMPANY (EDINBURGH) LTD
7 Albany Street
Edinburgh EH1 3UG

ISBN 1 85158 608 3

A catalogue record for this book is available from the British Library

All photographs © Hamish Brown Scottish Photographic, unless otherwise credited

Typeset in Great Britain by Litho Link Ltd, Welshpool, Powys
Printed in Great Britain by Butler & Tanner, Frome

There are no countries in the world
less known by the British than these
selfsame British Isles.
                    GEORGE BORROW

Two voices are there; one is of the
    sea,
One of the mountains; each a mighty
    Voice,
In both from age to age thou didst
    rejoice,
They were thy chosen music,
    Liberty!
                    WORDSWORTH

It taks a lang spoon tae sup wi' a Fifer.
                    TRADITIONAL

A beggar's mantle fringed with gold.
                    JAMES VI

O tell me what was on yer road, ye
    roarin' norlan' wind
As ye cam' blawin' frae the land that's
    niver frae my mind?
My feet they trayvel England, but
    I'm deein' for the north –
*My man, I heard the siller tides rin up the
    Firth o' Forth*
                    VIOLET JACOB

Contents

THE EAST NEUK

List of Maps

Introduction

When James VI described Scotland as being 'a beggar's mantle fringed with gold', the fringe referred to was the Fife coast with its important series of ports, which we link on this walk like a series of beads strung on a thread. The gold then was trade with the continent and the more local fishing industry, the former now dead and the latter on a life-support system. One reason I'm only too happy to describe this walk is that it might contribute in a small way to the local economy: gold in the pocket if not on the fringe. The ports have survived, giving glimpses of a past world scarcely seen elsewhere in Scotland, so they are invaluable for themselves, besides their attractiveness to visitors. The visitor on foot sees more and is more richly rewarded. The beggar's mantle still has a fringe of gold and the area lies within easy reach of half the population of Scotland and, with good travelling access via Edinburgh, of half the population of England as well.

A few years ago a magazine asked me to supply photographs of many local sites and to my shame I found I had very few in my files. I could supply plenty of pictures of far corners of the world but not of 'my ain back yaird'. I rushed off to take those needed pictures (hiding my deficiency) and in so doing was astonished to find all sorts of interesting things about the Fife coast where I'd lived – too literally on the fringe – for nearly 40 years.

That experience set me conscientiously exploring Fife and very soon I realised what an excellent walk could be had by following the Forth, beside which I lived – 'the Forth scrawled across Scotland like some exotic calligraphy'. I'd just completed *From the Pennines to the Highlands Walk* so working out a new route came as a welcome activity, both for the mind and limbs. I've always believed the best way of exploring any country, or any bit of a country, is on foot, and would recommend this walk as a walk, though the information on places can equally well be used by the car-borne visitor.

The route extended itself, too. Originally I saw it as a walk along The 'Castles Coast', as I call the miles from the old Queen's Ferry to Wemyss or Buckhaven, but beyond lay the 'East Neuk' (a very different world) and St

Andrews – so why not walk the whole way, I thought? Some parts were already popular walks and well maintained, other parts were strangely neglected I found, but every inch had to be explored, a task which took many months over all.

With such a scattering of castles and towns, bays and headlands and islands (do take in the islands!), wildlife and historical interest, I took far longer than expected to write this book. I had to learn a great deal myself. If footing it out is the best exploring, then that exploring is best enjoyed when allied to knowing something about what one sees. I've now quite a library of local books and the libraries and museums along the coast were most helpful, too; but especially useful was the series of booklets, describing the coast, bit by bit, produced by the Wemyss Environmental Centre. These were researched and written by Ann Watters, to whom I'm sure many curious travellers (or just nosy locals) are much indebted.

The walking is hardly strenuous but will fill the days with activity, so curiosity should kill the fat. The breakdown into separate days has been dictated by the need to find suitable accommodation and by how much there is to see in any section. There are few campsites and wild camping is not always convenient. I find a heavy pack annoying – and tiring – on coastal walking where the constant ups and downs forbid the loping rhythm of the hills and where there are so many places to explore as well. (Of course, you could try the challenge of finding a 'howff' each night, some shelter in a cave or such like . . .) But a special trip calls for some reward,

at the time, and some self-indulgence has the added benefit of meeting the locals. If you can make out the accents (East Neuk or Castles Coast) you will learn the 'crack o' the toon' and a lot more besides. 'All walking is adventure. On foot we take the time to see things whole. We see trees as well as forests, people as well as crowds,' wrote H. Borland. I once caught up an older man on the Pathhead Sands and he never stopped talking until I bought him a pint in Dysart. But how he knew his local history! Encounters like that are a delight, reminding me of Cory's old words:

> They told me, Heraclitus, they told
>   me you were dead,
> They brought me bitter news to hear
>   and bitter tears to shed.
> I wept as I remembered how often
>   you and I
> Had tired the sun with talking and
>   sent him down the sky.

This book, I trust, is your Heraclitus, and I hope you enjoy its gossip along the walk.

A coastal walk has simplified navigation. Whatever local vagaries crop up or whatever diversions occur (intentionally or otherwise) the direction of travel is clear throughout: the sea always lies on our right-hand side. So I've not over-described the route unless there is a real chance of going astray. (I think the most repeated phrase is 'walk on eastwards'.) Any changes can be discovered from the update sheet (see Appendix 1) for which contributions are always welcome from those who have just done the route. Changes can happen surprisingly quickly, both naturally and through man's activities. As far as the walking is concerned changes should be for the best, like the recent new path from the Frances Colliery to West Wemyss, and there are plans to improve the paths on the Fife Ness–St Andrews coastline. Demolition has seen the buildings of St David's Harbour completely disappear and rebuilding is happening there – and has already changed Dalgety Bay. In the 1952 *Third Statistical Account* there was an airfield where Dalgety Bay now sprawls. There were also 36 coal-mines in Fife. Seafield hadn't even been started yet we'll pass its site, also being developed for housing. Bottleworks at Pettycur are now 'luxury homes' and a landmark like the Chalmers Church in Anstruther disappeared while I was away for a holiday.

The importance of the Fife coast historically can be gauged from the fact that most of the towns we visit were royal burghs: Crail, Inverkeithing and Kinghorn became such as early as the twelfth century; Burntisland, Pittenweem, Anstruther and Dysart in the sixteenth century; St Andrews and Kirkcaldy in the seventeenth century (as did Queensferry). There is probably more to see of medieval life and architecture on this walk than in the rest of Scotland combined, and there is a tremendous proliferation of features such as churches, castles, tolbooths and doocots. (Fife had – indeed still has – more than any other county.) The shale and coal-mining industries have left their marks, other industries like shipbuilding, weaving and linoleum have all but disappeared.

Fife was criss-crossed with the comings and goings of history: Dunfermline was once the capital of Scotland; Falkland was a favourite royal palace; Inchcolm was the burial isle of kings when Iona became Viking-controlled; and St Andrews one of the most vital religious centres in Europe. The Forth and the Tay influenced that history, too, and ferries played a vital role until recently. As you can imagine, there is no lack of things to discover along the way. I've tried to mention the most important or the more improbable or the more amusing, but have still had to be frustratingly selective.

Fife also had a certain insularity historically. The only easy access was by bridges at Stirling or Perth, which explains why so many battles were fought near those towns or their approaches (and few actually *in* Fife). Even the Romans hardly touched Fife. There were ferries, of course, but they were at the mercy of the fickle elements. Queensferry and Ferryport-on-Craig (Tayport) were the major crossings, but others on the Forth at Burntisland, Pettycur, Dysart and Earlsferry played their part and lie on our route.

One thing that struck me on reading about the past along the coast was the constant change and perpetual evolution of industry that has always been. I can recall the outcry at the mining industry's collapse in the 1960s; Rosyth is another, current, case. But what of weaving, herring-fishing, salt-manufacturing? These disappeared long enough ago that they don't hurt. People tend to believe present agonies are unique or new, but life has always been tough – and life by the sea is never cosy.

Anyone seriously interested in architecture would have to carry the hefty *Fife* volume of the 'Buildings of Scotland' series. This work, by John Gifford, is incredibly thorough but full of delightful touches, and the glossary at the back is a boon. Many sites along the way have their own descriptive booklets which can be bought on the spot. Reading, before and after, can be helped by using the bibliography (see Appendix 5). Walking through so many towns of architectural interest (the East Neuk is famous for this) I was forced to learn something of the terms used to note interesting features. As some of these occur several times, rather than explain each time, I've added a glossary at the end; interesting in itself, I trust.

Because there are so many interesting places along the way I have given these the bulk of the photographic illustrations. Miles of sandy beach rejoice the heart but make poor pictures, I find, and given the choice of a picture of a tolbooth or a doocot (another Fife speciality) or just another bit of coastline, the former usually wins. I'm grateful to the many people who made it possible to use the historic pictures and aerial views. If you are carrying a camera, make sure you have plenty of spare film.

Heights of hills are given in metres as this is what the map now shows, and distances on the ground are given in kilometres (km). In giving the vital statistics of the Forth Bridges, however, I have left the figures in imperial measures and have also done so occasionally for buildings, these being clearer

to most readers. (As grid squares are 1km across, estimating distances is really very easy and a yard and a metre are near enough the same.) The maps needed are listed before each day's route description and a summary list is given in Appendix 2. Pathfinder maps are much more useful for coastal walking than are the Landranger series but, whichever is carried, do go over the OS maps with the text each night to ensure the coming day's route is understood beforehand. Time is always short. Blessed with OS maps we tend to take everything as settled and sure but there is a constant change going on – even with names. Running my eye along a 1645 map recently, our route took in Inverkythin, Dunabirsle, Dalgatie, Abyrdour, Bruntyland, Pretticurr, Kingorn, Weemis, Levin, Ely, Pitnaweem, Ansterrudder, Careill, Fyfe-Ness and Gearbridg.

I have used the word 'road' to imply a tarred surface and public use; 'track' implies an unsurfaced but motorable route which may or may not be private for car use but is clear for walking on; and 'path' implies a route only available for those on foot. Most of the route is on rights-of-way or created walking routes but there may be odd bits which are on private land. Whatever the situation, 'walk gently, take nothing but photographs and leave nothing but memories'. There are plenty of opportunities for walking on sandy beaches but, above the tideline, the dry sand makes for trying progress if one is walking for real progress (as we are) rather than just taking a short, local stroll. While some of the tide-out sands may prove irresistible, the text largely keeps to describing the popular, main paths and tracks which will lie above tidal dictation. The inter-tidal zone is there if wanted. And do take time to savour the sea. Get off early. No crack-of-noon starts. Then take time just to sit and stare. Have a paddle. Swim. Feel the flukies under your toes. Collect buckies for your tea. Marvel at the life of the rock-pools. Delight in the rich diversity of birdlife.

> This is the sin now:
> We adults do not lie back
> In scented grasses
> Under the lark's singing . . .
> And when did you
> Last curl toes in dewy cold
> Upon some summer morning hour?

I'm afraid, in the course of this walk, you will see some sorry sights. Vandalism seems simply to be part of the British way of life these days. Nothing is sacred. The day after I had been exploring the Wemyss Caves I went back with my camera and found the entrance to the Doo Cave had had paint poured all down its walls, a double act of vandalism, I suspect, for someone first dumped the cans of paint on the shore and then someone else found this game to play with them. (National or local bodies should long ago have saved the caves, so must bear responsibility too.) It is not only individuals who sin. The Frances or Randolph Collieries dumping their redd (spoil) straight into the sea were monstrous acts of vandalism. The abandoning of Ravenscraig Castle is disgraceful. The authorities have done little for the coast in the last ten years yet they have spent half a million on Kirkcaldy's High Street and Esplanade – which perhaps shows where our values lie. But then one can envisage urban tarting-up has more kudos, more votes, than tackling the damaged parts of the precious coastline. The Castles Coast does not compare favourably with the East Neuk – but it could.

The tidelines may well sadden you, too. The sea is simply treated as a rubbish dump and a sewer. They have built a super pool at the mouth of the Leven but the riverwater flowing by outside is polluted from Glenrothes and is not a spot for swimming. Beaches, many miles from the Frances, have coal strewn along them after certain storms and tides. Bottles, plastics and rubbish of all kinds is jettisoned by the 7,000 ships a year which use and misuse the River Forth. You'll see a distressing number of bird corpses on the tideline. Ironically, walking the Fife coast regularly as I had to in preparing this guide, I accumulated enough driftwood to keep me in house-warming fuel for the next two or three winters. (You try the Chain Walk with a rucksack full of fence posts on your back!)

This is a walk which is best done in spring or autumn. Many of the towns are popular summer holiday resorts when there could be difficulty finding accommodation. Given sharp, clear weather it would be equally good in winter, though some of the museums and other points of interest will not be open. With the reasonable linear transport services available it is also practical to follow the route as a series of day or weekend expeditions. There is really no hard and fast 'best' option. July and August are still pleasanter on the Fife coast than in more hilly regions. There are no midges for a start! In winter the birdlife on the coast is impressive.

The east coast can be surprisingly cold, especially if an east wind is howling in from Russia, so go prepared for this. Rainfall on the coast is mercifully light on the other hand, one reason I choose to live there, taking advice I heard as a youngster: 'Flirt with the west but marry the east.'

Become aware of the movement of the tides as soon as possible, for some stretches depend on low tide for the best route and you'll have to plan accordingly. The combination of high tide and a gale can mean wet progress if you haven't done this homework. As well as the evidence of your eyes, carry and use the Leith Tide Tables, available from most bookshops or from The Book House, 23 Tolbooth Street, Kirkcaldy, (0592) 265378. It is interesting seeing the progressive change as we walk east. The tide at Inverkeithing is +9 minutes, Aberdour +1, Burntisland is the same as Leith, then Kirkcaldy comes as −4, Dysart −6, Methil −9, Elie −17, Fifeness −21. Most places (where I warn about high tide blocking direct progress) will be passable an hour either side of high tide, so don't overreact to this problem.

Local weather forecasts can be obtained by telephoning Edinburgh (031) 246 8091 or, as useful, the Marine forecast: (031) 225 3232. Tide times can also be found by ringing the Forth Port Authority at Methil Docks: (0333) 426725; Kirkcaldy Docks (0592) 260176 or Burntisland Docks (0592) 872236.

The Fife coast is rich geologically (several sites are SSSIs) and this creates a varied and rich flora, to which is added a birdlife which is abundant, both for land and sea species. Fulmar or eider take on almost mascot status, as do seals. Do take time to explore something of this richness.

Book ahead for accommodation, even if it is only through a telephone call the night before. The days can be enjoyed more if there is a known haven at the end. Don't panic about accommodation, though: with the excellent coastal bus and train services one can always head for the next town forward – or the last town back. If one B&B is especially good you may like to return there for a second night – why not? This is a fun walk, remember. I've given telephone numbers of everything possible. (The occasional numbers in brackets will be six-figure grid references.) Make sure you note the name and address of any B&B booked by telephone and ask how you can most easily find it. I usually indicate accommodation in order of proximity to our route. Two is probably the best size of party – landladies are not always keen on singles. A last warning: if there is a championship golf tournament on at St Andrews every bed in the East Neuk is likely to be taken. Such events usually have national coverage but you can always check by telephoning the Tourist Information Centre, 70 Market Street, St Andrews KY16 9NU, (0334) 72021. They also could send an accommodation list; ask for that *and* the Burntisland–Kirkcaldy–Leven list from Tourist Information Centre, South Street, Leven, Fife KY8 4NT (0333) 429464. For the first two days you want the Forth Valley Tourist

Information Office, Burgh Halls, The Cross, Linlithgow, West Lothian EH49 7AH, (0506) 844600 or Kirkcaldy Tourist Information, 19 Whytecauseway, KY1 1XF, (0592) 267775.

Early closing is becoming less widely observed but the following apply:

Wednesday: Aberdour, Anstruther, Burntisland, Crail, Dysart, Elie, Inverkeithing, Kirkcaldy, North Queensferry, Pittenweem, Queensferry, St Monans.

Thursday: Buckhaven, Kinghorn, Leven, Methil and St Andrews.

In several places we walk along the edges of golf courses and it is only good manners not to be a nuisance to players. Stand still if you are likely to distract someone putting or driving – though knowing they are being watched can unsettle a golfer too! And watch out for flying golf balls.

While every possible care has been taken to ensure the accuracy of this guide the author does not accept responsibility regarding information or its interpretation by readers! Signposts vanish, brambles grow, housing schemes sprawl over fields, paths are bulldozed, accommodation changes – so to counter this, any information you can send in will be welcomed and passed on via the update sheet (see Appendix 1). Regretfully, I cannot enter into correspondence on points raised but they will be given respectful consideration. Those who venture on a multi-day walk must expect a bit of the unexpected. I hope you have an enjoyable journey. I look back on my exploration of the Fife Coast Walk with great content. So too did Robert Louis Stevenson, perhaps the finest writer to grow up with its smell in his nostrils. He once wrote:

I have but to see aligned on the page the words snell, flae, nirly, and scouthering and I think again that I can hear the great wind that comes tearing over the Forth from Burntisland and the northern hills. I can hear it howl in the chimney and if I turn my face northward I feel its icy kisses on my cheek.

Hamish Brown
Kinghorn
1994

THE CASTLES COAST

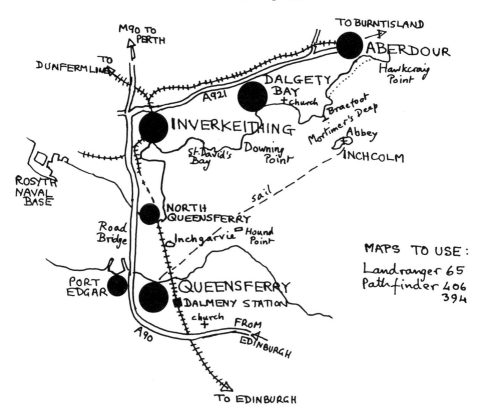

DAY 1 *Boat and Bridge*

Dalmeny–Queensferry–Inchcolm–Over the Bridge–North Queensferry

Maps to use: Bart 46, OSLR 65, OSPF 406 (NT 07/17) 394 (NT 08/18)
Walking distance: 7km

After travelling to Dalmeny/Queensferry the day is spent in local explorations, a sail to Inchcolm ('the Iona of the East') and then walking on across the vast suspension bridge to the Fife shore. A relaxing day to pick up the mood of quiet, historical villages and just being on the fresh Firth of Forth coast.

Note that accommodation in North Queensferry is fairly limited but it is easy to walk on to Inverkeithing, or even linger at South Queensferry – though Fife prices are probably more agreeable to walkers; whatever you do, you will find time flying, today, and every day.

TRAVEL TO DALMENY/ QUEENSFERRY

Edinburgh has a vast range of accommodation and may well encourage extra days at start or finish of the Fife Coast Walk. During the last two weeks of August and the first week of September Edinburgh has its annual International Festival, when finding accommodation becomes a major problem and, unless directly involved, Edinburgh then is not recommended. Quite a few exhibitions continue after the Festival so September is a good month, as is October when everything is much quieter but most facilities are still open. Most places open about Easter and, Easter holidays apart, April, May and June are good months for the walk. July sees summer crowds again.

Information on accommodation in Edinburgh can be obtained from the Tourist Information Office, 3 Princes Street, Edinburgh EH2 2QP, (031) 557 5118. This is sited just above Waverley Railway Station so is worth visiting on arrival anyway. Rail travellers will arrive at Waverley and onward trains also leave from there, so this would be my first choice for reaching the start. Waverley Enquiry Office: (031) 556 2451.

Trains run to Dalmeny. This is the station for Queensferry, south of the river, so called to avoid confusion with North Queensferry across the Forth but really creating confusion as the station is at sprawling Queensferry (South) rather than the tiny village of Dalmeny. Trains run from Edinburgh to Dalmeny about every half-hour. Pick up the Fife Region timetable at Waverley on arrival; it will also be useful for train times from Leuchars back to Edinburgh on the last day.

The main bus station is in St Andrew Square (a five-minute walk from Waverley; across Princes Street, up St Andrew Street, then second right) and intercity services will arrive there. Phoning the Enquiry Office (031) 556 8464 may be a lengthy or even fruitless game but buses to Queensferry and Dalmeny run frequently.

Edinburgh has two youth hostels (SYHA) Grade I: 7 Bruntsfield Crescent, EH10 4EZ, (031) 447 2994, and 18 Eglinton Crescent, EH12 5DD, (031) 337 1120. Haymarket Station, *en route* from Waverley to Dalmeny, is closer to these than Waverley itself. Eglinton is just five minutes from Haymarket, in fact. Two independent hostels only five to ten minutes from Waverley can be found at High Street Hostel, 8 Blackfriars Street, (031) 557 3984, and Cowgate Hostel, 112 Cowgate, (031) 226 2153. The Tourist Office accommodation runs into hundreds of establishments from homely B&Bs to five-star opulence. Send for a copy in advance or pick one up on arrival.

For train enquiries during walk, telephone Edinburgh Waverley (031) 556 2451 or Kirkcaldy Station (0592) 204771. Bus enquiries: Kirkcaldy (0592) 754411.

DALMENY

Coming out from Dalmeny Station descend the ramp and turn right, round the sandstone building, to reach the road which runs under the railway. Across this road is a bus stop and signs for the Forth Bridge visitor centre, Hawes Pier and the *Maid of the Forth*, all attractions deserving our attention. Before that, however, do take a walk out to see Dalmeny Kirk, one of the oldest, most historical, and attractive churches in Scotland.

To reach Dalmeny Kirk, follow the road under the Railway Bridge and on eastwards to a T-junction beside some cottages (signposted DALMENY). Turn right and Dalmeny is just over 500m ahead. Turn left (B924) when you reach the junction in the village (war memorial) and you'll find the church gates just beside you.

The church is dedicated to St Cuthbert (whose shrine is in Durham Cathedral) and dates back to the twelfth century. Approaching the building you'll notice a rather uninspired tower has been added, but the eye soon leaves this for the south doorway which some regard as the most beautiful in Scotland, being festooned with carvings and pictures from the Bestiary, zodiac signs, grotesque heads and the like. Though weathered, it is still beautiful. The interior of the church is richly ornate, too, with arches and vaulting looking fresh and new. Masons' marks abound showing links with Dunfermline and Durham. There are grave-slabs on the floor and, outside, by the door, there's a massive stone coffin, with a head cavity, which could be that of the founder. The churchyard has many really fine stones, quite a few showing symbols of trades, including the only one I've ever seen of two men 'rolling out the barrel'. There's also a big eagle on top of what looks like a cheese-press, and many others.

By odd coincidence, the only comparable Norman church architecture in Scotland is at Leuchars Church which we can see on our last day. If Dalmeny Kirk is locked the key can usually be obtained locally, as indicated.

Dalmeny village was built as a unit, hence its neat and spacious appearance. It dates back to the eighteenth century when the laird cleared other areas and settled the people here. Dalmeny estate goes back to the Moubrays who came across with William the Conqueror, but in 1661 the Primrose family bought the lands, later becoming Earls of Rosebery, one of whom was prime minister.

Our return to the station can be made by a different route, using an abandoned railway. Leaving the gates from the kirk, turn right and cross by the war memorial at the junction to head west through the village, houses in a row (left) and a farm (right) with an octagonal barn. The road swings left at The Glebe (sign for Royal Elizabeth Yard) but we continue straight on; ahead we can see a blue pedestrian

sign which indicates our route. If you walk on a few yards, onto railway bridge 27, you can see it spans an abandoned line as well as the busy line to the Forth Bridge and Fife. To gain this walkway turn off at the sign DALMENY STATION ½ etc. on a path which runs outside some back gardens and then descends steps, made of sleepers, to the track. Looking left, the first bridge in that direction carries the noisy A90 into Edinburgh. Turn right, however, to walk though the archway and along the old line which once ran to Port Edgar and closed in 1966 when the whisky connection was severed.

After ¾km we come on another bridge, with a pipeline across in front

Dalmeny Church: an old stone coffin outside the beautiful entrance

of it, and here we scramble up to join the road at the right corner of the bridge. Turn left over the bridge and along by a row of houses and under the main railway line bridge again with Dalmeny Station just round the corner. Now cross the road to take the footpath beside the bridge with its call to Forth Bridge visitor centre, Hawes Pier, and the *Maid of the Forth*.

The footpath runs alongside the railway (views to the Road Bridge) then crosses the abandoned line by a concrete bridge. After following along by the initial four stone arches of the Railway Bridge, the path passes under this centenarian marvel, crosses a track, and descends a flight of 120 steps (Jacob's Ladder) to reach the shore road. Turn left under the trellised girders of the high Railway Bridge – and we are in Queensferry.

The first building we come to is the Hawes Inn, where Robert Louis Stevenson set the start of that gem of a story, *Kidnapped*, the inspiration coming when R.L.S. was staying here in 1886, and keeping him in 'one unbroken round of pleasure of suspense'. Here he often walked the shores, watched the ships and went canoeing. The Hawes Inn was also described in Sir Walter Scott's *Antiquary*. The name 'Hawes' comes from Newhalls, as this part of the coast was called, though you may need a Scots accent to work out the connection. The garage beyond occupies the old stables of the inn. The Scotch Corner café lies beyond and, set back, the large brick Bridge House, was, in turn, offices and staff quarters for the bridgebuilders, then a sailors' home, and now flats.

INCHCOLM

Opposite the Hawes Inn is the lifeboat station and Hawes Pier, from which we can make an enjoyable visit to Inchcolm by the *Maid of the Forth*. Sailings vary but 2 p.m. is the commonest. Phone and check the day before and plan accordingly; (031) 331 1454 (operates July–September). This is a well-appointed 200-seater launch, with a friendly service. Sailings take half an hour each way, and up to 1½ hours ashore – which will pass in no time. Hawes Pier was designed by John Rennie and, latterly, was the only pier used by the car ferries. Note the light at the end of the pier as we slide past, and compare it with the equivalent one at North Queensferry later. Passing under the Railway Bridge brings home its massive size: it is 1½ miles long and towers 500ft (156m) above sea-level. A fuller description is given on the last day when we cross it, a splendid ending to our walk. If a tanker is unloading at the Hound Point terminal you'll realise how massive they are, too. The terminal sits out in the middle of the river. Look out for seals; they even haul out and sunbathe on the buoys. (On the promenade outside Hawes Pier is a sculpture of a mother seal and young one, by Kenneth Raeburn.) There is also a passenger ferry operating across to North Queensferry and if time is short or the sea calls this could be taken instead of walking across the bridge. Telephone, as above. Office on pier.

The four-mile journey will pass all too soon, as will the time ashore. 'Colm' is a form of Columba and that great saint was, rightly or wrongly, con-

Inchcolm Abbey, reached by a cruise from Queensferry

nected with the island. One of the island's earliest incidents is mentioned in Shakespeare's *Macbeth*, when Sueno, defeated by Macbeth at Kinghorn, was allowed to bury his dead on the island, after paying a hefty fee. One hogsback stone survives from then.

Alexander I was caught in a storm crossing the Forth in 1123, and vowed if saved to found an abbey in St Columba's name. He made the island and was succoured for several days by a hermit who lived in a cell, a 'desert' (hence the name Dysart), which still exists. Alexander's brother, David I, founded the priory and a century later it became an abbey. Sir William Mortimer, landowner in Aberdour, fell out with the monks but gave half his lands, and an endowment, so that he could be buried on the island. Somehow, on the way across, his lead coffin went overboard – hence Mortimer's Deep, for which modern supertankers, calling in to the Braefoot terminal, are grateful.

Columba's name was a powerful one. English raiders in 1335 bore off treasure from the abbey but, off Inchkeith, were overtaken by a storm and pleaded with the saint for mercy, promising to restore the stolen goods. The storm died away and they landed their haul at Kinghorn. The following year another raid penetrated to Dollar, under the Ochils, and the church valuables were stolen. On nearing Inchcolm the ship sank in Mortimer's Deep. Dollar Church was dedicated to St Columba.

More serious incursions by the English during the 'Rough Wooing' had the monks retreating to the mainland, but the Reformation brought the abbey's end, the last monk dying in 1578. Inchcolm is an impressive ruin (the most complete abbey in Scotland) because its island position largely stopped its fabric being pillaged for building stone, though Edinburgh's tolbooth was built of stone from the abbey. In 1854 workmen taking stone for one of the isle's forts came on a skeleton standing upright within a wall in the Abbot's House. The Earls of Moray owned the island from post-Reformation times till 1924 when it was presented to the Commissioners of Works.

At various times in history, too, the island was used as a quarantine station. The *William of Leith* with plague aboard (*c*.1582) was stuck there with most of the crew dying. As late as 1845 many of the sailors of Czar Nicholas I (during a fleet visit) died of fever. Heaps of skeletons have been unearthed all over the island.

Many of the more visible ruins are obviously from the last two World Wars but major fortifications were built in Napoleonic times as well. The most impressive are on the eastern end, the hill itself being worth a climb to gain an overall view of the island. In the Second World War a boom crossed the Forth, linking Inchcolm and Cramond Islands. There were defences on Inchmickery, Inchkeith and Cramond, as well as here, to protect the Forth Bridge and the naval base at Rosyth.

The island is now in state care and, on landing, there is a modest charge. At the end, if time is left, the tea-room over the ticket office may be welcome. There is an excellent guidebook on sale so I'll not describe the abbey itself in detail. Do make sure of climbing the tower which has its upper floors as a doocot. Up there the visitor is *almost* as high as the captain on the bridge of a supertanker! Those of more than average girth will find the climb interesting. A rare thirteenth-century mural

painting was discovered in the chancel, showing a procession of robed figures, swinging censers; sadly, the top half, with the heads, is missing.

QUEENSFERRY

Walking along towards Queensferry there is a reproduction Victorian pillar-box. Beside it once stood the geodesic dome of the Forth Bridges Exhibition, which was opened in 1990 when the Railway Bridge celebrated its centenary. The massive fireworks display, laser show, parachute jumping and the first floodlighting of the bridge all went off successfully. (The day before, gales and rain had lashed down all day!) Some feel the view of both bridges from here is the best of all. The view at night when the Railway Bridge is floodlit is quite fabulous, and, if there is darkness enough to do so, take an evening walk to some vantage-point (back up to the north end of the Road Bridge or onto one of the North Queensferry piers) to see this gentle giant spectacle.

Queensferry has been declared an 'Outstanding Conservation Area' and you soon see why. Beyond Seals Craig Hotel, site of the old East Port, we join a picturesque high street which has buildings going back to the sixteenth century, some terraced on top of others and separated by closes. The museum is a good port of call and will explain much of what we see – or don't see, such as the workings of the old shale-oil industry which honeycombs this area, underground and undersea. (The museum is open all year, Thu, Fri, Sat and Mon 10 a.m–1 p.m., 2.15–5 p.m., and Sun 2–5 p.m.) Almost opposite, in the shops under the houses of West Terrace, is the Bridges Bookstore and Coffee Shop, a good port of call.

East Terrace ends at Black Castle, which is dated 1626, and is painted that colour. The carved initials are of William Lowrie and Marion Speedie. Lowrie was a skipper, and he and his crew were lost at sea – which led to accusations of witchcraft and the burning of two local women. At least eight women were burnt in 1643–44 for witchcraft, the minister being a bit of a fanatic. Deprivation of sleep and other torture to force confessions sound more like this century. A secret stair goes up in the thickness of the walls of Black Castle.

Beside Black Castle the Vennel runs up to the 1633 Auld Kirk, now a YMCA day centre. The key for the Vennel graveyard is kept in the centre and is worth obtaining for there are some fine stones: one is of a ship under sail, another has navigation instruments, several depict trades, and there is a variety of skulls, lettering and so on. Bee-boles occupy one wall. (Along with Dalmeny and St Andrews, this is probably the best collection of gravestones on our walk.) The church still has its old bell, made in Holland and dated 1635. An inscription, 'Cursed be they that takes it', may have something to do with this. Queensferry was always fairly zealous; it had its own National Covenant (in the museum now), for instance.

West of the Vennel is the Forth Bridge Hotel, dated 1683. It is now only a pub and has no accommodation. Steps lead up onto Mid Terrace. Halfway along it, look in to Hamilton's

Close – where the atmosphere reels back two centuries. There is a short gap before the West Terrace. On the seaward side is a gap with steps leading down to the shore and the hidden Old Boathouse Restaurant. (There is a coffee house in the Kiltmakers.) The landward side gardens have a monument to John Reid, a Victorian provost of Queensferry. The Queensferry Arms and Staghorn Hotel are both old buildings. The latter is supposed to have been so named as a stag strayed into the village when the inn was being built and was hit by the stagecoach and killed. The former has an inn sign with the arms of the royal burgh. There were two coats-of-arms (like Linlithgow), one showing Queen Margaret aboard a ferry.

The old tolbooth dominates the scene here. The mercat cross, battered by growing traffic usage, was removed in 1764. The tolbooth had the usual run of uses (customs and tax office, court and prison, burgh chambers, weights and measures office, etc.). The clock on the tower replaced an earlier one and was erected to commemorate Queen Victoria's Jubilee. The Rosebery Hall was gifted in 1894 by the local laird, the fifth Earl, and replaced older buildings. The stairs were used for proclamations, etc, and on the street wall is a well dated 1817, a thank-you to the fourth Earl who had piped in water. The local war memorial is also sited at the tolbooth, still very much the heart of the town.

There is then a busy junction, the B907 heading up The Loan being the town's main approach road, but still plenty of points of interest. The fine building across The Loan is Plewlands

House which was given to the National Trust for Scotland and restored in 1955 as a group of seven flats. There is a marriage lintel with the motto *'spes mea Christus'*, an anchor, the initials SW, AP and date, 1641. ('Christ is my hope', Samuel Wilson and Anna Poulton.) Facing The Loan is the Bell Stane, the name now being used for a square of buildings. Originally a stone with a ring stood there, the western burgh boundary, and the site was used for ringing a bell to make announcements to what had become the market-place. A stone high on the building between Covenanter Lane and Harbour Lane has an owl perched on a bell, dated 1879. The shop on the right, probably a late encroachment into the market-square, carries an older stone of 1776. The name Covenanter refers to a 1680 fracas at an inn here. Donald Cargill and Henry Hall, wanted Covenanters, were nearly caught but escaped after a fight. Hall later died at the hands of Dalyell of the Binns, and Cargill was executed in Edinburgh.

Follow Harbour Lane down to the old harbour, a snug, narrow place, dry at low tide. The harbour was rebuilt about 1817 following plans by Hugh Baird (engineer of the Union Canal) and has one of the ferry slips. Herring boats crowded it for some winters, until the fish disappeared; coal, stone, potatoes and salt were exported, and grain was brought in for the distillery.

From the harbour walk west on a path past picnic tables to The Binks carpark. Inland lie the fine friary buildings, the oldest building in the town. The Dundas family is believed to have founded the friary here about 1330. After the Reformation it was the town church and Dundas burial-ground. The cloisters site was used by fishermen and nets hung to dry in the church. In 1890 the chancel, tower and south transept were restored to become an Episcopal church, which it still is today. The word 'bink' meant a ledge, the seaward rocks being cut to form a landing ledge; here and Sealscraig and Port Neuk (beyond Railway Bridge) were the original ferry points.

Walk up by the friary. On the corner is a bakery/tea-room which still has the old ovens and other features preserved. Turn right past it to a fork in the road. The right fork runs along under the bridge to Port Edgar, a vast marina and yachting centre named after the redundant Saxon prince who, with his sister Margaret, was chased out of England by the invader William (1066 and All That). Margaret, of course, had the ferry named after her. The present harbour dates from the nineteenth century. The navy had a destroyer base here in 1914–18 and a training school, HMS *Lochinvar*, later. They sold out in 1978. We bear left at the fork, on the road signposted LINLITHGOW and BO'NESS, and follow this up to the soaring Forth Road Bridge.

Whisky was manufactured, bottled and blended in Queensferry for over 150 years; the plant (left of here where there is now a supermarket) closed in 1985. A fire just after the war destroyed older works. I lived at Dollar then, 30km distant, and watched the flaring glow in the sky.

Queensferry was at its peak in the seventeenth century, its captains and merchants carrying coal, timber, wine, salt fish, etc., to the rest of Britain and having a lively trade with Scandinavia and the Baltic. Candlemaking was once important and both the local estates, the ferry operations and the navy yards used local workers. A constant change of working options is nothing new. Today the town's largest source of employment is connected with electronics and microchips (Hewlett-Packard). Queensferry was made a royal burgh and free port in 1636, by Charles I. Linlithgow, as the only royal burgh in the shire, had rather tried to impose on Queensferry and when an agent tried to extract taxes on Fair Day in 1628 there was a riot. After being fined, the town appealed to the king.

The first Friday in August (still the Fair) sees a very odd ritual when the 'burry man' walks the town. This strange figure, with floral staffs, is clothed entirely, from crown to ankles, in burdock burrs. Fraserburgh and Buckie once had a similar good luck ritual but now it is unique to Queensferry. The Fair was for long a feeing fair when farm labourers were signed on. Now it is just a holiday, with a Ferry Queen and so on.

OVER THE BRIDGE

Walk up, passing Plewlandscroft and Morison Gardens, to reach the Road Bridge. A footpath, rather misleadingly signed CYCLISTS ONLY, heads up and through below the bridge to meet a road. Turn left to go through under the bridge again and the road swings up to the complex of buildings servicing the bridge. (The millionaires' Moat House Hotel can be seen behind these build-

ings.) A pedestrian subway can take one to the west side with its view to the Rosyth Dockyard and upper river, backed by the Ochils, or one can stay on the east walkway with its view of 'the big red yin' and the Fife coast we will be walking. The east would be my choice. Give the queue of cars at the tolls a wee wave!

The earliest record of a ferry here is documented at the time Queen Margaret died. This refugee princess (Hungarian originally) was to marry Malcolm Canmore and have strong religious influence on husband and country which changed from its Celtic Christianity to that of Rome. Rome, in gratitude, created Margaret a saint. She was an early commuter between Fife and Edinburgh and the crossing took on the name Queen's Ferry, as did the town on the Lothian shore. The Fife side was known as North Ferry till last century. David I regularised services in 1129, but in 1275 the Church handed over its executive office to local seamen. They could be thrawn and even Charles II was to girn at their avaricious services. In 1810 the service was taken over by government-appointed trustees. Strong currents and erratic storms made the crossing hazardous at times (Alexander III crossed in a storm and rode on to his doom, and Alexander I, as explained earlier, was driven ashore on Inchcolm). Remember the boats were small and either rowed or sailed across. Even steam power, introduced in 1821, did not make for easy crossings. Several piers were created so ferries could reach the most convenient even in adverse circumstances. The opening of the bridge in 1964 brought an end to 800 years of regular ferry traf-

fic. Latterly 900,000 vehicles a year were crossing by ferry, compared to the 14 million vehicles which cross the bridge each year.

A bridge was first mooted after the First World War and a report prepared in 1929, but another war had to come and go before approval was granted. When built, though, it was the largest suspension bridge in Europe and fourth-largest in the world. The central span is 3,300ft long with 1,340ft side spans, a southern approach viaduct of 1,437ft and a northern of 842ft – a total of over 1½ miles. The cables are made of 12,000 galvanised steel wires each able to bear 100 tons; 314 wires made one strand and 37 strands made a cable. The wires were hung individually before being compacted into the single cable of enormous strength. The towers are 512ft high. In all, 39,000 tons of steel and 150,000 cubic feet of concrete were used in the bridge. The cost was £19.5 million.

If you are walking across towards dusk you will not fail to notice the starlings flying in to roost along the southern end of the bridge. Their din can be heard above other noises, even from inside a car. They are a notorious problem which strobe lights, bird-scarers, dummy birds of prey and broadcasting starling distress calls have all singularly failed to solve.

Motorists tend simply to treat the bridge as part of the road, so walking across gives a marvellous affinity with what is a superb feat of engineering. On a windy day you may be aware of the bridge swaying – relax, it is meant to, up to 22ft in big gales. And the bridge receives a fair ration of nasty weather. The tough, dedicated construction workers with experience of building bridges all over the world rated it 'a right dog'. It was an enormous undertaking. Only the Golden Gate Bridge or the Washington Bridge in New York could match it at the time and the collapse of the comparable Tacoma Bridge in a wind gust of only 42mph gave cause for thought.

I was lucky enough to see the bridge being built, over the years 1958–64, from the soaring, solitary towers, to the spinning of catwalks and cables and the suspension of the roadway. Waiting for the ferry was never dull. Working on the bridge was never dull either, I'm sure. Seven workers died during construction (the Rail Bridge cost 57 lives) including three who plunged into the river when a safety net collapsed while being moved. One man actually survived falling 180ft into the sea (the world high-dive record is 155ft!). A shaft at the south end was shut for six weeks after blasting; when it was opened again a dead sailor was found in it, a real puzzle. The only fatalities since the opening have been from traffic accidents or the odd suicide (not publicised to stop copycat attempts).

Just like the Rail Bridge (which is described at the end of the walk, when we cross it) work never stops on the Road Bridge. After all, it has the lighting, drainage, road surface, and financial complexities of a small town. Walkers see some of this effort –

The route into Fife – the Forth Road Bridge with North Queensferry and Inverkeithing beyond

motorists simply grunt at the toll-collectors and zoom off.

The view upstream takes in several landmarks from the nearby Port Edgar Marina and the Rosyth Dockyard, to Longannet Power Station (coal-fired, and fed directly from the pit 14km inland) whose chimney is quite a landmark, the sweep of the Ochils, the more distant Campsie Fells and Highland hills like Ben Ledi and Ben Lomond. Over 1¼ million people live round the Forth Estuary, yet it has quite a rural atmosphere. Wildfowl and waders flock to it as well, more than to any other estuary in Scotland. The flow of water into the estuary is 44.7 cubic metres per second and it widens out to a maximum width of 27km. In 1918 the German High Fleet was brought up and paraded between the ships of the Grand Fleet while the formal surrender was made at Rosyth. A few years later a parade showed warships anchored, row upon row, from Rosyth to Leith.

At the end of the bridge is a plaque commemorating its opening in 1964 by the Queen. After making the opening and first official crossing to Fife, she and Prince Philip returned to Hawes Pier on the last sailing of the *Queen Margaret*. St Margaret's Hope, where Queen Margaret first landed in Scotland as a refugee from William the Conqueror (the Saddam of the day), lies just west of the bridge.

Now turn down the pedestrian steps, but before descending to North Queensferry, turn right, under the bridge, and up the steps to gain the west side. A path leads off towards the hotel, left, and there's a viewing platform which offers a good look along the arc of bridge we have just crossed. The Queensferry Lodge Hotel, while probably out of most walkers' price range for an overnight stay, has good restaurant, café, bar and other services. There is a Tourist Information Office, (0383) 417759 (open: 11.30 a.m.–3 p.m.; 5.30–9.30 p.m.) and a shop which stocks only Scottish-made quality products. There is also a highly recommended interpretive display about the history of the Queensferry crossing. In the hall is a display of colour pictures showing the variety of merchant ships using the estuary. With the Rosyth Dockyard and Grangemouth with its oil refineries upstream, the traffic – 7,000 ships a year – is considerable.

NORTH QUEENSFERRY

Return to the bridge and go down the pedestrian steps under the bridge to rejoin the steps from the east side and so on down to the road into Queensferry, a road route as old as the ferry itself, linking as it did, the crossing and the royal palace at Dunfermline.

The road should be crossed with great care as cars come bombing down round a blind corner with no warning of a pedestrian hazard. On the other side, beside the North Queensferry town sign, turn off down a footpath and steps leading to a housing area below. The path runs between several back

North Queensferry and the Forth Bridge (© Cambridge University Collection of Air Photographs)

gardens and then turns right (just before it looks as if the path was ending) onto Ferry Barns Court (no name visible this end). Turn left down to the T-junction. The cables for the bridge are anchored just over on the right.

Turn left to walk up the road. After a few minutes, right, is the entrance to the Forth Yacht Marina, which is based at the pier from which the ferries operated until the bridge made them redundant. You can go down if you want and betray your age maybe by recalling the *Sir William Wallace*, *Robert the Bruce*, *Mary Queen of Scots* and *Queen Margaret*. It seems unbelievable that they once coped with all the pre-bridge traffic. They didn't in the end, I

suppose, and I can recall knowing the exact place in the queue where it was quicker simply to go and drive round by the Kincardine Bridge. (Originally the pier was built in 1877 as a railway link for Dunfermline and is still called the Railway Pier.)

Our road joins the main road down into North Queensferry and as we descend on the curve of road we have attractive views to the old village. The Fife authorities have been slow (compared to those on the Lothian side) to start tidying up the village and bringing out its attractiveness. The village is dominated by the Railway Bridge and the rhythm of passing trains is its heartbeat. Nearly opposite the police sta-

tion there is a footpath sign indicating FOOTPATH TO MAIN STREET. There are actually two flights of stairs and if you go down the right (west) stairs you will come on Willie's Well, which was built over by the new 1773 highway.

Return to the main road (rather than the footpath) and continue along towards the village. A steep hill road (just known as The Brae) comes in on the left and there is a group of wells. Most obvious is the painted Napoleon's hat-shaped Waterloo Monument, erected in 1816 and once much used by the horses that had to pull the stagecoaches. Above this well is a typical village well of Victorian times, painted black and in good order. Behind it is a plaque which makes yet another well and shows Europa and the Bull and what looks like a village woman struggling with a foreign sailor – as may have occurred in a clash of interests when water was in demand. Further up the road an ancient well was 'restored for the solace of wayfarers' to mark Queen Victoria's 60 years on the throne, 1837–97. The imposing school and North Queensferry Station are atop this hill.

A short description of the village follows. If staying here overnight, rucksacks could be left before wandering about. All the accommodation is central.

Swinging right onto Main Street, the Ferrybridge Hotel is the first building on the left. It and the houses running down to the Albert Hotel are dramatically dominated by the Railway Bridge. Walking down Main Street, note the alley of Post Office Lane, once a busy road leading up from St James' Harbour, then, on the

right, an arched way under the houses gives a view of the bay. A plaque points out that this was the start of the King's Way up till 1773. (The King's Way was simply the route to Dunfermline, often the royal home, and with the important abbey, founded in 1072.) The building beside the archway was once the Black Cat Inn and is dated 1693. The owners' names were placed on the lintel: Thomas Peastie and Bessie Craich. The Albert Hotel is opposite, and next to it is a stylish 1990 restoration of old buildings.

At the car turning area at the end of the road is an early nineteenth-century harbour light, a hexagonal building with a domed lantern. A flue exited from the top and originally the light was oil-fired.

If you walk out the harbour arm above the slip the last, castellated, house (with a splendid view) is the Tower House (or Mount Hooly), which was once ferry offices, waiting-room and lighthouse. Hooly is an obsolete word meaning canny or slow – which is how the masons worked on the building! There was an octagonal table on the second floor for the officials, to ensure that no one person could claim precedence.

Return by the Albert Hotel. Queen Victoria and Prince Albert landed at the Town Pier in 1842, so the name may have been given thereafter. An inn has stood here for hundreds of years. Behind the hotel is the Cadger's Slip where the cadgers (carters) met the fishing boats.

Turn right beyond the Albert Hotel and follow the road round the bay to the tastefully laid-out viewing-point below the bridge, beside one of its great supporting towers. There is a good view out the estuary and to Inchgarvie, bristling with old defensive structures. The Forth Bridge is simply one of the world's greatest engineering spectacles, and though I've been at this spot often, it still thrills. Maybe it's in the blood – one of my grandfathers spent his life building railways and bridges in what was then Siam. During summer terns may be diving in to the sea just beside the viewing-point, and seals are often spotted.

Inchgarvie's earliest mention is in connection with the Battle of Athelstaneford when the Anglian king Athelstane was killed by Hungus, King of the Picts. He set his enemy's head on a spear on the island as a warning not to encroach across the Forth into his territory. A state prison and fortress usually occupied the site – the forts of Burntisland, Inchgarvie and Rosyth were a thorn in the flesh to Cromwell's advance northwards. His fleet captured St Margaret's Hope, his army crossed to Charlestown, and one by one the castles fell and he won his victory of the Battle of Inverkeithing. Ironically, Rosyth Castle (now swallowed up in the navy yard) may have been the birthplace of Cromwell's mother, a Rosyth Stuart.

Something of the story of the bridge is told right at the end of the book but you might like to read it here, while sitting below those great red tubes arching out over the sea, with the next stepping-stone of Inchgarvie carrying another of the massive cantilever foundations. Inchgarvie can sometimes look like a ship, for it is long and low but with a superstructure of ruins, old and new, mostly built as defences – against fifteenth-century pirates or twentieth-century Nazi bombers. Rats and seabirds now fight for possession. Birds try and nest on the bridge and both mice and rabbits have been seen on it regularly. On one occasion a deer had to be shooed off from trying to cross the bridge. Trains pass overhead every few minutes, with a pulsing, rhythmic beat, a sound that I find a bit of a siren song to journey on to faraway places. We'll cross the bridge on our last day. Meanwhile, we have miles and days to walk, along the Castles Coast and the East Neuk.

Walk back to the village but turn right just before the Albert Hotel (footpath sign: HELEN PLACE AND ST JAMES' CHAPEL). Turning right again almost at once, the chapel, graveyard and gates are on the left. Locked because of vandals, the garden setting can be seen well enough. The chapel goes back 600 years and was dedicated to St James, patron saint of travellers. The graveyard dates to the seventeenth century. Much used by sailors and ferrymen, they added the wall round the site in 1752, as their plaque indicates. One stone has a very nautical tone:

'heier ue lay at anker with the manie
    in ouer fleet
in hopes to uay at the last day ouer
    admirel Christ to meet'.

Continue round to gain Helen Place and turn right along this narrow lane with its open drain. The cottage at the end is known as the Malinkie and was the village school till 1827. Turn left along the front of Yoll Cottage.

The lane we come out to is Post Office Lane (or North Lane, of Back Close). Just up it, left, is a 1776 lintel with the initials IM – MM. The continuation of the lane towards the sea is our route onwards for Inverkeithing (Helen Lane), the street further right has old quarrymen's houses, and both lead down to the small, tidal harbour of St James', well protected from the Forth's notorious westerlies, but now hardly used except for moorings or wintering yachts. There was one mighty change in 1993 – the opening of Deep Sea World, which claims to be the world's biggest aquarium. The million-gallon sea crater 'tank' is the old Battery Quarry and visitors travel along a moving walkway in a transparent tunnel through its depths to obtain unique views of ocean wildlife. There are exhibitions and audio-visual presentations, facilities for educational use and a large café. Not a place to be missed. There are sailings to it from Granton and Queensferry. It is open all year, 9 a.m.–6 p.m. Telephone (0383) 411411. The Battery Quarry was opened in 1764 and its whinstone has been used in the Forth Bridge foundations, the Forth and Clyde Canal and Leith Docks as well as in London, the Low Countries and even Russia. Quarrying ceased in 1924 when flooding by sea-water made it uneconomic. I wonder what anyone in 1764 or 1924 would have thought of a £4 million use for flooding sea-water.

After dark the Forth Bridge is flood-lit, so don't miss that spectacle, a memorable end to our beginning.

PRACTICAL INFORMATION / ACCOMMODATION

Telephone code for N Queensferry and Inverkeithing is 0383. S Queensferry is 031-331

Tourist Information Office: Queensferry Lodge Hotel, (0383) 417759, open 11.30 a.m.–3 p.m.; 5.30–9.30 p.m.

North Queensferry

Albert Hotel, Main Street	413562
Ferrybridge Hotel, Main Street	416292
Torback, Post Office Lane	414375
Bankton House, Main Street	415711
Queensferry Lodge Hotel (up to N end of Road Bridge – very expensive)	410000

The Queensferry ferry would also allow accommodation to be used south of the river. It plies from Town Pier to Hawes Pier, (031) 331 1454.

Inverkeithing is less than an hour's walk away and has considerably more accommodation. The route is described under tomorrow's itinerary, the undermentioned listed roughly in the order in which they are reached.

Forth Craig Private Hotel, Hope Street	418440
Niravaana, Hope Street	413876
The Poplars, 33 Hope Street	417645
Royal Hotel, High Street	412427
Queen's Hotel, Church Street	413075
9 King Street	416578
16 Bannerman Avenue	415049
Borland Lodge, Private Hotel, Borland Road	413792
96 Spittalfield Road	419590

South Queensferry: You can stay south of the river and walk over in the morning but, be warned, prices are much higher than on the Fife shore.

The only B&B is 18 Kirkliston Road
(up The Loan)   2550
Hotels, all about double most B&B prices:
Staghorn Hotel   1039
Sealscraig Hotel   1340
Queensferry Arms   1298
Hawes Inn   1990
Forth Bridges Moat House Hotel (up at end
of road bridge; very expensive)   1199

Edinburgh: With the regular transport
available, you could just return to the capital
for the night.

Taxi: Queensferry   (031) 331 1077, 331 3321
Inverkeithing   (0383) 411171, 415252,
    412998, 412911, 418666, 411111, 418638,
                                        412998

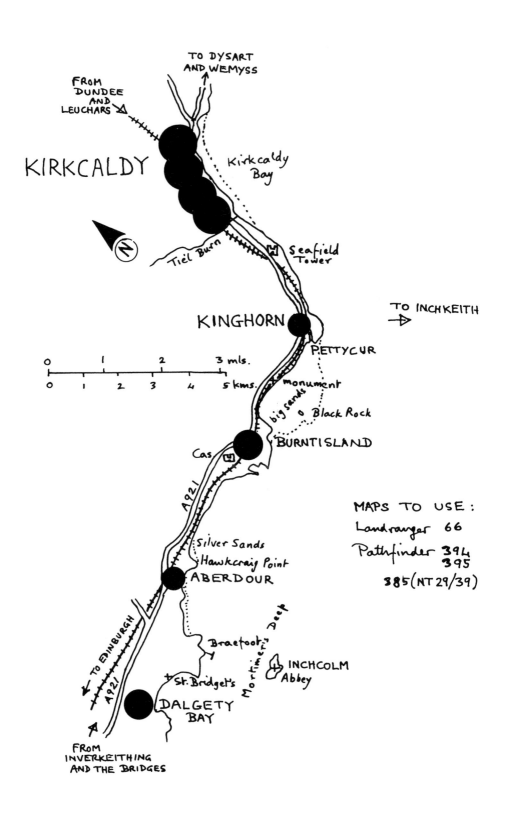

TO DYSART
AND WEMYSS

FROM
DUNDEE
AND
LEUCHARS

KIRKCALDY

Kirkcaldy
Bay

N

Tiel Burn

Seafield
Tower

KINGHORN

TO INCHKEITH

PETTYCUR

0   1   2   3 mls.

0   1   2   3   4   5 kms.

monument

big sands

Black Rock

Cas

BURNTISLAND

A921

Silver Sands

Hawkcraig Point

ABERDOUR

MAPS TO USE:
Landranger 66
Pathfinder 394
            395
385 (NT 29/39)

TO EDINBURGH

A921

Braefoot

Mortimer's Deep

INCHCOLM
Abbey

St. Bridget's

DALGETY
BAY

FROM
INVERKEITHING
AND THE BRIDGES

DAY 2 *Ower tae Aberdour*

Inverkeithing–Dalgety Bay–Aberdour

Maps to use: Bart 46, OSLR 65 and 66, OSPF 394 (NT 08/18)
Walking distance: 13km (20km)

Most of this day's walking is on footpaths or tracks, but do try and reach Aberdour in time to visit the castle. There is a constant alternating of quiet countryside and concentrations of industrial or urban housing areas. Aberdour, at the end, is a quiet village rather than a town, and an evening circuit is described to ensure you see the best of it. Inverkeithing, depite its heavy industry (interesting, too) has a few noteworthy antiquities and a friendly little museum. Dunfermline District Council have recently marked the path from North Queensferry to Aberdour with fingerposts and produced an outline leaflet. The only difference to this text lies beyond St Bridget's Kirk where they cut inland, road walking, where I suggest continuing to Braefoot Point.

NORTH QUEENSFERRY TO INVERKEITHING

Either head down Post Office Lane and along Helen Lane until there is a footpath sign pointing us up the hill for PORT LAING VIA CARLINGNOSE or start at the Waterloo Well (coastal path sign-post) – the two merge almost below the Railway Bridge (marker) then the path climbs slightly to contour round the crags of Carlingnose ('the witch's nose'; at Kinghorn there is Carlin Craig). This is an old industrial track we are following.

Look down onto St James' Harbour and the old quarry site which is now water-filled. Battery Hill beyond owes its name to a battery being set up there following the visit of John Paul Jones in 1779. The hill is still a forces establishment, as you may guess from the flag flying. The first German air-raid of the Second World War was aimed at the Forth Bridge in 1939. As we wend on we come to a large quarry area.

Keep right at all the forks to end on the cliff edge. The tanker berth (Hound Point) out in the middle of the river looks oddly marooned (especially if a tanker is berthed) but supertankers need deep water and the oil simply goes ashore by pipe, so to have an actual pier running out would be unnecessary. Along a bit below us is a bit of genuine detached pier. Some of it was probably taken down simply for safety. The rails can still be seen on it and this pier was the loading point for all the quarrying here. There have been something like seven quarries on the Carlingnose area.

The small cliff-edge path is too prickly for comfort, so head back and take the first track right which leads down to join a tiny tarred road where it bends sharply to take the hill. This leads down to the landward end of the now marooned section of pier. A few minutes' walk leads round to a quiet sandy bay, Port Laing, where we join another track curving down to the rubble-filled mess in the old wartime barracks compound. Walk along the rim of the bay. Looking back up you can just see the ruins of the Carlingnose batteries and barracks on top of the hill, along with new houses, which are now also threatened to be built down in the bay itself – as if the one secret, unspoilt place in a surrounding world of industrial use couldn't be left undeveloped for people to enjoy. Also on top of the hill is the duelling stone where a Captain Gurley was killed in 1824 by a Mr Westall after they'd squabbled over a gambling debt. The latter had to flee the country. There was only one other duel fought in the country thereafter, according to all the references.

They could do with cutting back some of the encroaching thorns on the footpath as we follow it from the bay, plunging into a jungly tunnel for a bit and popping out on to the gravelled drive of a house (dark whinstone) which we pass, then there's a white harled house, both sitting before another of the ancient quarries.

As we continue along a now wide, roughly tarred road, we look across the narrow entrance of Inverkeithing's Inner Bay to the large disused Preston-hill Quarry on the other shore. A large pier leads out from it, still in good order. As we turn left at the point (Cruickness or Crookness, the accurate older name) there are the remains of a pier on our side and a better one opposite (being north and south of each other, they are called West Ness and East Ness!). Also opposite is a wooden pier, ruinous, backed by a big works building. The steam-making works at the head of the bay are paper-mills and, ahead, we can see the cranes of the shipbreaking scrapyard. Before we reach that, though, we run the gamut of the Cruicks Quarry, which is still in operation. Walkers often tend to simply dismiss such a place as an eyesore but I think that is being shortsighted. It may not be beautiful but it is impressive – and it is *work*, it is livelihoods, it is history. I find it fascinating.

Cruicks Quarry opened in 1828 and Carlingnose a decade later. Pennant, on his tour in the 1770s, noted quarrying here, and other quarry names survive: Ferry Toll, Welldean, Lucknow, Jubilee, Battery. Stone from Cruicks, like that from Battery, went to the construction of the Forth and Clyde Canal, Leith Docks, London pavements,

Liverpool Docks and, abroad, as far as Russia, the hard whinstone (dolerite) being highly regarded for tough public use in setts, kerbs, pavements, harbours, etc. At the beginning of this century the quarrymen earned £1 for a six-day (ten hours a day) stint. The initial need for roads gave the quarries new life early this century, but now Tilcon's activities are much more localised. Nothing much goes off by sea any more, and, instead of a uniform chip, the crushers produce a range of sizes used for many purposes: road-surfacing still, and in cement mixes.

Somewhere over these slopes or near the quarry there was a battle in 1651, a small battle but one which had larger consequences. The extraordinary political-religious alliances of that period had reached a permutation where Cromwell (once an ally) had invaded Scotland, which had an active Royalist army. A battle at Dunbar led to the subjugation of Edinburgh and the South-East. The Royalist forces lay at Stirling, the vital bridging point on the Forth – a familiar enough situation. Cromwell, however, took advantage of Fife's vulnerability and crossed the Forth, scattered the ineffective opposition from the Ferry Hills at Inverkeithing and soon captured Perth. The Scots retaliated by invading England, hoping Cromwell would have to follow. He did, and destroyed the Scots at Worcester. General Monck, left behind in Scotland, captured most of the opposition leaders in a brilliant raid and, before long, all Scotland was mastered. Cromwell was nothing if not efficient.

There is a rather intimidatory notice as we approach the quarry but the route is a pedestrian right-of-way and safe enough unless one wilfully enters the quarrying area. The road swings left a bit by a wall, and goes on, passing under a conveyor; then, left, is the area of current activity, quarrying on a mighty scale. At the quarry entrance is Jamestown Pond, a local wildlife site for plants, amphibians and insects. (The azure damsel fly only breeds in one other place.) The bay is popular with wintering waders and wildfowl such as divers, grebes, goldeneye, etc.

As soon as we leave the Tilcon quarry the rest of the Inner Bay is taken up by shipbreaking and scrapyards, even less beautiful, I suppose, and both sad and fascinating as huge grabs grip piles of scrap and swing them onto ships, or oxyacetylene lights flicker as another craft is torn apart. There's something almost cannibalistic about having a ship cut up and then loaded onto another vessel. The real sadness is that this is the graveyard of some fine ships. I can remember two especially, the *Implacable*, a carrier which came here in 1955, and the famous 36,000-ton *Mauritania* in 1965.

Our curiosity is largely frustrated by the concrete walling along which we walk. This area is Jamestown, after a James Reid who converted chemical works into housing. If you turn and look back, the big block on the right fork is the only remaining building of character and, in its time, has been furniture warehouse, wartime naval store and a workmen's lodging-house. Industry coming and going is a constant factor of life. In the seventeenth century the bay had salt-pans, a wood-yard, a foundry, a limekiln and a bone-

The *Mauritania*, one of the many famous ships broken up at Inverkeithing (© Dunfermline Public Library Collection)

mill. At one time a railway ran out to Cruickness.

INVERKEITHING

Our road bears right and under the paper-mill railways and comes out to Hope Street just at the INVERKEITHING town sign. (Don't take the coast path as signed.) Turn right to walk up into town. On the right is an unusual Episcopal church which looks as if it had been imported from an alpine village. Beside it is Forth Craig Hotel and just before the Railway Bridge, right, is Niravaana (B&B) with its elephant gates. Further up there are allotments, right, with The Poplars (B&B) opposite. Catholic church and scout hall are passed, then a building (recently restored) with a more imposing front

and a date, MDCCCXXXIII. Beside it a lane breaks off, which will be our continuation after a brief walk round Inverkeithing.

On the right is the obviously old building of the friary, now the local museum (open Wed–Sun 11 a.m.–5 p.m.). The Grey Friars Monastery dates from about 1384 but the *hospitium* alone has survived. Behind are pleasant gardens where once, no doubt, the cloistered brethren took their exercise.

From the friary, continue along to the wide High Street. (It *has* to be High Street or Main Street, one feels.) The Royal Hotel is on the right and is the birthplace of one of Inverkeithing's more adventurous sons, Samuel Greig. He was born in 1735 and died as Grand Admiral of Russia, having won fame in war and as the creator of Catherine the

Part of the old Grey Friars Hospice, now the Inverkeithing Museum

Great's navy. He took a schoolboy trip to the Baltic on his father's vessel, *Thistle*, and his career was settled. He served with Hawke and was at the siege of Havana before volunteering for Russian service. He was largely responsible for destroying the hitherto invincible grand Turkish fleet in 1770 at the important Battle of Chesme (near Izmir). He then reorganised the navy in the Baltic, beat off a Swedish attack, and built the Kronstadt Fort so well that the attacking British navy under Napier, 85 years later, called it 'a hard nut to crack'. Not surprisingly – it had been built with whinstone from Carlingnose! One of his sons, Alexis, became a Russian admiral as well, and two others served in the British navy. His son Samuel was Russian Consul in Britain but died at the age of 29; his widow Mary then married a cousin, Dr Somerville, and Mary Somerville's distinguished career we'll describe when we reach Burntisland. William Roxburgh, a cousin and contemporary of Samuel Greig, was also one of the first small group sent to Catherine, and he too ended as an admiral in the Russian navy – as did the adventurous John Paul Jones, a Scot mostly honoured for founding the American navy, who appears in our story at Kirkcaldy.

Just along from the Royal Hotel is the Burgh Arms, dated 1664–1888 and with an attractive, appropriately painted sign. Beyond is a door with 1688 on the lintel, with the words 'God's providence is my inheritance. IB.' We then come to Bank Street and the mercat cross.

The superb mercat cross dates from the sixteenth century. The octagonal shaft is crowned with decorations, arms, a sundial and a unicorn holding the town's coat-of-arms, which was added in 1688. Some people dislike its being painted but often don't realise this was how it has always been – and how splendid the result is with this cross. You'll not see finer.

Bank Street is old: one marriage lintel has the date 1617 and besides the initials IT, BT there is a text: 'Except the Lord buildeth the house they labour in vain that build it'. Across Townhall Street lies the fine old town hall or tolbooth building with an outside stair, coat-of-arms, etc.

Inverkeithing is an ancient royal burgh, receiving its first charter from William the Lion. When exactly the original tolbooth went up we don't know, but in 1550 we read of a rent of 20/- being in hand from shops or booths on the ground floor of the Town House. The Council Chamber was on the first floor. There were several changes to the tolbooth in the eighteenth century, with the debtors' prison on the top floor (a bell, dated 1467, was hardly a congenial neighbour!), the Court Room on the middle floor and the 'black hole' (prison) at ground-level. This was the common enough use and history of our tolbooths. Most disappeared in the Victorian urge to 'improve'. The Fife coast has a good share of the survivors.

The mercat cross was likely to be near the tolbooth, and luckenbooths – stalls which could be left locked – were often set up there for security (like parking outside a police station!), as well as all the temporary booths and stalls of market-day. The scene must have been like a country Berber *souk*. The cross has been moved several times as traffic demands have increased. From 1799 till recently it was just outside the tolbooth, deviating all traffic going down Townhall Street. The traffic won and the cross moved aside into Bank Street.

It was only at the end of the fifteenth century that houses tended to be built entirely in stone so, naturally, little has survived from before then. (Even prehistoric houses are usually only traced by finding the holes left after the supporting poles have long ago disintegrated.) When houses along the Fife coast did move into this more permanent form, they were very simple keep-like buildings and, as time went on, they were added to, rebuilt and generally altered – so our walk is unusual in that we will see a great many of the surviving medieval buildings, by far the richest run of them in Scotland.

The forestair leading up to upper-level living areas was common and was partly defensive: a stair was a very effective defensive stance in pre-gunpowder days. It was also partly practical: below lay cellars for the traders, or room for hanging fishermen's nets or working in at a trade. Crowstep gables allowed beams to be laid across the roof for working on the thatch or pantiles, often at too steep a pitch for standing on. The size of rooms was dictated by the length of beam (tree) available.

Turn up to the High Street and, briefly, turn right on what becomes Church Street here. Queen's Hotel is across the road and, beyond it, facing the church, is another fine old building, now used as the church hall. The church hall is in the Fordell Lodging,

the town house of the Hendersons of Fordell Castle, who built it about 1670. (It was convenient to be 'in town' for the markets and other events and it made catching the ferry easier.) The church itself is not old but the tower is – when you see the weathering, it is rather apparent. There are gates on both sides of the church. Go in the south gate. Many of the gravestones have sunk deeply into the ground but it is worth a look around as there are quite a few stones with trade symbols on them: a weaver's shuttle, a sailor's anchor, a tailor's scissors, a butcher's chopper, a wright's square and compass, etc. On the way out peer in the window by the tower and you'll see the big, airy interior well enough. There's a brilliantly patterned window above the pulpit.

Walk back along the High Street (restaurants, cafés, pubs, chip shop and all the regular shops) and take the lane, Abbot Place, next to the MDCCCXXXIII building, which has been restored lately. The lane or path drops down steeply to cross the old dockyard railway track by a footbridge. Turn left once over the bridge, skirting the works (paper-mill) to come out at Ye Olde Foresters Arms beside the little harbour inlet.

Turn left to cross the apex of this inlet by a footbridge which leads to what is known as Ballast Bank. Bear right to pass behind the boatyard and through by some poplars to the large park and playing-field area. Cinder tracks skirt this or you can walk a red cinder road right by the sea. Waders congregate here in winter and there's a clear view over to the shipbreaking yard and the nearer mill. Caldwell's paper-mill was established in 1893 and in 1926 it became part of the Inveresk Group. Aim for the last house of the row at the far end of the park (Preston Crescent), passing a fenced-off works, right, and tennis courts and carpark, left. Turn right at the houses and continue on, dirt track now, past a row of wooden garages, with the works still on the right. The track then swings left to a large open space backed by the huge Prestonhill Quarry, with its pier to seaward. There's a good view to the Forth Bridge.

Across the open space take the track onwards, edged with lines of stone. Beyond a Pooh-trap it becomes a red cinder track rounding a point to St David's Bay and Harbour with the houses of Dalgety Bay (town) ahead. Dalgety Bay was started in the 1960s and has since sprawled on the hills to St David's Bay and inland, as the Donibristle and Hillend industrial estates, to the A921 coast road. It has the identikit look of any 'new town' and is no more Scottish than Margate. Fortunately, we avoid most of it. The whole area was important during the two World Wars with Donibristle Naval Base and HMS *Cochrane*, barracks and air defences – all completely gone.

The path runs tight by the sea, between wall and fence, but after a two-tone cairn the fence goes and there are good views out to sea, benches and a backing of woods. The cairn is painted white on the seaward side as a marker but it originally indicated the boundary of the Earl of Elgin's and the Fordell estates. Hidden inside the far end of the Letham Wood is Seafield House, a four-square building from the nineteenth century, rather austere in the dark local whinstone and with several blanked-out windows – no doubt filled in to dodge the window tax (another failed tax idea; abolished in 1868).

St David's Bay is in the process of being developed and will no doubt go into the amoebic spread of Dalgety Bay – which is perhaps better than nothing. The harbour was built (1752) to export coal from the Fordell mines, 7km inland from here. The coal was brought down on a wagon-way, along wooden rails and drawn by horses, the first 'railway' in Fife. Wood later gave way to iron and horses to steam-power. A similar line ran from Halbeath to Inverkeithing. The railway closed in 1946 but its line is still clear on the Pathfinder map (less so on the Landranger). Fordell Castle, as mentioned earlier, was built in 1580 by the Hendersons (it is now the home of the exotic MP, Sir Nicholas Fairbairn) and the people of the bay were little better than serfs until the 1755 and 1779 Emancipation Acts. Brick and tileworks were also established and the harbour was used for servicing minesweepers in the last war. The village was abandoned thereafter and now a more recent shipbreakers/scrapyard has also been demolished. An ambitious development has seen the harbour filled in to make a 'green' for St David's Harbour village, underway as this is published. Eventually there will be shops and a chance for refreshments in the village and a way on by the shore; meanwhile we walk along to a roundabout at the entrance: the road bending through houses of traditional character.

DALGETY BAY

Straight ahead is a stone wall, the original bounds of the policies of Donibristle House. There is an irony in such an old, bold symbol of public exclusion now surrounding the massive housing development of Dalgety Bay. Go through and turn right to wend through the wood (keep straight on where tracks cross) to come out at, and pass round behind, a small, sandy bay. Turn right at the road and then follow a footpath along the tall wall. More houses may well be built in this area up towards the small wood. The path comes out to the end of a street at present, heading off *behind* the first houses of this (Lumsdaine) road opposite where a footpath comes down from the east end of Crow Wood – and still following the cliff-top wall. The path doesn't follow the cliff edge, though, but runs along beside the back gardens of the houses. It then goes through a gap in the wall to descend by wide steps through Hopeward Wood back to sea-level before climbing again (wide steps, handrail) to a seat at a corner. From it, looking ahead, there is a longer point jutting out – Downing Point – marked by a marker pole at its end. This is where we are heading.

The path passes some more back gardens (or are they front gardens which are on the back side, or is the view side the front and the street side the back?) and climbs some more steps to reach beech trees at the start of Bathing House Wood. Here the path splits; don't take either fork but turn right and scramble up onto the knoll where you'll find a wartime gun and searchlight post. Continue down the spur and right out to the end of Downing Point. The tidal reef straight out is Thank Rock and the point aims at Inchcolm as well. Left of Inchcolm the end of Braefoot oil terminal can just be seen. If a supertanker is berthed you'll realise just how huge they are. The biggest can carry 300,000 tonnes of oil. We have a wide-angle view of the bridges in the other direction.

Looking to our immediate continuation you'll see houses rimming a bay and above the eastern end a tower or belfry sticks up. We head for this, so backtrack along the point and descend whinstone steps into Bathing House Wood (a small pine plantation) and along by the houses. If you walk the shore or grass edge, cut up a couple of houses from the end as we follow the tarred road (River View) as it makes an S-bend inland, turning off, right, to reach the obvious ruin with the tower or steeple, which is Donibristle Chapel, the Moray family vault.

The chapel was completed in 1732 as an Episcopalian chapel for the Moray family. 'The toffs not only sent their sons south to pick up the proper accent but to be correctly integrated in the religious hierarchy that has a person rather than God as its head' – the view of the socialist John Knox and Presbyterian Scotland. At least nine Earls of Moray are reputedly buried here. The architecture is strong, with bold quoins, and the west gable is topped by a bell tower which is in turn topped by a doocot, though I can't see it being very easily reached. The pigeons remain. The Moray arms and a Latin inscription lie above the entrance. The roof was removed in

49

1950, and in 1977 the vault entrance collapsed and it was possible to view the 17 lead coffins. The twelfth Earl was reputedly 7ft tall and an 8ft coffin rather confirms this.

Head on east through the pines and make down seaward as best as possible through current housing development past Donibristle House, a building which has had a fairly unfortunate history. Developers are taking on its restoration in grand scale but presumably a decent coastal path will be restored.

Donibristle House was first mentioned in the twelfth century as the residence of the Abbot of Inchcolm. At the Reformation it passed into the hands of the Commendator of Inchcolm. An Earl of Moray was the illegitimate son of James V and the half-brother of Mary Queen of Scots, but probably the best known was his grandson, the Bonnie Earl o' Moray of song and legend. He fell foul of James VI, so the Earl of Huntly and his cronies fired the house and murdered those escaping. Ironically, the murdered man's son was to marry the muderer's daughter.

That original house was destroyed in 1592. Two centuries later, in 1790, the west wing of a later house was destroyed and the main house burnt down in 1858. The shell of the mansion was pulled down in 1912, leaving the two 1720 wings we see, these being originally servants' quarters and connected by an underground tunnel with cells and a kitchen so big that they could garage several double-decker buses. The west wing had another fire in 1985. The navy used the east wing in the war and then it was the estate office. The crumbling central steps were crowned with ornate gates, described as one of the most beautiful pieces of ornamental ironwork in Scotland. They were removed by the council for safety and have disappeared from public view. I hope the new developers take out adequate fire insurance!

Walking on past the house we come out to trim surroundings again. There's a small point and the stones of an old pier can just be made out. This was the landing for Robert Moffat, the famous missionary (and father-in-law of David Livingstone) who once worked in the gardens of the big house and nearly lost his life pulling a fellow worker out of the sea. The next small bay is the New Harbour which ends at a sturdy harbour arm, recently renovated by the local sailing club. Overlooking the bay is the old stable block of Donibristle, with its circular windows and fine gateway. This had become a mere shell and its restoration as flats (Hopeward Court) is remarkable. The residents are hardly stable-lads and coachmen.

Beyond the harbour arm we come on the Dalgety Bay Sailing Club. Wend through the site to reach the start of Dalgety Bay itself. This is stony at high-waterlevel and becomes mudflats at low tide so is not attractive for humans – but birds love it. I spent an hour on the mudflats one day in winter and every inch was a web of wader footprints. (Don't be tempted to 'cut the corner' – waders of another sort are needed for that!) Inchcolm is closer and Braefoot is hidden and the walk round the bay is very pleasant. The woods of the Ross Plantation, marshy areas, the new gardens, Crow Hill

Historic St Bridget's Chapel, Dalgety Bay, which has an interesting graveyard close to the sea

Wood, as well as the shore and estuary, ensure a great variety of wildlife. Hearing woodpecker, bluetit, kestrel and eider all at once is typical. A treecreeper was working away, too. St Bridget's Chapel can be seen across at the back of the bay and we simply follow the paths nearest the sea to reach it.

There are often curlews working the mudflats here, probably the one browny-speckled wader that can be readily identified. Redshanks are as their name suggests and they tend to bob and have a distinctive '*pwee-wee-wee*' call and often work over lawns in the nearby gardens. The small sandpiper (common it never was!) is the real harbinger of spring, not the nasty cuckoo and, with its ceaseless bobbing and flitting flight and loud call '*willy-needy willy-needy willy-needy*', can soon

be recognised. The tiny ones are the problem. The ringed plover rushes everywhere, its legs turning to a blur as it darts in and out of the waves' sweep or skitters ahead of our passage. Dunlin and Sandeling can be confusing to the nascent ornithologist. Instantly recognisable is the oystercatcher (pied piper, as I knew it as a lad) with its waiter's garb and chef's voice. That bright orange beak is built for stabbing, and cockles and tellins are its prey. Some stab between the bivalves' halves, prising them apart; others simply batter through the shells, skills which are hereditary. You can tell the hammermen: their bills are blunt at the tip. Turnstones, being distinctly patterned, are easier, too, and they prefer rockier places or working along the tideline seaweed, tossing stones and weeds aside as they search for the

51

edible life underneath, their name quite suitable. All birds have something about their behaviour that is uniquely theirs. Had we eagle eyes we'd be better birdwatchers. All those difficult waders have different bills, of different lengths, so they can stab down into the sand for different prey, the razor-shells, cockles, tellins, the lugworms all being at different depths below the surface. Nature balances so well – except at the level of over-clever *Homo sapiens*.

St Bridget's Chapel entrance is on the landward side so turn up past the tiny watch-house to reach the gate. Watch-houses were used by guards overnight in early Victorian times to try and prevent body-snatching. With Edinburgh just across the water, the anatomy department no doubt found a few Fifers on the slab. Where the approach road comes in there is a small burn which flows through several basins, troughs for the horses bringing cortèges to the church.

St Bridget's is a delight in every way. It is old, receiving a charter from Inchcolm Abbey in 1178, and was dedicated to St Bridget in 1244. After the Reformation the local lairds built themselves 'lofts' (private pews in side wings) which still survive. One is quite a 'suite' and is reached by a winding stair. The graveyard, too, has plenty of interesting stones, including some dating from the seventeenth century, quite rare. The first stone on the right commemorates a drowning of a Liverpool lad of 13 in a shipwreck in the Forth in 1799. The bell from the church is now used in the church at Aberdour. It has the somewhat un-Presbyterian inscription, 'O mother of God remember me'.

Return to the shore path which runs along under the wall of the graveyard and above the shore. It is also the line of a sewage pipeline which breaks surface occasionally as it runs along Crow Hill plantation. The path leads to and skirts the seaward side of the sewage works to a vehicle turning area. Looking ahead, trees run down Ferny Hill to Braefoot Point at the end of the bay where there is a harbour arm, built for servicing the wartime defences which are situated on the hill. We work along the shore and then up by the trees to see these historical items. The shore is stony and, at full tide, one may have to scrabble along on the rough grass between tideline and the field fence. The islet in the Forth is the Haystack. The path switchbacks along the edge of the wood out to the harbour. If a very high tide rules out this route, walk up the tarred road from the turning area, turn first right and up towards the trees of Ferny Hill, rejoining the route there.

The pier is now unused. It was originally constructed by Irish navvies for landing ammunition during the First World War. A track heads up into the woods from it but we simply go up the slope overlooking the pier, between pine trees and gorse-edged cliff. As height is gained there are grand views upriver and also to Inchcolm and the Braefoot terminal.

The oil/natural gas terminal makes use of the safe water of Mortimer's Deep to allow supertankers to offload and, while there are tanks and other services here, the oil is basically just pumped up to Mossmorran for refining. That huge petro-chemical complex lies 6km northwards and, at night, looks like something out of a science-fiction fantasy. The ethylene gas is pumped onto tankers for export. A brick-built lookout-post tops our climb up. Don't be tempted to bear off left but take paths along, 20m in from, and parallel to, the cliff edge – and a diversion to the edge gives the most dramatic local view.

Before continuing along the cliff edge, walk directly inland and you'll find yourself on the massive concrete bastion of a gun emplacement hidden among the trees which are destroying the site. There are two circular settings and from the site you can see a narrow rail track heading off. If you follow this it leads to the magazine. When the big guns were first fired there were complaints from households in Leith who'd had their windows shattered. From the gun emplacement there is also an incline cut in the upper slopes which leads up to more wartime buildings and anti-aircraft guns, balloon anchorages, etc. There are more buildings on the summit itself, which is backed by a bite of quarry, so the easiest continuation is to return to the cliff-edge path. Just before another brick lookout-post in a hollow, the path swings left, inland, to run along by the oil terminal's security fence, there to guard the storage tanks below our route.

A stile leads to a small tarred road (the rejoining if the high-tide diversion has been used) which is simply crossed, and we continue in the same inland direction on a path strongly fenced off from the adjacent fields. There is an open sweep of view up to the bridges. Steps take us up onto a minor road, lined with daffodils in spring. Turn right and walk along past a communications mast in an enclosure. The clump of trees beyond it is called Tattie Knoll (a tumulus) and you'll notice all this area seems to be covered with dome-shaped hills, several lying beyond the approach road to the terminal. The big building ahead is St Colm's House, built in 1835 for the commissioner of the Moray estates.

A pedestrian underpass takes us below the oil terminal road. When we come to a T-junction, turn right along a private road which we follow right into Aberdour. Notice the fine avenue of trees coming in from the left to a crossroads where we head straight on. St Colm's House is off right. There are many fine trees: beech, yew, oak and young trees have been planted in plenty. Downan's Plantation is covered with my favourite flower each spring – the season's first flower, the snowdrop. Across the golf course, lying to our right all the way along, we can see the Bell Rock jutting out into the Forth. Beyond is Aberdour Bay and the wall of the Hawkcraig. (The white house is Hawkcraig House and the darker the Forth View Hotel – see Accommodation notes.)

After Downan's Plantation there is a superior but stereotyped housing estate on our left. Oaks line our route and away along the coast ahead we can pick out the big mast on the Binn above Burntisland. Nearer, there is an obelisk, just right of an obvious white house. This stands on Cuttle Hill and was built by the Mortons in 1744 as a landmark which could be picked out from their Midlothian estates at Dalmahoy.

ABERDOUR

Our avenue ends at a gate. Turn right along the road beyond which leads out to the east 'sundial' gates and lodge of the old St Colm estate, very splendid examples of their genre. Across the Aberdour High Street from the gates is the Woodside Hotel (expensive!). Over the entrance there is a bearded face, reputedly that of the Inverkeithing lad, Samuel Greig, who found fame with the Russian navy. It is almost certainly the face of the proprietor from a century ago when the Bell Inn was known as Greig's Hotel and, when he died, as the Late Greig's Hotel. By 1894 it was the Woodside Inn. The dominie was another Greig and Norway's great composer originally spelt his name so, being of Scots descent.

Those fascinated by doocots might like to take a quarter of an hour to see two on the western outskirts of Aberdour. Both are on private property, but you can see enough without trespassing.

Turn left from the gates and, after about 250m, just past the St Columba's Episcopalian church, there is a well-preserved round lectern doocot up in the garden of one of the houses. The owner has restored it beautifully. On the way back, behind a wall, you'll see a straightforward lectern doocot in a garden by a house, with a forestair and 1713 on the lintel. At Aberdour Castle there is one of the finest doocots in the country – of which more anon.

The centre of Aberdour lies along, right, from the gates. It is not a large town and is squeezed in awkwardly, one feels, due partly to the landscape and also there being two villages really, pushed to the edges of the Morton and Moray estates and split by the Dour Burn. There are several interesting things to see. Our route has, perforce, kept inland as the Braefoot terminal and spots like the Bell Rock bar effective coastal progress. Before calling it a day, a circular walk of Aberdour is recommended. If the day is wearing on, visit the castle first and also check the Accommodation notes so you can check in *en route* if possible.

Next to the hotel, now part of it, was Doune Hall and the date 1906 is still visible on a stone. Further along is St Fillan's church hall with its mural war memorial. This was the parish church till 1926 when the ancient church was restored and rededicated. Almost opposite, beside the Foresters Arms, is Shore Road, which leads down to the harbour. Poppies Coffee Shop (good home-cooking), Armando's Ristorante and the Cedar Inn lie just down here. The shopping area really ends at the bend marked by the Spence memorial clock, erected in 1910 to recall a long-serving GP. There is another tea-room (combined with an antiques shop) on the corner and the bakery next door has a curious 1739 stone above the lintel, 'Mr I.F.'.

The clock stands between the entrances of Aberdour Station and Aberdour Castle, both clearly signposted and both to be visited. Call in to the station first for a surprise. Not for nothing did stationmaster Andrew Philip's labours result in the Best-Kept Station in Britain Award in 1990. He'd already won the title for small stations but this was the ultimate, coming in ahead of 2,400 other competitors. The floral displays have even had a royal visit.

The entrance on the corner south of the clock leads to Aberdour House, acquired by the Earl of Morton in 1725 but dating to a century earlier. Twenty years ago it was largely gutted inside and desultory efforts to sell it failed. It is high time we had more effective legislation to prevent fine buildings being allowed to decay because owners won't do anything. Now it has been saved but at the cost of being surrounded by a claustrophobic housing scheme. A precious sundial in the grounds has been moved to the castle.

Walk on to the castle, which has had quite a lot of landscaping done of late, with the restoration of the south side terraces. In its heyday it was quite a grand place but in the early eighteenth century, following a fire, was allowed to go to ruin (the Earl of Morton bought Cuttlehill House, now Aberdour House, and resided there). A grateful Robert the Bruce granted Aberdour to his nephew Thomas Randolph after Bannockburn but his son sold it to a Douglas, in whose family it has been ever since. Their head became Earls of Morton, an earlier Earl being Regent for the infant James VI and having his head cut off by the Maiden (guillotine), and another being best remembered for imprisoning Mary Queen of Scots in Lochleven Castle. His eldest son never succeeded to the title as he was captured by the Barbary pirates. The Civil War nearly ruined the Mortons (but they were given Orkney and Shetland) but such things are relative; the bonny house and gardens survived, with a big walled area, terraces, orchards and, important for all, vegetable garden (and doocot). Not much of the original tower survives but central and eastern ranges have been preserved. The setting is perhaps more impressive than the actual buildings.

On one of the terraces is the sundial rescued from Aberdour House which I once heard described as 'a Roman altar standing precariously on four cannonballs'. Another sundial stands in the centre of the main walled garden and it was brought from Castle Wigg near Whithorn. On the south wall of the castle is a mural sundial, with Morton initials, so it hasn't come from anywhere. Being cut into the corner of the building gave longer hours of sunshine and a more effective clock.

Still very well preserved is a beehive-shaped doocot dating back to the sixteenth century. It is divided into four parts, outside, by string courses which served both as perches for the pigeons and as overhangs to keep out rats. A short flight of steps leads down to the interior, one of few open to the public. There are about 600 nesting boxes and in the centre of the floor you can see the foundation for the revolving structure of the ladders ('patence') which allowed the birds to be reached. Only the well-off were legally allowed to build doocots which produced a welcome addition of fresh meat when the common people were on salted beef, old mutton and haggis. The pigeons, of course, ate everybody's cereal crops. There are five doocots of this type in Fife. They were superseded by the lectern-shaped doocot, by far the commonest, which were usually rectangular with a single pitched roof, crowstep gables for perches and often had personal additions and adornments.

The fine old beehive-shaped doocot (dovecot) at Aberdour Castle

Sadly, most are now ruinous. Swank then saw the introduction of what could be termed architectural dove-cots, which come in all shapes and sizes, freestanding ('pepperpots') or incorporated into farmyards or gate-ways, a sort of practical folly in a way. I know of a church which was turned into a doocot and there's one combined with an ice house and at Wemyss Castle another took over an old wind-mill and Sir Andrew Wood's tower at Largo was used as a doocot.

Garden gates from the castle lead either directly to the church or to the Hawkcraig Road beside railway bridge 52. Ask the keeper to let you out one or other of these if possible, otherwise you'll have to walk back into town, and round by the main road. I'll describe it now for, even if the castle is closed, the church is not to be missed; the shore B&Bs can be conveniently approached that way and it is the continuation for the morrow for those staying in town. It makes an excellent circular walk.

From the clock tower continue along the main road (or go through the station again and over the footbridge to gain the main road). Walk eastwards. The big mansion up the slopes (with modern additions) is Hillside, once a D-listed school but now run privately. A James Stuart, who owned the house, is remembered as he fought the second-last duel in Fife. (This is our second 'second-last' duel of the day.) His opponent was Alexander Boswell, a son of Samuel Johnson's biographer, whom he killed.

At the black and white Drift Inn there is a sign pointing out SILVER SANDS ¼ and we follow this down Hawkcraig Road. Local pronunciation is 'Hawcraig' and an older name was Hallercraig; I reckon 'hawk' is a mod-ern corruption; there are plenty of hawthorns on the point. And I've a 1904 postcard (produced by the local butcher) which gives the name as Ha' Craig.

Just south of railway bridge 52 is the entrance to the church and castle gar-dens where we will come out if the cas-tle grounds were open, turning right onto the road. The church (St Fillan's) should be visited for it is both old and unusual, being first noted in 1178 and later becoming a great place of pil-grimage, there being a healing-well nearby. A stone, addressed to pilgrims, survives though its position blocks a leper window, a narrow slit which allowed lepers (kept outside) to hear and join in with the services. The architecture is unusual, with huge crowstep gables and roof. The roof was removed in 1796 when a church was built in the town. Now that building has gone and in 1926 the old church was fully restored. Several good grave-stones are on display at the entrance to the site; Revd Robert Blair, a famous Covenanter, is buried here, his stone inscribed in Latin. One gravestone has an inverted anchor and several have rhymes:

> My glass is run
> And yours is running
> Be feared to sin
> For death is coming

We continue down Hawkcraig Road. There are some pre-war houses (don't they look so much more com-fortable than their modern counter-parts?) and the newer Aberdour

Primary School. Just past Home Park is a fine house (now two) with a red roof and a turret-room. Looking past it, we can see the obelisk on Cuttle Hill.

Past the playing-field those coming this way tomorrow turn left for the Burntisland continuation – described in Day 3's text. The road swings slightly to the right along by a line of cottages before turning left, at a tiny dual-carriageway section, on the bend. After 100m turn in to the red-surfaced carpark and take the first track leading from its right-hand side. This puts in an S bend, passes a quarry and descends, at about the maximum gradient expected of a car, to reach Hawkcraig House and the Forth View Hotel (scenic B&Bs). The road ends at a ruined wooden pier, pointing to Inchcolm. Sadly, no sailings now run to Inchcolm from the closer, natural approach of the Fife shore.

Beyond the hotel are the red crags of the Hawkcraig, a popular rock-climbing venue. Before completing our circuit back to Aberdour it is worth heading to the top of the crags as the view is probably the best of the upper estuary. To do this (and it is also the route on tomorrow for those in Hawkcraig accommodation), backtrack to the start of the steep approach brae and, almost at once, turn off right up a twisty flight of pedestrian rock steps which will lead to the top of the cliff. Walk along the green path (with its giant's footprints) and turn off onto the highest point. Quite a viewpoint, isn't it?

Looking ahead we can see the Binn (the hill with the mast) above industrial-looking Burntisland, and Pettycur Point behind, all and more to be

A paddle steamer at Aberdour Harbour early this century (from an old postcard)

walked 'on the morn's morn'. The Silver Sands back the bay in front and, to reach them, the route tomorrow, for those coming this way, is to continue down the green path towards the sea-edge white and orange beacon, reaching the end of a tarred road (car turning area), which is then followed along, passing a small optics works unit, right, and various carparking areas on the left, to reach the Silver Sands Bay, and the coastal path beyond. Those continuing the circular walk will have to head back down the steps to the foot of the brae and then turn right along a well-made footpath that leads round to the harbour crossing the Dour Burn at the head of the bay.

The harbour is now purely used by yachties and there is a snack-bar in season. A wartime mine (a Shipwrecked Mariners' Society collection box!) graces the promenade, which is Shore Road, and leads up into town again. Manse Road (Fairways Hotel) is off left and several eating-places (as mentioned earlier) lie at the top end of Manse Road.

PRACTICAL INFORMATION / ACCOMMODATION

Telephone code: (0383)

Aberdour is only moderately equipped with accommodation but if there is any difficulty, as there may be in high summer, book ahead, even if only phoning the night before, or simply take a train or bus along to Burntisland where there is a fair range of digs available and where you could book in for two nights. Burntisland Accommodation is listed under Day 3.

Aberdour Hotel and Restaurant, High Street	860325
Cedar Inn, Shore Road	860310
Flock House, Seaside Place	860777

Dunraggie, Murrell Road (off Main Street, east)	860136
Hawkcraig House (Hawkcraig Point). Taste of Scotland Dinner. Super setting	860335
Forth View Hotel (Hawkcraig Point)	860402
Fairways Hotel, Manse St (off Shore Road). More expensive	860478
Woodside Hotel, High Street. Luxurious and expensive	860328
Moss Cottages East, 1½km west, on A921 (GR 174848)	860136

Taxi: Dalgety Bay   (0383) 824747, 822891
Inverkeithing (see under Day 1)
Burntisland (see under Day 3)

DAY 3 *Widening the View*

Burntisland–the Binn

Maps to use: Bart 46, OSLR 66, OSPF 394 (NT 08/18)/395 (NT 28)
Walking distance: 8km (28 km)

This is a short coastal day but recommended, on arrival, is a climb of the Binn, an exceptionally fine viewpoint; there would also be a second chance to explore anything in Aberdour missed the night before. The path to Burntisland is well made throughout.

ABERDOUR TO BURNTISLAND

The ballad of 'Sir Patrick Spens', which starts with the ringing:

> The King sits in Dunfermline toun,
> Drinking the blude-red wine;
> 'O whar will I get a skeely skipper
> To sail this guid ship o' mine?'

later has the grim lines:

> Half ower, half ower, tae Aberdour,
> It's fifty fathoms deep
> And thair lies guid Sir Patrick Spens
> Wi the Scots Lords at his feet.

This is generally given as the journey to fetch the Maid of Norway to succeed her grandfather, Alexander III (of which more shortly) but she was taken to Orkney and died there, nor would the king have despatched a vessel for that purpose, being still alive. Maybe this was a preliminary embassy. Wemyss of Wemyss and Michael Scot (the Wizard) are known to have made the journey. Anyway, the poem is irrevocably tied to Aberdour, and Alexander III was buried at Dunfermline. Burntisland is twinned with the Norwegian town of Flekkefjord, a modern link over that stormy sea. (Buckhaven and Methil together twin with Swedish Trelleborg, and Kirkcaldy and Levenmouth have German twins.)

If starting from Hawkcraig accommodation, the route on to the Silver Sands was described at the end of yesterday's write-up. If starting from the town, follow the main road east and then turn down Hawkcraig Road (also already described) till the sports ground is passed (left); then, just past it, a track bears off, marked by an old road-roller on one side and a rosebed on the other (backed with a NO GOLF ALLOWED sign). Follow this track which soon becomes a 'Burntisland red' cinder track. It swings left just beyond a large solitary tree (carparking in season) but go through a pedestrian opening and on in the same line right down to the sea, a route lined with cherry trees. Turn left at the foot to go through the gap in the wall, the start of the well-made coastal path to Burntisland.

The Silver Sands Bay is lined with a holiday-season array of toilets, cafés, playground and picnic areas, and can be busy at times. Two sewage pipes running into the sea mark this popular spot. To be fair, Fife's beaches have been undergoing a transformation – at the dictates of the EC, one may add – and its waters have become clean enough for the return of a rare fish, the sparling or cucumber-smelt, which, it is thought, abandoned most estuaries due to silting and pollution from sewage, industry and agriculture wastes. Excellent eating, the fish gains one of its names from its unlikely smell: a shoal could be noted from the shore by the strong smell of cucumber. Older maps show this area as Whitesands Bay but the Victorians changed its name to the more romantic Silver Sands – good for the tourist trade.

Once through the gap in the wall, look back now and then while walking on (something it is easy *not* to do) for there are good views to the Silver Sands. Burntisland will be reached in about an hour of pleasant walking.

The path is often on top of embankments built to protect the railway which is just over the wall on the inland side. At high tide in a westerly gale the path is apt to be splashed by spray. The first rocks past the initial embankment are known as the Hanging Craig. There are many jutting areas of sandstone, often veined with iron. Mature trees grow right to sea-level. A huge beech dominates the path just before it goes under railway bridge 54, a good place for a pause.

One Christmas Eve, a day of frosty clarity, I came this way (east–west) and in that sharp silence all I could hear were wildlife sounds: eiders and seals on the sea, two curlews and a whole bedlam of pied pipers (oyster-catchers) on the dark, seaweedy rocks, and a cawing of rooks beyond the dead elms. Two herons flew past on their newspaper wings. One advantage of the winter day was that, once through the tunnel, the bare trees didn't mask the view as they tend to in leafy summer. Not that I could see much with the sun a golden dazzle over Edinburgh and the Forth sheeted silver. This is one of the best woodland sections of our whole trip.

There's yet another geological hiccup, the first indications being a certain dampness and water leaking onto the path. We have hit a line of limestone crags. You'll note the spout of a well ('well' in Scotland often means a

61

spring) and, shortly, come on a castel-lated bridge over a burn which comes down as a fall above the path level. The Starley has a high lime content. Locals call this the Fossil Falls as objects placed in the burn will soon be coated with lime, as are the crags where water seeps down their face.

The path runs along a curve of wall and then pops out onto a corkscrew of road which has descended by several Victorian mansions and runs down to Carron Harbour. Our path onwards is clear enough, but do first cross railway bridge 55 to look at the view – upstream you will recognise all the headlands back to the bridges. The grassy point beside the harbour is a pleasant spot for a picnic. On the west is a ruined harbour arm, Starley Harbour, while on the east is the revived Carron Harbour. Up above the former, the battlements of a seemingly old castle may be seen. This is not what it appears, for it was only built after the last war and is tiny. Much of it is authentic material as the builder had collected bits and pieces from all sorts of derelict buildings and ruins and incorporated them in his plans. Easterheughs stands just off the A92 and can be clearly seen near the top of a brae on that road.

Both Starley and Carron Harbours supplied limestone to Falkirk (hence the name Carron), the original centre of Scotland's iron industry. A carronade was one form of gun named after the boom town, and used by the British navy to good effect. The harbour now has minor boatyards and slips. Starting off along the path you'll notice the wall leans ominously, despite being strapped up. A bridge under our path,

various cuttings, abutments and other stonework point to the busier days of Carron Harbour when trains brought the limestone in from Ninelums Quarry. Now it is all a tangle of ivy, brambles and trees.

The next landmark is a huge radio mast in the big field above the path which here is shut in between walls on both sides, with the railway cut in below on the seaward side. The view out to sea looks across to Arthur's Seat and the silhouette of Old Edinburgh running up to the castle; the Pentland Hills crest behind like some dark breaker about to engulf the capital. The path drops in an S-bend and a mesh fence with a decaying notice about trespassers is the start of the most industrial mile of the whole walk – Burntisland's aluminium-processing plant.

BURNTISLAND

The red bauxite ore is imported to Burntisland from Ghana by sea (about the only current use of the harbour), bulk-carrying lighters ferrying it from the large vessels anchored offshore. Alumina is extracted from this and sent on for further processing to produce the actual metal. Being an electrical process, works were built at Fort William and Kinlochleven where cheap hydro-power was available. There is a great deal of waste with the first step in the process and red is the colour of Burntisland. You'll see a red mountain above the works and, behind that long seaside wall on the right, the whole green area is land reclaimed from the sea by dumping the red

Rossend Castle above Burntisland Harbour, from an old photograph
(© Kirkcaldy Museum Collection)

waste. It was landscaped in 1982 and has changed from red to green. Aluminium itself has not been made since 1972 but the alumina and dried hydrates are used in a hundred products, from spark plugs to toothpaste, from pottery to fire retardants.

Well along the works area the path dips and there is a pedestrian tunnel under the railway; take this. It leads out to a red-stained settling-pond round which we wend, coming out onto a dirt track. Over right from here you can see the tidal mill building: obviously old walls but a brick gable and modern roof. Turn left along to the tarred road at a multiple crossroads at the foot of a hill. Opposite is Haddow Grove. Take the steps up behind the Haddow Grove sign, beside the houses, and then turn left up what is Melville Gardens. At the top, on the right, is a range of buildings, now private houses but once the stables of Rossend Castle when it was an affluent mansion. A plaque has the date 1816 and the initials ESB.

Rossend Castle itself stands back from our road as it swings left again (still Melville Gardens), a fine example of what can be done to restore an historic building and use it in a practical way. It is the base of the Hurd Rolland Partnership of restoration architects. I wonder what Mary Queen of Scots would make of drawing-boards and fax machines in her bedroom?

In the corner of the grounds there is a small folly/gazebo which is actually a listed building and dates to 1800. There is a fine view over the harbour. Tradition has it that Agricola used the port and built a fort inland on Dunearn Hill.

Burntisland is another of those corrupted names. Explaining it as land burnt to improve the soil is nonsense, an attempt to make sense of a modern name. Brint Iland, Bruntisland, Bertiland and other forms pre-dated that, and for most of history it was simply Wester Kinghorn, Kinghorn originally being the more important place (royal burgh twelfth century as against Burntisland, sixteenth century). Railway ferry, shipbuilding and the aluminium works in turn have meant Burntisland has long outgrown Kinghorn. The town is now utterly tied to the aluminium works, a dangerous case of all the eggs being in one basket.

Continuing, we pass swings and an old drinking-fountain and come to an archway on the road. On the east face there are coats-of-arms and several dates. Just beyond the gateway we cross the railway again: left we see the aluminium works for the last time, right we look along the track and the harbour area, the West Dock below us. Right of it lay Cromwell's Dyke, a defence built in the 1657 occupation. (Cromwell seems to rival Mary Queen of Scots and Bonnie Prince Charlie for the number of places he visited.) Cromwell thought very highly of Burntisland as a port – but then it was *portus gratiae* in Roman times, when Agricola landed here.

Burntisland was once an important ferry port, passengers crossing to Granton and Edinburgh. From 1850 to 1890 there was a train ferry, the world's first, designed by Thomas Bouch who is apt only to be remembered by the disaster of his Tay Bridge. The actual wagons were shipped across, a rare experience which ended completely with the building of the Forth Bridge, rather as the Queensferry car ferry came to a dead stop when the Road Bridge was opened. And now they are thinking of another road bridge! A passenger ferry operated until 1952 and in 1991 a hydrofoil passenger service commenced, but sadly proved uneconomical.

Just 20m on from the bridge is a gap in the wall, right (lamp-standard), with steps leading down. Take this and go on down the broad steps of the alley to go under the railway. (Along to the right there is a good view of the castle.) Turn left to go under the railway again and you are at the start of the High Street.

Across on the right (Harbour Place) is a restored group of old buildings with crowstepped gables and other features. The Green Tree on the corner has a decorative lintel sign and a stone, higher up, dated 1884. The Smugglers Inn (Harbour Place) is much older. Not far along the High Street, left, is the oldest building in Burntisland, the Star Tavern (established in 1671) which has a painted sign which is a self-portrait. Not far past where Lothian Road comes in you'll see a cross marked in the middle of the road. This marks the site of the old town mercat cross which had to give way to growing traffic demands.

Continuing along the High Street, the 1907 Carnegie Library and the old municipal building with its clock spire are the next features. There is a museum upstairs, reached from the library and open during library hours. They will switch on the audio show for you – a most enjoyable recreation of last century. A back room has displays on the town's major historical interests. Telephone (0592) 260732. Round the corner, first right, in the Kirkgate, is the Tourist Information Office, (0592) 872667.

Walk along the Kirkgate to Somerville Square, the south side of which is a notable row of old buildings which have been carefully restored and with which the modern developments have been well blended. (Contrast the jagged concrete reef of houses along Somerville Street.) The Somerville name commemorates Mary Somerville, daughter of Sir William Fairfax who fought at Camperdown. She married Samuel, the son of Samuel Greig, the Russian Grand Admiral. Largely through determined self-education Mary became a notable scientist, with publications on such topics as the 'Mechanics of the Heavens' and 'Molecular and Microscopic Science'. As a girl she was fascinated by the fossils she saw in the local limestone being exported at the harbour. She taught herself algebra but got into trouble as the servants 'clyped' on her as the one using up so many candles. Actively discouraged by well-meaning parents, she gradually found books and mentors to help her before being married to her cousin and moving to London. He died within three years and she later married another cousin,

an army doctor who became a great supporter, and she was able to do all she wanted – on top of being a full-time mother and homemaker. She was well into her nineties when she died, a quite remarkable person. Somerville College in Oxford is named in her honour. The Fairfax home was in the Watson tenement on the south side of the street.

At the top of Kirkgate stands the church hall. Turn left onto East Leven Street and there is the solid, famous parish church. Before considering it go down the lane beside the attractive new gates to a viewing terrace overlooking the harbour, a harbour which is pretty well devoid of activity other than the aluminium company's bulk-handling operations. Lime, herring, vitriol (sulphuric acid), oil and, above all else, coal were once exported. At the end of last century something like three-quarters of a million tons a year were exported, but Methil gradually won an exporting 'war'. The 1914–18 War saw shipbuilding boom and over 420 ships were built here in all; in the 1939–45 War it was mostly aircraft-carriers. Shipbuilding ended in 1968 but oil-rig construction has had some success since.

Head back (you don't really have much option!). Across East Leven Street is a recent architectural 'creation', using the belfry and frontage which was all that remained of the Free church which was destroyed by fire in 1978. The siting of the Free church right opposite the parish church could be called provocative. The parish church gates will be locked (vandals, alas, are no respecters of precious places) but the curator will be pleased to rendezvous with you if you

65

phone beforehand (even on reaching Burntisland – there's a phone box at Rossend Castle.) At present the curator is W.B. Mackie, tel: (0592) 873275. A notice informs us that St Columba's is the oldest Scottish post-Reformation church still in use. Many would rate it the most interesting church building we'll see on our whole walk, so don't miss it. The gates, erected in 1992, celebrate the church's 400th anniversary.

Building a church was a precondition of James V's charter for Burntisland. (The 1243 Kirktoun building was inadequate.) The new church was built as a rectangle with the pulpit in the centre, to emphasise 'the equality of believers' but merchants and members of the craft guilds (hammermen, bakers, masons, etc.) soon took seats in the gallery and decorated them with panels showing their arms. These were painted over in 1822 but rediscovered in 1907. The inordinately splendid laird's pew became the magistrates' pew latterly. James VI, unable to travel, called a General Assembly to Burntisland and it was here, in 1601, that the plans for a translation of the Bible into English were put in hand: the King James Version, as it was to be called.

The balcony is also reached by an outside stair which can be seen from the churchyard. This allowed fishermen to join the congregation with minimal disturbance. On the loft door and above the main door (dated 1592) are anchors, apparently shown

Burntisland Church, one of the most historical on the walk. The outside stair leads to the sailors' loft

upside down but in reality indicating 'anchored in heaven'. The big tower was added in 1749. The weather-vane is a gilded cockerel. On a window-sill is a model of the church with a removable roof to show the interior fittings, all complete. At a scale of a quarter-inch to one foot it took 700 hours of work — and 28,000 matchsticks. There is no stained glass in the church so the light floods in over the box pews.

Take time to wander about the churchyard. Right round in the far corner is the impressive Watson family monument, with a horizontal skeleton along the foot. There are several fine inscriptions. Note the ⯿ (reversed four), an old symbol used by merchants, some suggesting it represents the four corners of the world.

Continue along East Leven Street. After a narrow section on the right is a building of ecclesiastical interest, called the Parsonage (now flats for the elderly). It was built in 1854 by the Revd George Hay Forbes, a Victorian 'Episcopal liturgist and publisher', a rather bony entry and worth fleshing out. Forbes, newly ordained, came to Burntisland in 1848 and started a school (in what is now the Inchview Hotel) which soon had 90 pupils, so expansion was needed. But first he needed a house and built the Parsonage, not hesitating to help dress stone himself though crippled (with polio?). Early in life he'd spent years in bed though active mentally – he eventually spoke 20 languages and could read 30 more. To assist moving about the house he fixed a rope on the top floor and simply abseiled down. To save climbing stairs a speaking tube led up from the basement where he set up the Pitsligo Printing Press. A huge translation scheme with different people translating individual books of the Bible had Forbes tackling Ecclesiastes. He didn't just translate the book, he *printed* it as well, in 41 languages at least, including Hebrew, Arabic, Ethiopic, Syriac, Peshitto, Persian and Greek – a typesetter's nightmare! When he arrived in Burntisland, nobody would help the incomer priest when he fell after his crutches slipped on the street, but 21 years later he was the town's provost. This dynamo could relax and there is a delightful picture of his way of indulging his pleasure in paddling. He used to hire a two-wheeled cart and horse and be taken down at half tide and sat at the back, feet dangling in the sea.

We come out onto the old common, known as the Links (Lammerlaws Road, right), where we turn left back to the High Street. Facing us is a highly decorative building in two-toned sandstone which stands on the site of the East Port when the town was walled in the days of Charles I. The Old Port has decorative balconies and above the corner entrance is a whole succession of features, right up to the pointed turret roof. Flanking the door arch are two 'golden salamanders' (or 'yellow lizards', if you are less romantic); then, over the door, there are stone figures holding a shield and, higher, a *triple* sundial, the faces with inscriptions: 'Time Flies'; 'I mark Time, Dost thou?'; 'I only count the Sunny Hours'.

Opposite the port at the Links entrance (behind a phone box) is a charming 1887 fountain with a canopied cherub figure, daubed by vandals probably, but look inside the canopy for the crocodiles, a unique feature. The fountain once stood across the road where Cromwell Road heads up, the site now occupied by the town's war memorial.

The Links had a golf course as early as 1668. (The club is, after St Andrews and Crail, the oldest in Fife.) In sunny summer this is a popular picnic area and the shows (travelling fair) may be in full swing. Highland Games are held in the third week in July; finding accommodation then may be difficult. Over towards the Lammerlaws (west end of the bay) there used to be a sea-water swimming pool (1935) but it closed in 1979 and the site was demolished in 1990. The prow of the Lammerlaws has lime kilns and Cromwell built a fort there in 1651. Criminals were once hung on that windy headland. In 1608 lodges were erected on the Links to isolate plague victims and in 1746 there were 3,000 Hessian troops encamped there thanks to the doings of Bonnie Prince Charlie. The church with the large steeple along the Kinghorn Road is the Erskine United Free Church, a denomination that split off in 1733.

Much of the Burntisland accommodation overlooks the Links. (If a quieter village atmosphere is wanted then a bus or train to Kinghorn is possible.) Once accommodation is fixed up, the second part of the day can be undertaken. The evening (sunset, early or late in the season) can be rewarding as colours sweep over the widening estuary, especially if seen from the height of the Binn: a wee hill with a big view. Allow two hours at least for the ascent and return.

THE BINN

From the East Port/fountain/war memorial head up Cromwell Road to a roundabout (the East Toll) and straight on beyond on what is the A909 Cowdenbeath Road. The Binn dominates the houses and playing-fields, right, built on the grounds of the now demolished Binn House.

The Binn is part of an old volcano and the crumbly lavas are still exposed on the flank as you can see. The same rock breaks through on the Kinghorn Road between the cemetery and the Kingswood Hotel on tomorrow's route.

Walk right out of the town. The houses on the right are followed by a long field and then woodland where, 25m on, there is a sign for the path we want: PUBLIC FOOTPATH TO STANDING STANES ROAD. Go up the worn steps and follow the path up a woody dell which is, in reality, the waste from a quarry, part of which you'll see off left. At the top of the wood a gate leads into a field which is crossed to another gate/stile and, 25m beyond that, turn right. There's another sign, PUBLIC FOOTPATH TO THE BIN (sic). We pass a small dam which is the home of coots and ducks. The woods, in spring, echo to the sound of the yaffle, the apt Scots word for the green woodpecker.

A green road leads on from the gate, curving up towards the big mast. Looking down the way you can see where a refuse tip has filled a considerable area of the old quarry. Leave the green track to climb steeply by the edge of the wood to gain the easy crest of the crags, a grand scenic ridgewalk.

There are stiles at all the field fences and a vandalised view indicator.

Inchkeith and Burntisland from the summit of the Binn

The mast lies inland a bit, a real beacon of a landmark, with the Lomond Hills (cones of their volcanoes showing) sprawled right of the mast. The cliffs above the houses have been draped with wire mesh and there are avalanche barriers just like they have in the Alps for snow; in places the rock is buttressed with concrete supports and trees have been left to grow – all pointers to a certain lack of adhesion in the rock. In odd places there are hints of basaltic columns. Most of our high points of the walk are volcanic intrusions in a world of softer sandstones and shales – and, of course, coal measures. The promontories of Queensferry and Hound Point, the islands of Inchkeith and the Hay, Pettycur, Kincraig Point, the Binn and Largo Law are all volcanic.

If the tide is out you will see the sweep of sand leading out to the Black Rocks – tomorrow's best route. The whole river up to the bridges lies spread like a map and on the other side the eye can range from Edinburgh right along to the bold hump of the Bass Rock. Fife Ness is east of that so you can gauge our future progress. We begin to lose height again and, ahead, can't but notice red spoil heaps with pipes and roads, the current site for dealing with the waste from the aluminium works. The waste is brought here for settling on what was once the site of a shale-oil works, another industry which has come and completely gone. The shale-oil industry was better known on the Lothian side but tunnels ran under the Forth and in 1878 oil was discovered on the Binn. A village to house a thousand men was built, with a school, mission hall, etc. A fire in the huge works in 1892 was a setback, then American oil undercut prices and the company went into liquidation in 1905.

There's a larger wooden stile out the last field and we walk along by concrete posts (fence supports *sans* fence) to the start of the spoil area which is well fenced off with big notices warning of the unsafe ground. A few ruined buildings on the left are all that is left of the Binnend works and village. We turn right, through the line of an old wall, to angle down concrete steps onto a gritty whinstone-grey path. This is on the line of an older works road – you can see masonry edging it, right, while below is a tangle of brambles and willowherb which love growing on derelict sites. There are a couple of 'Pooh-traps' to stop kids rushing out onto the road which is joined just before the Burntisland golf clubhouse. Simply turn right and walk back down to the East Toll roundabout and into Burntisland.

PRACTICAL INFORMATION / ACCOMMODATION

Telephone code: (0592)

Tourist Information Office, 4 Kirkgate
872667
1 South View, Lammerlaws (seaside)
873270
39 Cromwell Road (up from East Port)
873838
67 Cromwell Road   872108
27 Craigkennochie Terrace
(off Cromwell Rd)   874471
28 Kirkton Road   873320
45 Kinghorn Road   984037
93 Kinghorn Road   873288
103 Kinghorn Road   872193
127 Kinghorn Road   873165
148 Kinghorn Road   873877

Inchview Hotel, 69 Kinghorn Rd
(expensive)   872239
Orcadia Hotel, Lochies Rd
(off Kinghorn Rd)   872230
Charene Hotel, 241 High Street   872617
2 Grange Road (off Aberdour Rd/top of
town)   874223
Kingswood Hotel, Kinghorn Rd (halfway
to Kinghorn, expensive)   872329

Kinghorn Accommodation is listed under Day 4, and could be reached by bus/train or an hour's walk along the sands.

Taxi: (0592) 872408, 874474, 872224
Tide Times: Tel. (0592) 872236 (Burntisland Docks)

DAY 4 *Lang Toon, Lang Syne*

Pettycur–Kinghorn–Kirkcaldy

Maps to use: Bart 46, OSLR 66 and 59, OSPF 395 (NT 28)/385 (NT 29/39)
Walking distance: 10km (38km)

This is a short day in terms of miles but there is a great deal to see and do so don't slitter. If the tide is out, the sands to Kinghorn offer an unusual walk. Kinghorn is a quiet but friendly place, and the walk on to Kirkcaldy has plenty of geological interest. Do make sure of reaching the museum there at least an hour before its 5 p.m. closing time.

Kirkcaldy is one of those names which is sure to catch the unwary with its pronunciation. Try *Cur-coddy*. (The meaning is not very clear.) The day is described right through to the far end of Kirkcaldy but this is for textual tidiness: where you stop will depend on your chosen accommodation.

TO PETTYCUR

Wherever you are staying in Burntisland, head down to the shore. From the cherub fountain cut across the Links, more or less in line with some poles, aiming for a bridge (no. 67) under the railway – just right of swings and a blue-painted shelter. This will bring you out onto the Promenade, which is followed to its end (seasonal tea-room and small pier). If staying out the Kinghorn Road, walk across the Links (from a phone box) to a bridge (no. 68) under the railway. If staying on the Kinghorn Road beyond the Links, cut down Lochies Road (beside the Orcadia Hotel) and under a low bridge (no. 69) to a small pier, beside the tearoom at the end of the Promenade. And here the route onwards has to be decided.

When the tide is lapping up against the railway embankment there is no choice; you retreat under the railway to the A921 which has to be followed most of the way to Kinghorn, passing the Kingswood Hotel and the monument to Alexander III. There is another tunnel (bridge no. 70) under the railway opposite the cemetery, so you can always have a second look at the tide level. If the sea is lapping against the railway embankment, keep to the A921.

If at all possible try to avoid high tide, for the Burntisland–Kinghorn sands are some of the most extensive we'll meet. After days by the sea we should be aware of tides, and it would be easy enough to linger an hour in Burntisland to make the sands walk possible. At low tide do walk the 1km out to the Black Rocks and then along the margin of the sea. The Black Rocks become covered at highest tides but can safely be taken in at low tide on our walk. An old book on Burntisland shows this area as proper land 200 years ago, all eroded and won by the sea since then. Salmon-fishing posts can still be seen in the sands, another industry which has disappeared. I'm always torn between wanting to walk the sea's edge and wanting to go along the high-tide mark; ornithologists will prefer the former, beachcombers the latter. In 1652 the Burntisland magistrates organised a horse-race along the sands to Pettycur.

Either way, halfway along the great sands, note the obelisk-like monument above the railway beside the A92 (no access from the shore). There is actually a granite cross on top of a long pillar set on a wider base with pictorial and explanatory plaques. It is a memorial to Alexander III, last of the Celtic

The monument to Alexander III who rode his horse over the cliffs here and was killed in 1286

kings, who died in a riding accident hereabouts in 1286 and thereby produced one of the great speculative *if*s of history. He was hurrying, on a dark and stormy night, to reach Kinghorn Castle and his new wife, Yolande, and was either thrown from his horse or it went over the rotten cliffs. They were found dead at the bottom the next day. His heir was a granddaughter, the Maid of Norway, and she died in Orkney on the way back to Scotland, thereby leaving the succession open to claimants. Edward I of England was asked to arbitrate; instead, he tried to take over, which led to the Wars of Independence, to Bruce and his successors, the Stewarts, who in turn became kings of both countries. *If* Alexander had not been so desperate to get home, *if* he had lived and sired a male heir again, *if* he had not crossed the ferry to Fife (several tried to deter him), *if* he had not gone on in the dark (several tried to stay him) . . . well, the whole history of the world would have been different, wouldn't it?

A bluff over the sands with caravans on it (not the huge array of Pettycur Bay caravan park tiered up beyond the monument) has rocks at its foot known as Wallispaw, and if the tide is up to these you'll have to scramble a rough switchback path along under the bluff. Beyond these rocks is Pettycur Bay, another superb bathing beach, safe and clean (even to EC standards) with its eastern end marked by a harbour arm. Rather pretentious houses now range the back of the bay.

If high tide has forced you to walk along the A92 then it is possible to walk down again to the sands here. On the left of the A921, Pettycur Bay car-avan park dominates the road (there is a restaurant and an area for camping); then, reached by the Lochty Bridge (no. 71, over the railway), is the Sandhills caravan park. Turn in here and, at once, turn left on a fenced-off pedestrian right-of-way down to Pettycur Bay (well signposted).

The area of new houses along to the harbour was originally the site of a salt-works (1870) and, in 1902, became a bottleworks. The sand from the shore was used for this but it became so dirty with coal dust (from the spoil being tipped into the sea further along the coast) that this stopped in 1961. Thus Kinghorn's sole industry, a profitable industry, was eventually gobbled up by a big firm with loss-making works in the south. Kinghorn was then shut down – an all too familiar story – and was eventually demolished. You may still pick up tiny green or brown beads of glass in the sand.

The very obvious prow overlooking Pettycur Bay is the Witches' Point or Hill so called as poor women were burnt there (the last in 1644), just outside what is now a fairly crowded cemetery. I've read that if a witch was dealt with leniently she was only partly burned then tossed over the cliff-face still tied by the long chain to the iron ring in the rock (still in place) thereby giving a quick end to her suffering. At one time the cemetery was the site of the Leech Loch which mysteriously drained away in the eighteenth century, long before the road was put in along the coast in 1842 or the railway burrowed through the hillside. The seemingly empty green area is full of unmarked paupers' graves. The most noteworthy stone is to local author

Annie S. Swan, and one corner has many Polish names. You can learn a great deal of local history just wandering round a cemetery. A lot of the stones are flat, not from vandalism, but the big gale of February 1968. A path cuts up from the road behind the new houses if the curious want to explore. A few fulmars nest on the crumbling volcanic crags, an SSSI for its flora, including Scotland's only wild clary site. Clustered bellflower, hairy rocket, quaking grass, cowslip, several stonecrops, thrift and campion also grow on the slope.

One of Fife's old Pettycur Milestones, indicating the once important Forth ferry terminal

The harbour arm at the end of the bay gives shelter for a collection of small craft used for pleasure and fishing, but it dries out at low tide and has had little done to it in the way of upkeep since it was last rebuilt in 1760.

How badly silted-up the harbour is can be seen from the corner steps down to the sands. There are 17 of them – but how many show? One of the problems was keeping the sand out of the harbour, and, slogging-labour being neither popular nor efficient, a brilliant solution was found. A big tidal pool was created where the carpark is now sited and when the tide receded a sluice was opened and this poured out onto the harbour side, removing the sand.

Originally Kinghorn was the town above the next bay east, set high and inland, while Pettycur was just the harbour. The fulmar-busy heights overlooking Pettycur Harbour were called Crying or Crying-oot Hill (Shouting Hill), the reason being, I suspect, that someone was always being sent up there when the ferry was spotted to yell the news up to Kinghorn where the passengers would be ensconced in the pubs waiting. Another tradition says the yells were from those watching for shoals of herring out in the firth and shouting their tidings down to the fishing boats in the harbour. Crying Hill, now built over, was the likely site of the castle of Alexander III and an important royal residence in the thirteenth century. Living on Crying-oot Hill as I do gives me a spooky feel for history. Sticking out further than anything else between the bridges and Elie Point we catch every gale that blows. The worst (February 1968) took off our garage roof, and a milk bottle carrier with two empties, left outside the landward door, was found inside the garage – having come in via the roof. We never found the bottles.

The Kinghorn name has a complex derivation. (There's also a Kinghornie on the coast south of Stonehaven.) In a document of 1374 it is given as Kyngorn and is locally pronounced *Kin-gorn* with the stress on the second syllable. It means 'boghead' and near Kirkcaldy there's a Myregornie, an example of a name in one language then linked with a translation. It is interesting to see the latest dictionary of Scottish place-names giving 'head of muddy ground' (which is all right) but then saying this is because 'the town overlooks the mudflats of the Firth of Forth', whereas the old boghead was inland (Kinghorn Loch backs the town). *'Cean-gorm'*, meaning 'blue head', is often given as a derivation, illustrating the dangers of picking too easy a solution. Pettycur I've seen given as *petit coeur* (French: 'little heart') but it is one of the many Pictish names with the *pit*, *pet*, *petty* prefix (Pitlochry, Petercultur, Pethymuick) and meant 'a parcel of land, a place'. The same root has *peth* in Cornwall, *piece* or *patch* in English and, from Latin, *petit* in French.

INCHKEITH

My southside windows look out to Inchkeith Island. (All the Forth Islands are inches, another word for island; Keith comes from the northern family of that name.) The island, unlike Inchcolm or the May Island, has no sailings so will probably have to remain temptingly visible but unreachable. It is part of Kinghorn parish so I have a proprietary interest in it and have canoed out to the island many times. The beam of its summit lighthouse flickers across my bedroom walls in comforting fashion.

The name Inchkeith is ancient. Malcolm II, hard pressed by Danish attacks, rewarded the Caithness Catli chief, Robert de Keith, with the island – though the Earl Marischal family did not hold it for long. For most of its life it was a fortress island and remained so till it was sold by the government a decade ago. Schemes to turn it into a children's adventure playground or an exclusive commuters' suburb for Edinburgh fell through, but for a few years it was an animal sanctuary. Odd schemes are not new: James IV housed a dumb woman with two infants on the island to see what language they would come to speak. Both 'languages of God' (Hebrew and Gaelic) were claimed, but the truth was that the children didn't speak at all.

There were many experiments made with the lighthouse as it was so accessible. The dioptric system was first tried there, for instance. In 1899 when the foghorn was installed it sounded almost non-stop for 130 hours, so people living on the Fife coast were driven bonkers. It was turned to face seawards thereafter. The old familiar roar has gone, replaced by a shrill bleep, and now the light has been made automatic while the mixture of ruins, jungle and gulls dying of botulism from scavenging in Edinburgh's rubbish dumps hardly makes Inchkeith a cheerful place. Weekend yachts and boats enjoy visiting the harbour but it would be nicer if the vandals only left spray paint behind. Despite the light and foghorn there is a modern wreck on the eastern reefs, the *Switha* (a fisheries cruiser, ex-trawler) which 'took the ground' in

1980. If you overnight within sight of the light you can check its rhythm: one long every 30 seconds.

Inchkeith was the first lighthouse built solely by Robert Stevenson, in 1804. The Bell Rock (1811) and Isle of May (1816) were to follow. The Stevenson family provided four generations of lighthouse engineers. A Thomas Smith began the family tradition. In the late eighteenth century, life was pretty precarious and he lost two wives and several children. He married a third time, a lady herself twice widowed and the mother of Robert Stevenson, who became Thomas Smith's partner and successor – and married his stepfather's daughter. Their sons, Alan, David and Thomas (father of R.L.S.), were all lighthouse engineers, as were David's two sons, David A. and Charles. Charles's son, D. Alan, followed the tradition and only died in 1971, thus ending the 200-year story. Kirkcaldy, Leven, Anstruther, Crail and St Andrews all had harbour work undertaken by the Stevensons. Thomas Smith, the founder, was a wealthy man (from providing most of Edinburgh's street-lighting) and bought an Elie-built sloop for the Northern Lights Trust, fitting it out with comforts few seamen enjoyed in those days. It was called the *Pharos*, a name which has been used right to the present for one of the servicing vessels.

KINGHORN

Take the road up from Pettycur Harbour. There's a carpark on the right and, below it, a jetty still runs out, once an alternative low-tide landing spot for the ferries. The first building on the right is older than it looks as it was a ferry inn, then a temperance hotel, then soldiers' billets before being turned into flats which were rebuilt in 1991. Immediately after this is the Longboat Inn and Restaurant. There is also a bar, The Hideaway, where meals can be had round on the seaward side by their home-made pier. All the rooms have sea views out to the island of Inchkeith. From The Hideaway, if you look round the corner, westwards, on the seaward side you'll see the main house is perched above a mini Giant's Causeway of columnar basalt formations.

Turn off Pettycur Road, right, at the odd-sounding Doodells Lane (a corruption of 'two delfs', an old measure used in this area), a footpath that wends along above attractive Kinghorn Bay, with its houses and yachts, parish church and striding railway arches. Quarrel Brae refers to the battle when Macbeth and Banquo defeated an invading Danish army. A more serious quarrel was Henry VIII's 'Rough Wooing' and, following the Battle of Pinkie (1547), the English burnt Kinghorn and killed over 400 people. As did Cromwell's forces.

The path comes out at Harbour Road. Turn down this, but almost at once head up the steps and over the bridge at Kinghorn Station. This was once an attractive wee station (gas-lit till not so long ago) but has been crassly modernised, though the north front of the main building is pleasant. Turn left once out the station and you are in the town centre: health centre (right), post office (left), war memorial and church hall (ahead) and the High Street shops when you turn right.

The High Street has lost all character with many buildings demolished and replaced with 1960s economy concrete blocks. The south side retains something of its Victorian character, several of the buildings having date stones, arms and other decorations. Cross Buildings (no. 29) is the only indication that Kinghorn once had a mercat cross here.

There are a surprising number of traditional rhymes about Kinghorn (none very flattering):

Burntisland for salted herring
Kinghorn for cursing and swearing.

or

Dysart for coal and saut,
Pathhead for meal and maut,
Kirkcaldy for lasses braw,
Kinghorn for breaking the law.

but, at least,

The deil's deid and buried in Kirkcaldy.

Round an S-bend stands the Elizabethan-style sandstone building, the 1826 town hall. Its turrets and battlements and transomed windows are rather out of place on the Castles Coast. At one time gaol and burgh offices, the building has stood empty for decades. Turn left onto North Overgate, the only part of the town to hint at what it once looked like, with some pantiles, outside stairs, crowstep gables, pends, etc. Look into Glamis Road (off left) for further glimpses of the old. The joiner's shop was originally a plash-mill where flax was 'retted' before spinning. The dell holds the Loch Burn which once drove several mills. (Where has all the water gone?)

Return to the North Overgate and, further up, take the road to the right – the Eastgate. The house on the corner is a fine example of the period: 1728 on the inscribed lintel. The other side has Templars Walk and Bleaching Hill to point to forgotten history. There's an Edwardian post box, still in use. Just before the main road is reached lies Bow Butts House. Bow butts were the archery practising area in ancient days. The house is an interesting mansion and in the grounds is a fancy octagonal doocot, the base of which may have been an ice house. The house and grounds are private but glimpses can be had as one walks round, right, onto and along the main road back into Kinghorn.

The empty church on the right was originally the Free church, then a school and then the RC church. On the other side of the road a housing area occupies the lands of one-time Abden House, the 'big house' of the town, where the king would expect to stay when he crossed the ferry; then there is the Caberfeidh Nursing Home and a pub.

The Ship Tavern building dates back to the seventeenth century and, turning left to go down the South Overgate, you can see a marriage lintel dated 1668. John Bruce, 'Bible Bruce', was the King's Printer in Scotland. There's a mason's mark on the left side of the stone. The South Overgate meets the Trongate and becomes the

Bow Butts doocot, Kinghorn, which once incorporated an ice house

Nethergate – the resonant old names at least survive and the Nethergate was picturesque till the '60s building 'clearances'. The burns once powered flax-mills and there was a net factory. The modern flats stand over the Loch Burn. Pass under the huge railway arches. At the foot of the Nethergate a few more old houses survive; no. 34 has a 1733 marriage lintel. The road ends at Kinghorn Bay (Bayview Hotel), a lively place in summer, and is dominated by the parish church of St Leonard's. The church dates back at least to the thirteenth century but the present building is mostly dated 1774. There are ruins of older periods in the churchyard but proximity to the sea has badly weathered most gravestones. One verse reads:

> Though raging seas and blustering winds
> Have tossed me to and fro
> Yet here I lye at anchor safe
> At anchor safe below.

Local seamen had a right to use the south aisle, not only during services but also for secular gatherings and social occasions if the weather was bad. Fishing has long gone and the south aisle is now a side chapel, but a 1567 ship model (the *Unicorn*) still hangs from the ceiling. The north aisle is the Balmuto Isle, the lairds for centuries being Boswells of Balmuto. One died at Flodden, another was surgeon to James VI, another Lord of Session (positions of sane security, one feels) and the present family head is a law professor in America who has rebuilt the old house.

KINGHORN TO KIRKCALDY

Head back up the Nethergate under the railway arches and then turn right at the top of the children's play area on a path which soon goes through an underpass below the railway, then runs along between the railway line and a caravan park. At the end of this stretch keep a look out for a well (spring) under some rocks to the left of the path. Packhorses were no doubt once glad of its waters and cattle once grazed the East Braes.

The first bay we come to has several interesting names and features. The inlet ahead at the end of the bay is Hoch-ma-toch and at the Kinghorn end, beyond the concrete slab of embankment, is Bellypuff. Beyond Bellypuff you may just see the remains of a slip, all that is left of a once considerable shipbuilding industry. John Key and Sons opened in 1864. There was no dock so ships had to be launched complete and with steam raised. The engines were brought from Kirkcaldy by train and the works' overhead crane was made of girders from the ill-fated Tay Bridge – recycling I think is the term. The last ship was SS *Kinghorn*. (The shipyard closed in 1922.) Among other ships, they built three ferries for the North British Railway Granton–Burntisland crossing. The last, the *William Muir*, ran from 1879 till 1937, making about 80,000 crossings. The *Thane of Fife* ran from 1937 till 1952 when the service ceased.

The rocks at the end of the bay are a geological showpiece, for one can see the lavas as if they had just stopped flowing into the sea and curdled yesterday; under them are pale limestone bands and then shale layers – all marvellously displayed. (The coast from Kinghorn to the Tyrie Burn is a listed area of special geological interest.) The shore is rich in fossil coral. The lava flows originated on the Binn above Burntisland.

A small stream marks the parish boundary. Further on there is a jut of land with the basalt weathered into what looks like huge balls. Kiln Rocks, the name given on the Pathfinder map, points to lime kilns being active here once, using the Abden limestones. The path then climbs, putting in an elbow bend along opposite Abden Home, now flats but having been an old folk's home and a poor law house back in 1854.

After being forced close to the railway boundary fence the path climbs up to cross a wall, the height so gained opening up an extensive panorama over the Forth Estuary. If the flowers had been interesting in the last section (bloody cranesbill, ox-eye daisy, scabious, thyme, sweet cicely and wild rose, amongst others), here we are suddenly in knee-deep grass, often in motion with the stroking patterns of the plentiful winds. When the slope dips we are looking down to the dramatically sited Seafield Tower.

When a path joins ours, turn back on this lower alternative and round the first bend there are several lime kilns in evidence. Walk on westwards across a flat area, once the limestone quarry, now backed by blackthorn and wild roses, and then there is a deeply cut cave running 40m into the cliff with a metal bridge spanning the outer beach

of well-rounded stones. The Seafield cave once ran in further but the railway construction in 1827 collapsed the innermost section. Low tide and a torch are needed to go in between those basalt jaws. Turn back here and on past the lime kiln ruins again. Note the slab of limestone at the top of the shore: it is so smooth that many take it for a concrete embankment. Offshore the limestone runs in sweeping lines parallel to the shore – rather attractive effects. The rocks offshore are favourite hauling-out places for seals.

Just before the hollow ruin of Seafield Tower is reached go down onto the top edge of the shore and you'll see a vigorous spring of freshwater. I've never known it run dry. Scramble up a band of delicately lined and tinted sandstone to reach the ruin, built in the early sixteenth century by the Moultry family. A Moultry died at Flodden. The castle was abandoned in 1733 then it passed into the ownership of Melville of Raith.

A rough track leads from the tower (above was the Tyrie bleachfield) and the next landmark/seamark is a fairly ruinous harbour arm which seems to guard no harbour – and anyway who'd want a harbour with all those reefs offshore? It was built in 1889 but local disputes prevented it ever being used, and a big storm in 1898 began its demise. The brick culvert takes the Tyrie Burn to the sea. Last century bleachworks (employing 70 people, who walked to work from Kinghorn or Kirkcaldy) and ropeworks occupied the area inland but the site was cleared for the building of the Seafield Colliery, itself now cleared. When the sea-wall and culvert decayed, a once popular sandy beach here (there was a café and Punch and Judy shows) was washed away, leaving the long ribs of rock exposed.

The track is full of potholes but you can walk along nearer the shore. The slopes above were once dominated by the twin hammerhead-shaped winding towers of the Seafield Colliery which only opened in 1954. Seams worked extend miles out under the sea and along to the Frances (Dysart) and Michael (East Wemyss) Collieries. Spoil was not tipped into the sea either, and the mine was linked by rail. This showpiece closed in 1988. A gate leads onto a seaside area which has been landscaped into a picnic area and carparks, the latter laid with a familiar red material.

In 1993 the go-ahead was given for a huge housing development in this area, so what is described below may not be exact any longer. Whatever happens, keep along by the sea and you will reach Kirkcaldy's promenade beyond the Tiel Burn.

Out to sea we can make out a clutch of horizon lumps – the Bass, Fidra and Berwick Law – while, opposite, the Cockenzie power station chimneys are a landmark. Edinburgh is marked by Arthur's Seat and, at night, the floodlit artificial ski slopes on the Pentlands.

At the end of the grassy area (a raised beach) is a small, mostly defunct industrial estate. At mid to low tide take to the sands and bypass this. A big stream, the Tiel Burn, will bar the way thereafter, but turn up its bank and

Seafield Tower and the sweep of coast round to Largo Law, extreme right

cross the wall onto the main road. An alternative is to walk through the estate from the picnic-grounds, a road marked by two white bollards, but this area is likely to be redeveloped so may change. From 1845 to 1973 a rope-works lay to the left – a building 400m long, the standard length required for twisting the strands (hawsers for the Queens). Right lay a sweet factory on what had been a sea-water swimming pool on the site of old chemical works.

The road comes out at a big bus depot (they bring London Underground trains here for painting!) but walk on, in the direction of the block of flats. The Tiel Burn bridge is crossed and, right, lies a big carpark with a snack bar, the start of the 2km-long esplanade, what Thomas Carlyle described as 'a mile of smoother sand, with one long wave coming on gently … beautifully sounding and advancing from the West [Tiel] Burn to Kirkcaldy Harbour'.

THROUGH KIRKCALDY

One or two B&Bs are found at this end of Kirkcaldy, in what was once the separate village of Linktown. Starks Park (Raith Rovers' ground) is one of its landmarks. I indicate the position of most B&B options so you can stop wherever you've chosen. For convenience I take the route description to the eastern end of Kirkcaldy under today's section. As the Museum and Art Gallery only opens at 10.30 a.m., try and fit it in before it closes, 5 p.m. Raith lies further inland, the site of a battle in AD 596 when Aidan was discomfited by invading Angles.

The Esplanade has recently had work done to make it more attractive. Each spring (a week in April, but it takes a week to set up and a week to dismantle) this area is the setting for the Links Market, Europe's largest street fair, which originated in a plea to Edward I of England who had Scotland under his hammer in 1304. Now a glorified fun-fair rather than traders' market, it marks the start of the showmen's season.

One thing I'll *not* go into much concerning Kirkcaldy is its proliferation of churches and religious denominations. From the eighteenth century onwards the churches split and joined up constantly over various points of dogma, so new buildings were constantly appearing. Now many are empty or taken over by a range of modern sects and even commercial enterprises. I made a tally once and had 17 different affiliations listed.

On the landward side, an area once full of mills and works, there have been recent improvements, too. On this side lies the Volunteers' Green, now a garden area, once the training area for what could be regarded as the then Territorial Army. There were even cannons facing out over the estuary. There were potteries in Linktown and, if you walk the sands at low tide, there are distinctive bits of china to be found, along with the 'craw's taes', the pointed stands that kept the stacked wares apart so their glazes didn't fuse together.

Walk along the Esplanade as far as the first set of traffic lights. Just 30m beyond, on the side of the sea-wall, there is a plaque commemorating the building of the Esplanade in 1923,

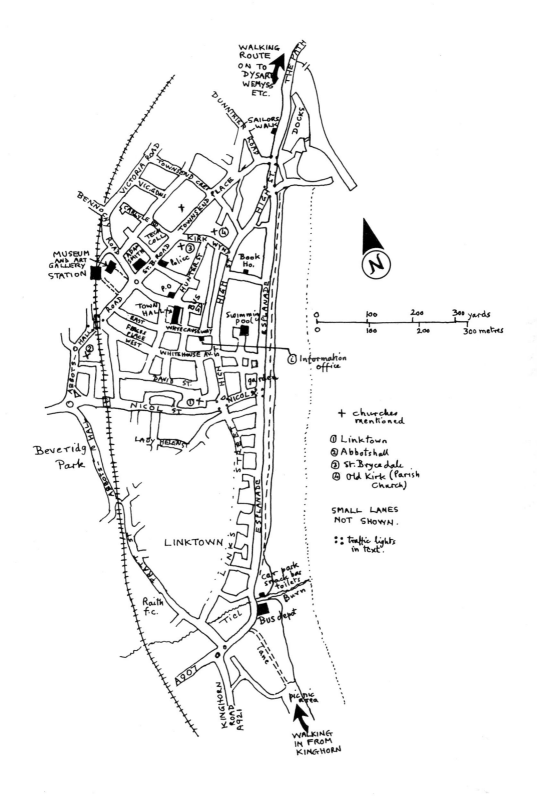

work which was created to alleviate unemployment at the time.

In 1778 during the American War of Independence John Paul Jones (who harried as far north as Orkney) anchored off Kirkcaldy and threatened to open fire on it unless bought off – for £200,000. The minister, the Revd Robert Shirra, came down to the Pathhead Sands and led prayers for the town's deliverance and an off-shore gale rose soon after to drive the American raider out to sea. There's a 49-stanza ballad on the event, which I'll refrain from quoting.

All the way from Kinghorn we have been walking north, something which even locals forget. So ingrained is the idea of the Forth running west–east that it is assumed the Esplanade does likewise, and I bet you'll check it on a map when I say that Kirkcaldy lies *west* of Carlisle.

Cross at the lights to go up Nicol Street to the next set of lights. Across on the right is the Wemyss Buildings which features an arcade, originally there for loading linen cloth. (Frank's Stores now stock all manner of outdoor equipment.) Keep on again, with the big Linktown (Bethalfield) church on the right and the Abbotshall Hotel visible, left. Other B&Bs are nearby. Walk right up Nicol Street, passing under the main railway line (bridge no. 84, counting from Edinburgh) towards a roundabout. As we will be turning right, before reaching the roundabout, cut the corner (Falloden Cres) onto Abbotshall Road. On the other side of the roundabout lies the huge Beveridge Park, a gift to the town from one of its many manufacturing benefactors. Walking along we reach Abbotshall church, built in 1790 (the crypt is reputedly eighth century). Malcolm III gifted Kirkcaladunt (sic) to the church of Dunfermline in 1075 whose abbots built a 'hall' (residence) in this part of the town.

On entering the gate, if you turn right before reaching the church and walk on 50m, you should find the grave of 'Pet Marjorie', a child who died at the age of eight. Marjory Fleming had kept a diary (fascinating to us) but could have been forgotten if Dr John Brown (of *Rab and His Friends*, *Minchmoor*, etc.) had not thoroughly romanticised her story, made her an intimate of Sir Walter Scott, and given her the 'Pet' name. She is certainly Scotland's youngest literary figure of note.

One stone has crossed rake and spade symbols, showing a member of the Gardeners' Guild. There are many yew trees in the graveyard. Needed for making bows in centuries past, yet poisonous to cattle, in pre-enclosure days the only safe place to grow yews was in the graveyards. They are aptly lugubrious, though, for their setting.

Turn right when leaving the church-yard and continue along past a mini-roundabout (Parkway Hotel) and traffic lights (and under the railway bridge) to reach a major roundabout beside a filling station. Cross before reaching it and, at the roundabout, you'll see the main entrance to the Memorial Gardens. Walk up through the gardens to the war memorial with its horrifyingly large displays of names (900 and 450 respectively for the two World Wars). A cenotaph has interesting sculpted bronze plaques to the three services. Behind is the museum, art gallery and library: the whole created as an integrated memorial after the First World War, the gift of John Nairn, the linoleum manufacturer. Behind the museum is the station, a new, modern building thanks to vandals having burnt down its predecessor.

There is a Victorian post box in the station wall behind the museum. The linoleum smell at one time was all-pervasive; in certain winds we could smell it in Kinghorn; in others it could reach Buckhaven. Just occasionally we still catch a whiff for a minimal amount is still produced in the old fashion that gave rise to a recitation poem that ended:

> For I ken mysel' by the queer-like smell
> That the next stop's Kirkcaddy!

Behind the station stood the Barry, Ostlere and Shepherd linoleum works, now demolished. There were acres of works beyond the station, in fact, an industry that dominated the town till the 1960s. Nairn's lay at the other, Pathhead, end of Kirkcaldy.

The museum's award-winning displays are presented in a lively manner and cover all the major local interests (don't miss the table, chair and dressing-table all made of coal). The Wemyss Ware collection is displayed in the café, a glittering show. Up the stairs hung with E.A. Hornel works is the art gallery with a room of contrasting portraits, a room of William McTaggart paintings and many works by S.J. Peploe. There are half a dozen temporary exhibitions each year so there is always a serendipity element, however

often you visit. There is also a useful gift shop and bookstall. Be prepared to spend at least an hour here: it will be one of the highlights of your Kirkcaldy visit. Open: weekdays 10.30 a.m.–5 p.m., afternoons on Sunday. (0592) 260732.

Walk down the gardens to the roundabout entrance again. Straight ahead you'll see the green spire of the Town House, a pleasing building started in 1939 and completed after the war, with sculptures on the walls and a large stair mural, able to hold its own with the thrusting Victorian swank of this area of Kirkcaldy. Behind the Town House is the bus station. Also behind the Town House, facing the bus station, are the Provost's lamps from six of the seven burghs which formed the new Kirkcaldy District in 1975. Buckhaven and Methil's is easy to spot; then, clockwise, are Markinch, Burntisland, Kirkcaldy, Leven and Kinghorn. (Leslie had no lamp.)

To our left (at the big roundabout) is the Adam Smith Centre, a theatre complex and café, while beyond (right) the slender, tall (200ft) spire of St Brycedale's Church can be seen. We walk along to it but first you may want to pop into the Adam Smith Centre to check if there is something appealing on for the night as they do plays, every kind of music, panto and films. The Adam Smith Centre flank is as imposing as the front, while across the road is the equally confident Victorian police HQ building. Next, on the left, is the Kirkcaldy Technical College and then St Brycedale's Church, which has been completely rebuilt inside. There is a pleasant tea-room in the east aisle, much appreciated by staff and stu-

85

dents from across the road. There are stained-glass windows by Burne-Jones and William Morris.

We turn right into Kirk Wynd, but note the B&B signs further ahead (Townsend Place). Left is Carlyle Road and next left along Townsend Place is Townsend Crescent, leading to Victoria Road (and along it, right, Glebe Park) – all places with B&Bs. Bennochy Road is the one leading up between Memorial Gardens and the Adam Smith Centre (it swings left at traffic lights).

Kirk Wynd is the only street in Kirkcaldy to have kept its ancient character. The Old Parish Kirk was consecrated in 1244, though only the bold tower dates back so far. It is best viewed from across Kirk Wynd. Below it is a super-ornate house of 1890 which tries to incorporate everything: battlements, turrets, a coat-of-arms and even a dragon on the gully box. Next is a classical old house with crowstep gables and red pantiles. It has a painted 1637 marriage stone for MA (Matthew Anderson) and ML (Margaret Livingstone). He was a corn merchant and important enough to have a coat-of-arms. On the same side, further on, is a plaque inscribed 'Thomas Carlyle lodged here 1816–1818 His school is opposite'. This was the (long-gone) old burgh school where he taught for a while as, probably, did Edward Irving, the preacher. The tabloids would have enjoyed the tangled web of their lives. Irving graduated at 17 and took up a teaching post at Haddington. He tutored Jane Welsh, the doctor's daughter, and fell in love with her when she was only 13. Already engaged, and not being released from

that tie, he left for Kirkcaldy. Irving introduced Jane to Carlyle, whom she eventually married, Irving having after 12 years grudgingly fulfilled his original engagement. Irving was Thomas Chalmers' assistant but moved to London and became a famous preacher. He eventually went 'over the top' and, excommunicated, formed his own Church. His flaming meteoric passage touched Kirkcaldy once more too. The Old Kirk had a horseshoe balcony in those days and, for his 1828 preaching visit, the church was packed out to such an extent that the balcony collapsed under the weight and 28 people died in the accident and the panic that followed.

The Old Church is just that, the original ecclesiastical building of the area, and has always had close links with the town, many of whose notables have stones in the graveyard. Lofts for guilds became a huge horseshoe gallery in a 1807 rebuilding of the church but the north gallery collapsed, the 'national disaster' mentioned above. On Christmas Eve 1900 the spire blew off the tower. In 1968 the church was remodelled inside, the galleries being removed, but in 1986 much of this work had to be redone when vandals fired the church. Luckily a taxi-driver heading along the prom saw smoke coming from the tower in the early hours of the morning. The chancel windows are by Burne-Jones. More striking are the contemporary west windows, slender columns of colour and light, erected to mark the last restoration of the church. A portrait of Revd George Gillespie, minister of Wemyss and a member of the Westminster Assembly, is one of the earliest surviving portraits in Scotland. The bell dates from 1553 but has been recast twice. If the tower is open it gives a splendid view over town and coast. The full scale of the spire of the nearby St Brycedale's Church becomes clear as it dwarfs the technical college buildings. Town House, roof-top carparks and old linoleum works all catch the eye. Eastwards, Ravenscraig Castle can be seen – on our route onwards along the coast.

The graveyard is rather uninteresting but there are stones of local philanthropists like Robert Philp and Michael Nairn. Philp (*d*.1828) left a trust to help provide education for the poor of the district. He was a wealthy bachelor linen manufacturer with no heirs. The Kinghorn school was in use till 1986, the Kirkcaldy one exists, as a restaurant, but the Linktown and Pathhead schools have gone.

When Kirk Wynd reaches the High Street (pedestrianised to the right), across the High Street there is a pillared wynd entrance and a plaque indicating that this was the site of the house of Adam Smith's mother and where he was living (1767–76) when he completed his *Wealth of Nations*, one of the most seminal books of all time. He was born in Kirkcaldy in 1723. At the age of three he was kidnapped from Strathendry Castle by tinkers. He studied at Glasgow and Oxford Universities, travelled on the continent and returned to Glasgow as a professor, before coming to live here to write his book. Very much part of the Scottish Enlightenment, he was a friend of people like David Hume and Robert Adam, another Kirkcaldy chiel.

The Adam dynasty had its start in Kirkcaldy for William Adam, born 1689, was son of a Kirkcaldy mason, and the prototype of the poor man making good. From being a mason he became involved in coal, salt, land, milling, brewing and farming activities as well as designing or working on such famous houses as Haddo, Mellerstain, House of Dun, Tingwall, Hopetoun and Craigdarroch. Even so, he was to be overshadowed by his son Robert (and Robert's three brothers).

Robert Adam was born in Kirkcaldy in 1728. His education was interrupted by the Jacobite Rising of 1745–46 and his father died in 1748. He spent three years on the continent and by the time he died, in 1792, his buildings, monuments and fortifications (over 80 major works) ranged from Kent to Antrim and Cornwall to Fort George. If there is time to spare on the last day (or you have an extra day in Edinburgh) do visit Charlotte Square, another Adam showpiece, where the National Trust for Scotland's Georgian House is open to the public and would give an idea of the sumptuous interiors he created as part of his all-embracing building projects.

Kirkcaldy had one much earlier famous son. Michael Scot was one of the most talented men of the thirteenth century, a scholar successively at Oxford, Paris and Toledo, professor of Rhetoric at Bologna for some years, a philosopher, doctor, Arab scholar, mathematician and chemist. In the popular imagination he was turned into a magician (the fate of many poor 'witches' who knew more than was good for them) and incredible stories are attached to Michael Scot, such as his splitting the Eildons in three (though a thousand years before the Romans had called them Trimontium!). He was one of the envoys sent to bring the Maid of Norway home after Alexander III had gone over the cliffs near Kinghorn.

A lesser known son of Kirkcaldy was Sir Sandford Fleming (1827–1915) who became a Canadian engineer (surveying for the Canadian Pacific transcontinental route) and the inventor of world Standard Time. Less known, too, is the greatest sportsman born in Kirkcaldy, the footballer John Thomson. As a young miner playing for Wellesley FC he was signed up by a scout who had come to watch the opposing goalkeeper. An unassuming person who was brilliant on the field, he was a great star in the best tradition, playing in several cup-winning teams. Playing for Celtic in an Old Firm game in 1931, he dived at the feet of a Rangers attacker and received an accidental kick – and died that night as a result.

Scots were great soldiers of fortune and the great Marshal Keith (a Jacobite exile) was once involved in peace negotiations with the Turks. The solemn meeting of the commissioners, with appropriate translators, was duly carried through. Formalities over, the Turkish vizier took the Marshal by the hand and, in a rich Fife accent, welcomed him, explaining that his father had been bellman in Kirkcaldy and he'd seen Keith and his brother, the Earl Marischal passing on occasions.

In the Town House is a plaque mentioning six famous sons of Kirkcaldy, Robert Adam, Adam Smith, Robert Philp, Sandford Fleming, Dr John Philip and John McDouall Stuart. The last-named will be mentioned under Dysart. The fifth, Dr John Philip, was a missionary, the first superintendent of the London Missionary Society and to whom one Dr David Livingstone reported on his arrival in South Africa. Philip was the nearest relative of the philanthropist, Robert Philp, who was very annoyed at his relatives changing the spelling of their names: 'If ma name isna guid enough for them then neither is ma siller.'

The High Street, while maintaining most of its original buildings, has undergone pedestrianisation (with the usual common denominator of boring shops) but is redeemed by having trees planted along it. The first street, shorewards, south (west) along the High Street, is Tolbooth Street. There is no tolbooth but the Book House is an excellent bookshop and the gift shop next door has a tea-room.

There is nothing to hold us otherwise, so head off along the High Street – the north (east) end (not pedestrianised) has better buildings on the left side so walk on the right, passing the cinema, then cross over at the Gate of India to use pedestrian-controlled traffic lights to cross where High Street meets the Esplanade. Technically Esplanade meets High Street, for the A955 coast road is still the High Street as we walk on east (NE), passing Funkies DIY, Pillan's Pie Shop and other shops to reach the harbour area.

Between Funkies and the harbour there used to be salt-pans but these were killed off after the Union of the Parliaments when the then predominantly English body imposed swingeing salt taxes on Scotland. At the end of the Esplanade there once stood a pool known as the Bucket Patts, a storage tank for sea-water for the salt-pans if they needed topping-up at low tide. It was a popular paddling pool thereafter. The carpark at Funkies was the site of a church till it was demolished in 1970.

Coal Wynd, Fish Wynd and Malcolm's Wynd run steeply up the hillside facing the harbour. There is one exceptional building, the Sailors' Walk – obviously old, with white walls, crowstep gables and red pantiles. It is the oldest surviving building in Kirkcaldy, dating to *c.*1460 and restored in 1952. It houses a secondhand bookshop, Book Ends (open Tues–Sat). The harbour as we see it now only dates to 1840 and was

built for whaling rather than fishing. Grain for the nearby Hutchison mills is the major import now and you may see heaps of scrap iron being loaded for export. In 1644 Kirkcaldy had 100 ships registered but then came the Civil War: 200 Kirkcaldy men fell at the Battle of Kilsyth in 1645, during the Montrose campaigns for the king. Five years later Cromwell's troops killed 480 Kirkcaldy defenders and destroyed 50 ships. A year or two later only 12 were registered. The port never really recovered from this downturn. 'Fire, pestilence and sword' were much in people's prayers. In 1584 over 300 died of plague. A century ago, however, you could catch a twice-

The collection of Provosts' lamps behind Kirkcaldy Town House

weekly sailing to London. Now you'll be lucky to see a ship.

Here we must leave our description of Kirkcaldy. Most will have found a resting place before now, I trust, otherwise the Pathhead and Dysart B&Bs lie one to two kilometres along the A955 from the harbour. Just follow the road to reach them and, in the morning, walk back to rejoin the route at Ravenscraig Castle, which is well signposted.

PRACTICAL INFORMATION / ACCOMMODATION

Telephone code: (0592)

Tourist Information Office, 19
Whytecauseway, Kirkcaldy   267775
Tourist Information Office, Kirkgate,
Burntisland   872667

Kirkcaldy:
Parkway Hotel, Abbotshall Road   262143
30 Townsend Place   262713
49 Townsend Place   269588
25 Townsend Place   203874
26 Carlyle Road   262460
26a Carlyle Road   200733
16 Carlyle Road   267710
34 Victoria Road   261258
Victoria Hotel, 28 Victoria Road 260117
Ollerton Hotel, Victoria Road   264286
143 Victoria Road   268864
32 Glebe Park   264656
44 Glebe Park   264531
19 Bennochy Road   205932
44 Bennochy Road   202147
113 High Street   260855
2A Lady Helen Street (next south
of Nicol St)   269243
Abbotshall Hotel (visible from start
of Nicol Street)   640803
21 Pratt St (first right, inland from
Bus Depot)   264849
2 Kinghorn Road (first left, inland
from Bus Depot)   262658
King's Hotel (Overlooking docks,
go up wynds)   266589
213 Nicol Street   268596

Pathhead/Dysart: (on tomorrow's
continuation; most on A955 coast road)

17 Dysart Road
(near Ravenscraig Castle)   269275
69 Lady Nairn Avenue (next inland to
Dysart Road)   52806
Strathearn Hotel
(facing Ravenscraig Park)   52210
Royal Hotel, Townhead
(Dysart Road continuation)   52109
59 Normand Road
(Townhead continuation)   52804
8 Normand Road   53133
Ravenscraig Hotel, St Clair Street 54950

One could also train or bus from Kirkcaldy back to Kinghorn if a village, rather than town setting, appeals.

Kinghorn:
9 Rossland Place   890592
45 Pettycur Road   890527
61 Pettycur Road   890138
66 Pettycur Road   890755
Longboat Inn, 107 Pettycur Road
(more expensive)   890625
Rossland Hotel, Pettycur Road
(top end)   890577
Bayview Hotel
(right on Kinghorn Bay)   890228

Camping: The nearest is the Pettycur Bay Holiday Park, Kinghorn, 890321. Open March–Oct. (Bus best, or train to Kinghorn.)
Swimming Pool: The Esplanade, Kirkcaldy
                                 265366
Adam Smith Centre (Theatre):   260498
Kirkcaldy Cinema: 260143
Bus station Hill Street (behind Town Hall)
642394

Railway Station (behind Museum)   204771
Taxis: Kirkcaldy   54449, 641414, 202020,
          206206, 204048, 200900, 202040

Dysart: 55455, 260260, 266888
Tide Times: Tel. (0592) 260176 (Kirkcaldy
Docks)

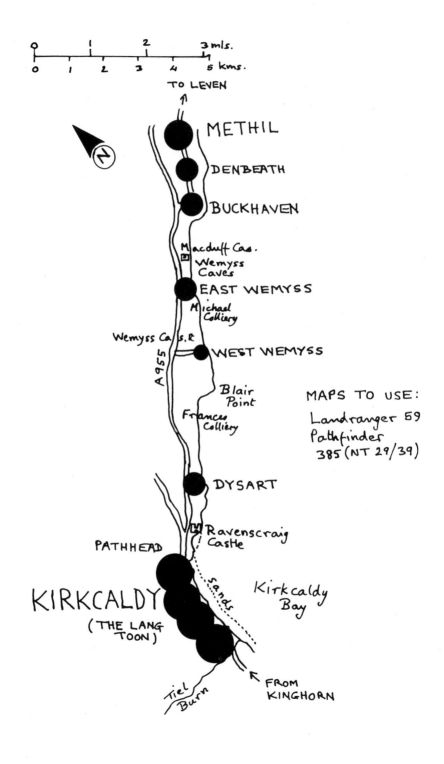

0   1   2   3 mls.

0   1   2   3   4   5 kms.

TO LEVEN

N

METHIL

DENBEATH

BUCKHAVEN

Macduff Cas.
Wemyss Caves

EAST WEMYSS

Michael Colliery

Wemyss Ca/s.R.

A955

WEST WEMYSS

Blair Point

Frances Colliery

MAPS TO USE:
Landranger 59
Pathfinder
385 (NT 29/39)

DYSART

Ravenscraig Castle

PATHHEAD

KIRKCALDY

(THE LANG TOON)

sands

Kirkcaldy Bay

Tiel Burn

FROM KINGHORN

DAY 5 *The Coal Coast*

Dysart–Wemyss–Buckhaven–Leven

Maps to use: Bart 46, OSLR 59, OSPF 385 (NT 29/39)/373 (NO 20/30)
Walking distance: 15km (53 km)

This is a remarkably varied day, quite a long one in distance so the suggested places to visit *en route* have been reduced by selecting the most interesting. Ravenscraig Castle is important, Dysart a delight, the Wemyss Caves unique, then the day ends with the longest, inescapable, continuously built-up area, through Buckhaven, Denbeath and Methil to Leven. Most of the route is on paths but there are three short breaks where evasive action may be required if the tide is high. Macduff Castle concludes the Castles Coast and, willy nilly, the above towns give us our only real stretch of road walking. Variety is the spice of Fife.

Part of today's route description may be in yesterday's notes, depending where you found accommodation, but we'll pick up the new text at the Kirkcaldy harbour area.

PATHHEAD AND DYSART

Walk on east from the Sailors' Walk building and note, after passing several pubs (sailors were aye thirsty), there is the listed frontage of Nairn's linoelum works. Much is only a front wall now – there is nothing behind. William Nairn founded his weaving business in 1828 and continually expanded into new areas. With sail-cloth sales dropping as ships turned to steam, he went to all the floor-cloth factories in England and won orders for the canvas backing. Later he took up the patented process of linoleum manufacturing and brought it to Kirkcaldy (1847). Cork boats used to crowd the harbour and the carts then had to face The Path, a hill they didn't dare stop on going up, and down which trams hurtled, unable to stop either.

The ecclesiastical wall before the brae is part of one of the many 'splinter' churches. The road has been built up to window-sill level. Its original bends straightened, the road climbs steeply up The Path (pronounced *Peth*), with the large flour-mills of Robert Hutchison either side, beside a hidden burn, the East Burn which, just inland, creates quite a den, where the young John Buchan once played. His father was a minister at Pathhead and only left for Glasgow when John was 14. The opening scene of *Prester John* is set on Pathhead Sands, just below, while *The Free Fishers* starts with the nail-makers and weavers of Pathhead, and there are claims that the old steps down to the beach numbered 39. John's sister Anna was a popular romantic fiction writer under the pen name of O. Douglas.

At the top of The Path is another fine old building, Path House, the seventeenth-century town house of the Oswald family. Note the two-faced sundial on the corner. New housing here has been tastefully designed to fit in with the traditional, unlike the three huge tower blocks which are an eyesore from all round the bay. Behind and in front of Path House there were acres of huge buildings involved in the linoleum industry, most of which have gone now. Some still standing have been given Listed Building status and the open spaces are being redeveloped as the pretentiously titled Pathhead Village. One of Philp's schools stood in the middle of all this industry and was demolished with the rest. The distinctive, not unpleasant hot linseed oil smell is noticed only occasionally now, for there is but one linoleum manufac-

turer left. Vinyl and plastics have ousted the real solid, indestructible lino but some has to be produced still for restoration work or for those who can afford the real thing.

Inland from Path House lies the Feuars burial-ground which has a link with the Porteous Riots. Andrew Wilson was a baker in Flesh Wynd and also something of a smuggler. ('English' taxes on Scotland after the 1707 Union made smuggling widespread.) Wilson and a friend, Robertson, robbed a customs officer at Pittenweem, were caught and condemned to be hanged in Edinburgh. Taken to church for their last service Wilson seized his guards and yelled for Robertson to run. With some assistance from the congregation he dashed out and made a successful escape. Next day Wilson was hanged and the irate mob stoned the guards. Captain Porteous, a weak, lazy fellow, fired on the crowd and killed several people. He was tried for this and condemned to hang but was reprieved. This so infuriated public opinion that a mob broke into his quarters, dragged him off and hanged him from a dyestaff in the Grassmarket. Wilson is buried here. We must not explore Pathhead, however, so cross over seawards from Path House. A plaque in the adjacent carpark shows where Michael Nairn established his works in 1847.

On a jutting crag of sandstone ending the bay is the stark outline of Ravenscraig Castle, the romantic castle of Scott's *Lay of the Last Minstrel*, from which the unfortunate Rosabelle set off over the Forth only to be drowned. The grassy area is largely artificial, being built up from all the

Ravenscraig Castle, the showpiece of the Castles Coast

rubble of demolition and then land-scaped. Chemical works, a naphtha factory, a whaling factory and Nairn's Folly all crowded in here at one time. Nairn's was a huge building which dropped from street-level to sea-level. It even had its own power station. People mocked this vast development but it was the start of a century 'when most of Kirkcaldy's bread was spread with linseed oil'.

Drop down the road towards the foot of the Ravenscraig. A concrete footpath with a handrail leads round the foot of the prow of the castle point. On the other side there is a small, noxious cave and, just beyond, a bit of walling, broken at its left end where it is possible to scramble up to the castle. This, though hardly an official entrance, saves a frustrating detour to reach the castle, which is of consider-

able historical interest and worth see-ing. It is described below, after the more circuitous, easier and official approach is explained. The apparently little cave actually runs deep into the crag but was blocked up following a tragedy in 1740 when a group of ten young boys died inside when the roof caved in. Continue along beside the wall/cliffs of the bay which terminates in a small capped tower and, halfway along, has another sixteenth-century beehive doocot. A flight of steps leads up to the doocot and a path through the park which is the best option onwards. We saw a similar doocot at Aberdour Castle, and will see others, but these beehive-shaped specimens are rarer than the lectern-type doocots.

Steps lead up from the doocot to the Ravenscraig Park and if you walk on up the drive you will come on a sign pointing along to the castle, which is eventually reached by a modern non-drawing bridge. In 1992, in a gesture of dereliction of duty, Historic Scotland handed over the castle to Kirkcaldy District Council, the custodian was withdrawn and, as forecast, the vandals moved in. In what state you will find the castle is unknown. Its sacrifice to market forces is a sad affair.

Ravenscraig was the first castle built specifically to deal with the new danger of cannon attack. The walls are 14ft thick in places (if you can enter to see them; despite promises much is locked up these days) and the slanting roof was planned to deflect cannonballs. James II, the initiator of the castle, was – ironically – killed by an exploding cannon when he was besieging Roxburgh Castle in the Borders, and Ravenscraig was completed by his widow, Mary of Gueldres. It soon passed to the Sinclair family (in exchange for Orkney rights) and it stayed in their possession till 1896. The setting is superb and many standard castle features can be seen. There is a well in a cellar down a dark flight of stairs. A great spot, deserving better than its present official neglect.

Once you have finished exploring the castle return to the park and its doocot simply to follow a path which wends along parallel to the sea. It is separated from the sea by the park wall which angles in and out of every wee bay in a way I've never seen anywhere else. If the wall was intended to keep people out, why all the doorways to each bay? This anti-social act so incensed the masons building the wall that they returned at night to destroy their own handiwork. Not long after

the wall was finally completed (c.1900) the park was gifted to the town by the Nairn family of linoleum fame and fortune. The English brick housing development behind the castle is on the site of a cottage hospital donated to the town by Michael Nairn. My father once spent some time in one of its circular wards. It closed in 1967.

The little watch tower we could see from the castle juts out and can be a good hide to see autumn or winter waders on the rocks below. It gives a last view of Kirkcaldy. The crazy wall then follows, built by the local laird to stop the miners walking along the shore to work. Keep to the main path. Eventually there are grassy areas on the reclaimed land between wall and sea but still follow the path, taking right options to keep along the coast. Eventually we are forced uphill onto a bigger track. Keep right and from a prow (the Fort) look over to see Dysart Harbour immediately below, St Serf's Tower and Pan Ha' beyond – one of the best surprise views of the walk, Dysart being easily the most picturesque port on our Castles Coast.

Keep along the wall for another 70m or so then turn right at some steps (rather hidden by a jutting wall) to gain a fine balcony path with railings. This is known as the Sailors' Walk, which circles the cliff of the inner harbour. Turn right along this, passing under the viewpoint of just a few minutes before and then twisting down steps to the harbour. Immediately on the left is a 20m tunnel leading out west onto a grassy area. Originally it allowed cart access to and from the harbour.

Walk across the harbour area. The large stone building under the cliff was

Dysart Harbour today, with the keep-like church tower and the restored houses of Pan Ha'

restored in 1990. Built in the 1830s it was the oil shed for processing whale oil but in fact never operated as the Earl of Rosslyn stopped the project because he considered it too close to his Dysart home. Cross the metal footbridge over the entrance to the inner harbour and bear leftish along the inner harbour quay to another fine old building.

The inner harbour was cut down into solid rock (on the site of a quarry) and opened in 1831, the first such basin on the east coast. Much of the rubble was dumped beyond the tunnel, as was ballast from the ships, so there are some strange geological specimens found hereabouts. The sea promptly washed much of the material into the harbour mouth. Coal was the major export and carts would queue up to fill the holds – a cargo being up to 250 cart-loads.

On the east wall of this old harbour building is the first of several intriguing street names: Hot Pot Wynd. This curves up outside the grounds of a monastery but we keep along at seaside level. The name comes from the Dutch word for a brae (*het pat*) which sounded just the way locals would say 'hot pot'. The Dutch connection was strong enough for Dysart folk to be nicknamed Little Hollanders. The Carmelite monastery is in Dysart House, once home of the Earl of Rosslyn. Bridges led across the wynd to Ravenscraig's Park (his demesne) but he had to sell up to clear huge gambling debts. The newly rich Nairns bought the house and gave the park to the council.

The first house has the Shore Road sign on it, and the next has a double sundial on the corner. The shore here has been tidied up with carparks and grassy areas. Once it was the site of extensive salt-works. Salt was a major industry along the Fife coast, and a laborious one. Water was pumped from the sea into huge pans and boiled till the water evaporated, leaving the salt. Salt, coal, beer and fish all went to Holland, and in return imports included cartwheels, Delftware, kegs of Holland's, pipes of Rhenish, and pantiles. In about 1700 a ship sailing to France was captured by Barbary pirates. There was also extensive trade with northern Germany and Sweden. In many ways Scotland, for centuries, was far more European in outlook than England, and some would say this is still the case.

St Serf's Tower (80ft) dominates this end of Dysart, a strangely warlike church tower. Little of the church remains but its walls. The north aisle was removed so Shore Road could reach the shore. When the Nairns bought Dysart House work was done on the tower, such as adding a doocot on top, before they donated it to Kirkcaldy. The first two floors are of barrel-vaulted stone, the upper levels of wood, very much as in any tower house. The first church could well have been the cave (a sea-worn cavern on one of the raised beach levels) to which St Serf came from Loch Leven when he was abbot on what is now St Serf's Island. The church survived the Reformation though a local priest, Walter Myln, was arrested and burnt at the stake at St Andrews for heresy. The present parish church still bears the name of St Serf. Access to the tower may be possible; ask locally. The cave, in the grounds of Dysart House, is not open to the public.

In 1642 a Margaret Young was kept imprisoned in the Tower for ten weeks on a charge of witchcraft. It was not a pleasant period. The town minutes for 17 December 1633 record a total 'debursement for William Coke and Alison Dick, Witches' of £14 4s. 6d. and detailed the items: 'For 10 loads of coal to burn them, For a tar barrell, For towes, To the executioner, To him that brought the executioner, For the executioner's expenses.' In 1649 the Dysart minister, an 'expert' no doubt, was called to Burntisland to test a suspect witch, Janet Brown. He pushed a pin into a marked spot and when she did not react this was taken as proof of guilt; she was burnt the same day.

The first road off Shore Road is Pan Ha' (Pan Haugh, the level ground where the salt-pans stood), a name hinting back to the days when salt-pans rather than grass occupied the seafront, and we walk along this sparkling restored area of old Dysart. The 1960s were not just a tale of woe. As elsewhere on our route the National Trust for Scotland in those years did a great deal of rescue and restoration work through its Little Houses Scheme. Look out for their plaques when you see areas like this. The first building, free-standing, was once the Bay Horse Inn and dates back to 1583. There are heads (Mary Queen of Scots and Darnley?) on the skew putts. If you walk in by the east end of the house there is a doorway behind (part of the old manse) with the date 1583 on the lintel, and the words 'My hoip is in the Lord'. Offshore is a reef, the Partan Craig, 'partan' being a local word for the edible crab. Saut Girnal Wynd (salt store lane) and Hie Gate (high lane) are alleys leading up through the restored houses. Take the Hie Gate and climb steeply up to a junction, passing the attractive 1582 house, the Anchorage. The road heading off up, opposite (Rectory Lane), has a museum in the first building on the right which tells the story of John McDouall Stuart, the first person known to have crossed the deserts of central Australia from south to north, in 1861–62. He was born in Dysart in 1815 and emigrated in 1839. Five years later he was on Captain Sturt's expedition before mounting expeditions of his own to Lake Eyre and the centre of Australia. Hardships and illness defeated two previous south–north attempts, so his ultimate 2,000-mile success was a triumph. He returned by the same route. The museum is only open June–August, 2–5 p.m. Telephone (0592) 260732.

Walk on up Rectory Lane and turn first right onto the High Street. The building on the corner is the Normand Hall, assuming it is still there for it is abandoned and due for demolition, which seems sad. A memorial hall, it has seen everything from Queen Victoria's Jubilee celebrations to concerts and plays, boxing, youth club and cinema.

Dysart's centre (the Cross) actually has a Jubilee lamp erected in 1887 to celebrate Queen Victoria's 50th year on the throne. Dominating the Cross is the beautiful old tolbooth (not so beautiful, I'm sure, for those in gaol there). There is an outside stair and a date, 1576, when it was probably first erected. The 1617 date on the Town

House stair next door shows a simplified version of the town's crest – a bare tree, the roots exposed. The date 1617 on the forestair is that of major renovations grudgingly made by local taxation. The bell chamber was added in the eighteenth century. In 1840 the ancient prison was still being used, a report commenting on it being 'quite unsuitable... dry, but not very secure'.

Some rebuilding had to be done when one of Cromwell's troops 'blowed off the roofe . . . so there scarcely remained a sclait'. They'd stored gunpowder in the tower. Beside the tolbooth is the 1874 Mechanics Institute, now used for social events. Some of the attractive buildings at the Cross are modern, just to show local

authorities can be sensitive, sometimes. When you turn up Cross Street you may think otherwise, for over on the left is a hideous 'prison' block of houses. And why are so many buildings painted black? Cross Street meets Quality Street, and across, right, is another superbly restored building, the Towers, which dates to 1586. The house next to it also has a marriage lintel of 1610.

Return to the Cross and straight on, Victoria Street, then turn right (modern flats) to return to Shore Road. On one of the flats there is a fine ornate stone dating to 1585, the year of the plague when 400 people (over half the population) died. IV and IK no doubt chose the motto with feeling; they sur-

Dysart harbour last century when shipbuilding, mining and fishing were still industries
(© Kirkcaldy Central Library Collection)

vived. Shore Road here was once dominated by the wheelhouse of the Lady Blanche Pit and old photographs show several tall chimneys in Dysart. All gone.

Drop down to the seafront again at the Pan Ha' and head eastwards once more. When the tarmac ends there are some garages, then the track continuation passes a length of stone wall with a brick arch in it which was the entrance to the middle-of-town Lady Blanche Pit (closed in 1928, demolished 1954). Just along a bit used to be the site of gasworks. The track leads to grassy slopes, the old Dubbie Braes where people played, picnicked, walked in the woods and enjoyed Dysart's sandy beach. Religious and political meetings were also held on the braes and the Volunteers practised firing cannon at targets anchored out to sea. Wash-houses were removed and everything smartened up for the celebrations marking Queen Victoria's Jubilee. The present mess of the Frances Colliery lies ahead, for years a serious obstacle to walking the coast. Remedial work has improved things a bit.

At low tide it is possible to walk along the shore but this is probably less enjoyable than using the path through the Frances. Looking along, you can see our objective, West Wemyss, on the far point and, halfway, the Red Rocks of Blair Point, then a nearer sweep with old war defensive concrete blocks below the black redd (mining waste). These points would have to be clear to attempt walking the shore. It seems extraordinary that tipping redd into the sea was ever allowed, and this may well have changed currents and

caused problems up and down the coast as well as being a dirty pollutant (Aberdour's Silver Sands can sometimes still have a black coal rim as a result).

Coal made Dysart prosper for several centuries but at a cost: the seams often ignited (the one at the harbour was Europe's thickest at 33ft). In 1476 the town nearly vanished in an explosion; there was another in 1578 and multiple deaths in 1662, 1700, 1791 . . . In 1912 over 900 people were employed by Dysart's three pits, the Lady Blanche, the Frances (Sinclair names) and the Randolph (a Wemyss name). Around 86,000 tons of coal were shipped from the harbour. A tunnel brought the coal direct from the Lady Blanche and also provided ventilation as did an older stair pit, the Violet. A stair pit was just that: the coal was 'putted' (pulled) and carried up on the backs of women and children who worked a 12-hour day. Miners were no better than serfs till the 1799 laws gave them some rights. At about that time, too, something like 6 million nails were exported, made in Pathhead and Gallatown, a trade then lost due to the Carron ironworks' cheaper methods.

For the best route, continue along on the grass till at the end of the playing-fields we come on the spoil area of the Frances Colliery, now fenced off. Turn up left on a footpath (the fence stupidly crosses it and has been cut open by locals needing *their* access). It swings left to lead up to a street where we turn right and walk along to reach the right-of-way path through the Frances. It starts right of the last council houses.

The pit is mothballed rather than

completely closed; pumps are still working to prevent flooding and there are plans mooted periodically for reopening the mine. This would be a boon locally, and modern regulations would prevent a repetition of tipping redd into the sea. In its last years both the Frances and the Michael (3km ahead) were worked from the super-modern Seafield Colliery – itself completely gone. The Frances was opened in 1850, was nationalised in 1946, and was one of the most successful pits in the country. It began to tap into the Michael's 20-year reserves, broke records – and was closed, because of a fire at the main face in 1985.

The path goes through by the Frances then drops to contour through the woods beyond, a section of path constructed in the last few years as a job-creation scheme. At a wall, where the path turns steeply up to the top edge of the wood, there is a bit of old walling and a path on to a viewpoint above the Red Rocks of Blair Point, an area of considerable slippage. The rocks we see have pulled off from the main cliff and, on the seaward side, there have been several further falls, another reason I don't recommend the shore route: it's a bit of a slippery obstacle course.

Return and take the steps up to the top edge of the wood and then continue eastwards. The path leads onto a prow with a sudden view of the bay sweeping on to West Wemyss. As so often, all our upward climbs seem to be rewarded with views far beyond the normal foot-poundage payment. The bay ahead is shingly but the line is clear along the grass backing the shore. Steps twist down onto the shore. If you are interested in seeing the fallen Red Rocks, they can be inspected in a few minutes by walking round to Blair Point if the tide is out. The sycamore wood along the hillside backing the bay is Chapel Wood. Water runs out from the trees, a rusty colour, probably from having flowed through old mine-workings, with which the area is riddled. Flints on the shore are 'imported', from ballast off-loaded at West Wemyss harbour.

THE WEMYSS TOWNS

Our path joins a rough drive at a walled-off garden and then there is an area which could have been the setting for *The Secret Garden*. There is an old tower hidden behind arched walls and guardian turrets, everything smothered in trees and crumbling with decay – yet there are glimpses of trim lawns for the garden is the family burial-ground of the Wemyss family. Hitchcock could have used it splendidly.

A chapel may have been first built here in the fifteenth century by Spaniards fleeing the Inquisition. Sir Patrick Jackson spent £1,000 on chapel and manse in 1536 and the Wemyss family granted it some land and free coal for use with its salt-pan. The tower at the east end of the arched wall was a doocot then. The chapel was destroyed and abandoned at the Reformation but in 1627 Lord Elcho (later second Earl of Wemyss) turned it into a house and it was lived in till the middle of the eighteenth century. Admiral of the Fleet, Lord Wemyss, who was First Sea Lord at the end of the 1914–18 War, is probably the most notable modern person to be buried here.

West Wemyss Harbour is silted up and as we approach it, tide permitting, head over to the steps up onto the end of the harbour arm – quite the best viewpoint. At high tide keep to the drive which passes behind a white house to reach a grassy area and carparks (which are actually built on the infilled inner harbour), and then walk out on to the harbour arm. West Wemyss Harbour dates back to the early sixteenth century at least. One of the earliest mentions of the harbour is in 1590, when a barque from plague-infested England put in here and passed on the dread epidemic which then raged throughout Fife.

The white building under the fulmar cliff (Shorehead House) has a Dutch gable and is often attractively mirrored in the trapped water of the harbour. It is the old pilot's house and was always painted white to act as a seamark. A light was also hung at the end of the harbour arm. Recognising a coast is never easy as even I know from canoeing in this area, and in the days of sail it was crucial to note landmarks early. Just west of it an area of capped walling marks the site of yet another old pit, the Victoria (named after the queen), which opened in 1824, ran out of coal in 1914 and was used as an entrance for miners till 1940. A tramway ran from it to the harbour.

East of Shorehead House you can see a series of five bricked-up arches, the site of stables for the pit ponies, while the richly coloured sandstone building beside it used to be the smiddy. Beside it and rather hidden is a bricked-up archway which blocks a tunnel which runs for 1km up to the Hugo Mine at Coaltown of Wemyss. This in turn was linked by rail with Methil Docks. The tunnel kept the mining activity decently out of sight from Wemyss Castle. It was bricked up after some schoolkids got lost in it and nearly suffocated.

Another Dutch gable on a big building above this area is the Belvedere Hotel (good bar meals), a modern conversion of what was the Miners' Institute and one excellent saving of a traditional building. The Institute was built in 1927 (striking miners were glad to turn builders then), closed in 1952 and was renovated in 1979. The Wemyss family built several villages for their miners: the Coaltown up on the A955 and East and West Wemyss. Sadly, following the end of mining on the Fife coast, West Wemyss largely slipped into decay and only now is its architectural worth being recognised and efforts made to preserve the village. The houses looking on to the harbour (Coxstool) are a fine example of restoration work. Several of the houses had to be rebuilt after a great storm in 1898 (pictures showing the damage can be seen at the Environmental Centre later and the Belvedere Hotel has an interesting collection on its walls).

Coal was the main export from West Wemyss, much of it going to Middlesbrough, Amsterdam and Hamburg. The coal industry caused the town's population to expand to 1,300 in 1901 (by 1981 it was 379) and the harbour was increased in size. The boom coal years saw a tidal basin and dock built; a second dock was started but never completed as the long decline had begun. Methil Docks, opened in 1887, larger, deeper and taking the new steamships, rather overtook Wemyss Harbour. The latter fell into a sorry state and in the 1960s the inner harbour was filled in with rubble (from demolished houses) and grassed over. Such harbour as is left is too silted up to be usable, and the few local fishermen simply keep their wee boats on the coal-tinted beach, a pattern we'll see repeated at Buckhaven.

On leaving our harbour arm viewpoint, head along past the restored buildings of the Coxstool to join the Main Street. The big red building overlooking the junction was once a manse. Outside the top Coxstool house is a loupin-on stone, with the Belvedere Hotel just beyond. At present, the seaward houses along Main Road are all boarded up; the apparent windows are fake, though the walls and roofs have been worked on. West Wemyss has another graceful tolbooth, in which Dutch architectural influences are strong. The present building is early eighteenth century but records report one long before then. There is a pend (passage) through beside it, with the original prison doors sealed now. Walk through onto what was Duke Street (another corruption of Scots: *joug* means jail). It has been demolished and on the main houses you can see all openings are bricked up and the old stairs have been removed. (To such measures do we have to go to keep vandals at bay!) Hopefully, one day, West Wemyss will be fully restored and lived in. Its potential is tremendous, as can be seen from the parts which are modernised. It is one of my favourite Fife coast towns.

Walk back through the pend. Note how the corner is cut away and a spur stone (pal stone) protects the corner from being bumped by traffic. Head up Broad Wynd opposite. The village store was sited on the corner and hopefully may be opened again. Look back at the tolbooth, noting the swan weather-vane and the oft-repeated Wemyss family symbol as is seen on the arms and the initials of the fourth Earl (1678–1720). Broad Wynd leads to the Cross, an area of both sad and saved buildings. Turn down the landscaped steps (Narrow Wynd) beside the Church Street sign. The church was succeeded by St Adrian's so has disappeared. The manse lies beyond the old school. Turn left where we join Main Street again, the corner site being the Wemyss Arms/Cluny's Cave Restaurant, famed for its fresh, reasonably priced seafood. This last stretch of Main Street is fully residential and ends at the local war memorial. I like the name Happies Close (right, near the end). The war memorial is set in the original gateway to the churchyard, hence the unconnected date on the pillars. The road swings right to a bus turning area/carpark but we can turn left initially to go into the churchyard by a more recent gateway.

St Adrian's was built in 1895 of the local sandstone. On the eye-catching round west window the sandstone is peeling off like the skin from a tangerine. There are several gravestones of note.

Once out the seaward gate, head over to walk along just above the shoreline. You will see Wemyss Castle perched on the cliffs above, the Michael winding tower ahead, the prow of Buckhaven, Methil's oil-rig construction work and the far sweep of Largo Bay.

The first crag has a walled-up cave (and a walled-up window in the wall) which is known as Green Jean's Cave, after the ghost who appears when anyone dies in the castle. She appeared rather often during the wars when the castle was a hospital. Above the castle site is a tower which was originally a wind pump for mine-workings, then became a doocot, and now is purely ornamental.

Up through the trees beyond the castle you may see a row of 'caves' in the cliff which have clearly been carved out by humans. These are given as being old stables or a piggery. The Red House above was the Victorian residence of the castle chaplain and is now part of the estate offices. The cottage by the shore was originally the laundry (kept well away from the toffs) and then the keeper's house.

Just past the cottage turn in the gateway, and then turn right immediately to follow a path along the edge of the wood. An isolated rock on the seaward side is known as the Lady Rock, supposedly because it was a favourite picnic spot for the ladies from the castle. The top is hollow and the rock curls over like a cowl. A wall runs out to sea, presumably the castle boundary at one time. Eastwards, along to the colliery workings, was once the site of a golf course, opened in 1850 but abandoned before the end of the century. The pit waste has been piled along here and you can see how the sea is cutting back into it, forming a miniature cliff. Eventually our wood-edge path starts to climb upwards.

Just round the corner, near the pit (nothing to see now), is the Glass Cave, so called from its long association with glassmaking. Sir George Hay established one of Scotland's earliest glassworks in the cave in 1610, and it is mentioned over the next century before finally going bust in the early eighteenth century. In 1901 the cave collapsed due to the workings of the Michael Colliery – named after Captain Michael Wemyss (1889–1982) of Wemyss Castle – and, for safety, was filled with redd from the pit. Opened in 1898, it overlooked the last hole of the unhappy Wemyss golf course.

In the colliery there is another ruined cave. The Michael Cave was discovered in 1929 when the ground below a boiler cracked and investigation revealed a cave below. (There was a graffiti date 1690 on its wall.) Archaeologists were given a brief, grudged period to investigate before the cave was filled with concrete. A cup and ring mark and a hunting scene with an elk were noted, and the last, extinct before the time of Christ, gives interesting speculation as to the date of the drawings. In 1951 the population of East Wemyss was 3,673, a big change from the small fishing village it once was. The fishing declined but linen manufacturing then became important (one fabrics factory still operates) and then came king coal.

The flat area has been planted with beech, ash and other deciduous trees, and on the left is a wall and an old road that led to the castle. We pass along by a row of houses, built for the pit managers, and a buzzing transformer to turn left at a footpath sign onto the road

105

leading to the houses of Victoria Avenue. This heads round the old foundations to pass seawards of the next house east, so cut over directly.

There is a view down onto the Michael colliery – or what is left of it. The main Dysart seam was inclined to ignite spontaneously, and in 1967 a disastrous fire saw nine lives lost (fathers of the children I was teaching at Buckhaven at the time) and the Michael closed, a local tragedy as it was regarded as a long-life colliery. The resultant population fall led to our school being shut down, too, for all these things have effects which tremble outwards, hurting many innocent people. Most of the buildings have been removed, as has the big chimney, but the winding tower remains. Beyond the row of sheds, water, red-staining the rocks on the shore, is still being pumped out of the workings. They might just, one day, be reopened for there are vast reserves left. For a while coal was still mined but taken out via Seafield. The Fife coast and under the Forth must be like a rabbit warren.

Ahead of us, on this higher level, are long streets of miners' houses, 'rows' as they were called. These have been carefully modernised and are still occupied, so full marks to Kirkcaldy District Council for saving such a historic site. The first row which we look along is Randolph Street (Randolph from one of the Wemyss family, of course. The new council houses of Macduff include Alexander, Rolland and William, but these are names of councillors, there being no monopoly of vanity). Don't walk along the row but, before the first house, descend

steps right onto St Mary's Terrace and an open green area. Cross this to a gap between the beds with show trees and dogwood to reach Approach Row, which we walk along. I wonder what the original miners would think of the modern comforts inside the cottages and the cars lined along outside? Turn first left, first right, and on down to the main coast road (A955). The post box at the top of West Brae (right) is of Edward VII vintage.

On the landward side, set back between two identical houses, is the bowling green. The houses were built after the First World War as homes for retired miners who, I'm sure, appreciated the Latin inscription on the gables: '*Nisi Dominus Trusti*' (Put your trust in the Lord) and '*Deus Adest Laborantibus*' (God helps those who work). Left, as we reach the A955, is a wee shop by a bus stop. The building is called the Carshed for it was originally a shelter for passengers waiting for the tramcars which operated between Gallatown (Kirkcaldy) and Leven in the years 1906 to 1932.

Turning right we walk along the main road. On our right is the Den (local word for 'dell') with the milky-coloured Back Burn flowing through it, this colouring being the result of the burn's origins in the old Randolph Colliery. The flat area in the Den was once a quoiting ground and, flooded in winter, became a curling rink. Across the road is the red sandstone St George's Parish Church, built in 1937 with a harder stone than the local type, brought from North Yorkshire. A pillar by the church wall has a bench-mark on it. The road up east of the church led to the station, on an 1854 branch line from Thornton to Leven, which closed in 1964. A garage and wee shop are passed and across the road is a row of turn-of-century houses which have a nice range of chimney pots. We then reach the Wemyss Environmental Centre, which is in the basement of the large, attractive East Wemyss Primary School building. The centre is a mine of information on all aspects of life in the area, past and present, so do go in; there are plenty of displays, reference sources, and publications (see note at the start of the Bibliography, Appendix 4). It is open on weekdays, 9 a.m. –4 p.m. Telephone (0592) 714479. The key for Jonathan's Cave may be obtained here (see p.110).

When you leave the centre/school, turn left at the gates to go down what is School Wynd. It passes the abandoned Ex-Servicemen's Club and a small shop and runs down beside waste-ground (the site of the public hall) to reach Main Street. The spur stone on the corner is of parrot coal and just along, right, is the Wemyss Hotel, an old inn rebuilt in 1907 as a roundel shows, still with a carriage entrance from the days of horse transport. Across Main Street is an old school building, the Back Dykes road and another war memorial set in an original churchyard gateway, this one with an attractive small figure of a soldier, signed Tweed, 1921. Seventy names (no ranks) are listed. (The memorial to the 17 who died in the Second World War is in the parish church.)

St Mary's-by-the-Sea used to be the parish church and a church is recorded on this site back in the days of David I (twelfth century). The church was closed in 1976. Part of the building is a private house. Most of the stones in the graveyard have weathered away but on the landward wall there is one from 1646, an unusually early date. Further along is a 1761 stone where all the letter Ns have been incised in mirror image – И. Many stones have an anchor on them, several being fisher feuars from Buckhaven, one hammerman's has a gun and powder horn, one has a sharply incised plough (1821) and graceful calligraphy while another has several types of writing all mixed and run together. The manse (1791) faces the church across Main Street. Walk seawards along Main Street. Off it (left) is Kingslaw, then beyond Weavers Court, it becomes East Brae and pulls up steeply past a black and white building which was once a famous brewery.

THE WEMYSS CAVES

Turn onto the foreshore, passing restored cottages, to reach the famous Wemyss Caves which came to the notice of archaeologists in 1865 when symbols matching those on the better-known Pictish stones were discovered. Here they are more primitive so could be some of the earliest Pictish work.

There is a track along the shore but it was severely damaged in winter '93-'94 storms. The caves have great archaeological importance and, after decades of neglect and vandalism (both by man and the elements), may be turned into something of a showplace. Meanwhile, the road along below the cliffs has been patchily strengthened – the sea has washed it away more than once and we'll have to wait for developments. The caves at present are *very* dangerous and, without a strong torch and expert guidance, their treasures are largely invisible. They are best appreciated from one of the guide booklets available at the Environmental Centre (Frank Rankin's 1989 *Guide to the Wemyss Caves* is the best). I used to know the caves well when I taught at a Buckhaven school, so a description as we walk along may be helpful.

The first complex cave is the Court Cave, so called because baronial courts may have been held there. It lies just beyond the last house on the shore: a rectangular opening of a side passage being noted, then the main entrances

The Wemyss Caves, showing the Court Cave at the turn of the century (© Kirkcaldy Central Library Collection)

which are now wired off, and notices warn one to keep out. Several pillars were installed when mining made the cave unstable in the 1930s but this did not stop a major collapse in 1970. The rubble still almost fills the entrance. There are drawings in the cave. The one referred to as Thor and the Sacred Goat is very clear, in that little side passage. Facing it is a cluster of cup marks, going back long before even the Picts.

The next cave along is labelled Dovecot Cave. More traditionally, it is the more easterly of the two Doo Caves, the other (inner) having collapsed. The pigeon-holes at the back and right side are easily seen, though mud coming through from the West Doo Cave is rising to obscure them a bit. The large cave collapsed during the First World War, the result of guns being fired from a battery built above

The Doo Cave is so called because it has two walls carved with pigeon nest holes. Now much silted-up and needing remedial work

the cave. A lot of interesting drawings were lost, including the swimming elephant, a Z rod and other similar Pictish symbols. There is nothing visible now except a hollow if you scramble up the hill. A storm in 1945 took away a brick wall which had been built across the East Doo Cave mouth, which is reasonably safe to enter. Any drawings were destroyed when the roof was smoothed off and the nest boxes (70 to 90 of them) cut out. Vandals have poured paint down the wall near the entrance.

A storm also took away a shoreline doocot which appears in so many old pictures of Macduff Castle. It stood near where the track narrows and was built up on a concrete wall. Beyond is a large grassy bay, ringed with cliff and with the castle above. A path leads up to the castle, which is rapidly decaying from persistent neglect and vandalism. If you scramble inside there is a stairway down to the cellar, lit by a gun loop, or up to tottery heights. The exterior stonework is reduced to a dramatic honeycomb in places due to the weathering of the soft sandstone. Old pictures show two towers; now there is

only one, thanks to the local council blowing up the east tower in 1967 'for safety'.

Macduff Castle is connected with the Thane of Fife, slayer of Macbeth. Tradition has it he escaped down an underground passage to the Well Cave and made along to the east and crossed to North Berwick from Earlsferry, which supposedly took its name from the event. He took refuge in England and eventually defeated Macbeth at Dunsinane. (A castle of that vintage would have been constructed of wood, however.)

The stonework immediately above the cliff is the remains of the castle burnt on the orders of Edward I. This castle passed through various hands before being bought back into the Wemyss family in 1630. They, however, owned Wemyss Castle and so Macduff Castle was allowed to fall into decay.

Several caves lie along the base of the cliff under Macduff Castle. The Fern Cave, left, is blocked off; nothing to see. The Well Cave is fenced off and visitors warned not to enter. You'd need proper gear to explore fully, anyway, for the entrance cave, after sloping down, becomes a narrow passage through to the huge, domed cave proper. A dried-out well lies at the back and a passage (silted up) supposedly leads up to the castle. The interior is now heaped with stone from rockfalls, so the dangers are real. There is nothing in the way of prehistoric art to lure one in. The walls are covered with generations of carved initials and dates. The earliest I've noted is 1742. Some from last century were superbly carved and one seems to be the work of the Wemyss family. The well has prehistoric festive associations, the Celtic New Year Festival (Samhain) being eventually taken over by Christianity when a Hansel Monday torchlight procession was held by the young people of East Wemyss.

The lower, smaller cave next door has no name and can be entered, not that there is much to see. The rock of the cliff has attractive colours and textures, however. Outside the caves you may see chervil growing. The Scots name is alexanders and a tea made from the leaves was supposedly used to cure lust! The next 'bay' has no caves, at least none that we know about. I feel every inch along under the crags should be dug away – who knows what could turn up? It's astonishing how little has been done here by archaeologists. It should be an Historic Scotland showpiece, instead of a disgrace. In 1991 archaeologists from the Royal Museum in Edinburgh did take casts of all visible carvings and these may be on show at the Kirkcaldy Museum or the Wemyss Environment Centre. But there must be perfect carvings in the West Doo Cave which only needs digging out (no danger) and there may be other treasures, too.

An access road comes down this bay and, if it is full tide, after exploring Jonathan's Cave, return to this track and go up it until able to traverse along the edge of the fields, descending again just beyond a bite of quarry, right, down a gentle tree-clad slope. If the tide is very high this access road can be followed inland to a track junction. Turn right there to walk along what was once railway track. At the first houses of Buckhaven (Viewforth) turn down steps, along Viewforth for 50m, then cross the road to take steps down to the shore. Head over to pass all the huts on the seaward side.

Let us return to the caves, and the best of them. The track continues but soon ends at the iron grilles that indicate the superlative Jonathan's Cave, said to be named after a one-time resident nailmaker. In 1988 the sea cut back nearly 6m of banking to threaten the cave. The OS gives Cat Cave and it was also called the Factor's Cave as that man once received the East Wemyss rents here. Jonathan's has more drawings than all the other surviving caves combined. All but one of these drawings are found on the west wall. The very first is a graceful swan. Could the Wemyss family have taken their crest symbol from here as well as their name? At the levelling of the floor you may see a graffiti name, STAN. On the bulge, above left, is a boar; then 1m right, a fish; 1m right again (low down), an area with all sorts of symbols and geometrical patterns. (The obvious long fish is modern.) What looks like a bird pecking the ground is next (probably it is a figure as there is one left of it); then there is the most impressive figure of a bull (a horse does not carry its tail as shown). About 3m beyond, on the last bit of wall before the undercut begins, is another animal, perhaps a dog or fox, and several tridents. And on the east wall, opposite, is the drawing of an oared ship (Viking galley?) which may well be picked out in chalk, or you can trace it with your finger. This is the oldest known drawing of a ship in Scotland. At the back, a ledge ('Jonathan's bed') has some pecked crosses or swastikas. The grilles at the entrance were installed to keep vandals out, but jacks were used to break the bars and the heavily padlocked gate simply disappeared. In 1986 a car was set alight in the cave and flaked off some rare drawings. A Save the Wemyss Ancient Caves Society has been formed (SWAC) and looks for support from visitors. Details are available from the Wemyss Environment Centre or telephone (0592) 712815 or (0592) 266361.

The sea has destroyed the track beyond, so climb down onto the beach (or return for the high tide options already mentioned) and walk along under the 2m cliff being exposed by the sea's erosion. Clays and soils and shells (some are from cave middens) form distinctive bands. Scramble up again as soon as is practicable. The even nature of the cliffs behind betray this as an old quarry. Wend back westwards, and just when you feel you are about to be nudged over the edge you'll come on the Sloping Cave, the entrance a rather narrow slot as a landslide in 1888 almost blocked it. The effort of squeezing in is rewarded: the cave is the longest. There's a double disc symbol at knee height on the left and, on the right, rectangles ('comb cases'?) and many holes/holdfasts. If you go right to the back a torch is handy. Scramble out and head east again. Beside the path, below where the quarry wall angles back, there is a depression with a small hole of an entrance. This is the White Cave, of

which little is known beyond the fact that it is big – some suggest it runs miles inland to Kennoway. A dig would be interesting. The quarry provided stone for Buckhaven's harbour, and a temporary mineral line carried it along the bay.

What looks a bit like an old harbour is simply the walled-off area of an old gasworks which has now been scooped out by the sea. The eroded edge of the bank is dangerous, so keep further in, or, tide permitting, along the shore. A curved brick wall on the landward side and a concrete circle, making the gasometer base, are obvious landmarks, and from the latter the entrance to the large Gasworks Cave is obvious. A rockfall in 1959 clutters the floor and has buried a prehistoric quern. Professor Simpson (of chloroform fame) and Dewar (thermos flask inventor) were the first explorers. The cave was originally paved but was wrecked by treasure-hunters. There is a row of holdfasts on the east wall.

BUCKHAVEN AND METHIL

Beyond the gasworks site (it was demolished in the 1960s I seem to remember) there is a sweep of bay round to Buckhaven, with houses clear against the sky above the Ness Braes. The bay ends at the old harbour of Buckhaven – or Buckhyne, as the locals more correctly call it. The anglicising of Scottish place-names riles me: Glendowan becomes Glendevon, Kingorn becomes Kinghorn, and Buckhyne becomes Buckhaven. A *hyne* or *hynd* was a harbour arm; *buc* was 'to roar' (both Norse words, and medieval maps sometimes had it Hynd of Buck). The beach along is mostly stony but it is preferable to the slopes above, which are tearing and slipping in an astonishing fashion. At very high tides you may have to go higher, but don't otherwise. There's a clear path to start, then the bank is cut into by the sea's erosion. Take to the shore, which is slabby or bouldery, and the banks sliding on to it are vividly coloured – reds, purples, ochres – and they can be treacherously glutinous. There's a sandier section (lots of coal traces) and then below the Ness Braes you can gain the grass-sown area above the higher, eroded banking. All this slipping is recent, probably set in motion by the sea's undercutting. The Rosie Colliery lay up the hill but has been cleared completely. An old net factory and smiddy have gone too.

Daniel Defoe came spying out the land here in 1700. He called Buckhaven 'miserable', but he'd been fooled by the locals and was unforgiving. Tradition has it that the real founders of the town were shipwrecked Dutchmen (*c.*1500) who stayed on, married locally and soon integrated into the fishing community. Defoe again writes that the populace were employed wholly in catching fresh fish every day in the Firth, and carrying them to Leith and Edinburgh markets. He said that, despite appearances, 'there were scarce a poor man' in Buckhaven, but 'they are so generally clownish that to be of the village is become a proverb'. One of the clowns took 6d. off Defoe!

At the end of the bay there seems to be masonry jutting out to sea. This is the filled-in harbour, a rather sad spot which marks so much of Buckhaven's past. We won't see much of Buckhaven but its history is worth touching on and I've fond memories of it as I taught at Braehead School there under the 'prophet', headmaster R.F. Mackenzie. Many a time we launched our canoes off these boulders or banged piton routes up the few cracks in the sandstone walls near the caves. People gleaned 'sea coal' in those hard years of the early 1960s. Where we walk on grass along to the fishermen's huts there used to be a bandstand, bathing-pond, putting green and campsite, and Victorian postcards depict pierrot shows and crowds on a white, sandy beach. But the Wellesley pit tipped its waste into the sea – after it had already tipped the redd *over the houses* of the Links, destroying much of Buckhyne's old character and starting the building up on the bluff. Things have gone full circle for we will walk along past huge concrete blocks of flats erected in the 1960s on this wasteland. Braehead School closed because the mining industry failed, but the mines were a godsend a hundred years ago because the once important weaving industry had collapsed and the fishing industry was declining. The failing, closure and changing of industrial patterns is not a modern phenomenon.

It is interesting to see how tenaciously the huts and fishing cling to this exposed spot. Everything from old vans to garden sheds are used, roofed with anything, boats in between stacks of lobster creels, lums reeking – a world quite timeless. Men go out to sea not only of necessity but to satisfy some ancient pull that cannot be denied. In 1831 Buckhaven had 198 boats and an 1866 parochial directory lists 100 boats, owners and boats' names. There are only 12 different family names (40 Thomsons, 14 Robertsons and 13 Deases being the most common). There was not much inter-marrying between fisherfolk and weaving folk, but this was really just for practical reasons: a weaver lass would find it rather difficult baiting hooks for a fisherman husband. Even the weaving had a nautical angle, though, the last fishing net factory closed in 1945 and a local mill supplied the yarn for the first Atlantic cable.

The sea was both benefactor and enemy. In the nineteenth century there were tragedies, usually 'lost with all hands', to Buckhaven boats at Stornoway, Wick, Fraserburgh, the Forth, outside Buckhyne itself, Dunbar, twice at North Shields, and Great Yarmouth – which also illustrates the 'drave' the boats followed. At Whitby a Byckhyne boat helped save an English boat; the latter took up a collection, but the Fifers refused to accept it on the grounds that it might have been the other way round. The Whitby fishermen presented a barometer instead. A lifeboat station was established in 1900. Two years later they saved the crew of the barque *Norman* of Kristiansand. The service closed in 1932 as the harbour had silted up.

Leave the old harbour area and head towards the obtrusive concrete blocks of houses. West Wynd heads uphill, and if you walk up it as far as the first house on the right, you will see this is an old remnant of the scores of similar buildings which once ran along the Links. There are red pantiles and a loft door at roof-level was probably an old sail loft. Return down the brae again and turn left (east) along West High Street, a name far older than the ugly cubist erections of the 1960s, which, unfathomably, were given a Civic Trust award!

The West High Street (now only a side-street) heads off up steeply, a street where the houses have retained some character, so I hope they survive. When you come to a T-junction at the top turn left (Church Street) to reach a crossroads, with the parish church, St David's (1869) across the road. Walk on past this to what appears to be another church. This was St Andrews, the old Free church, and the name is appropriate for the church once stood in St Andrews. Bought at a knock-down price it was shipped to Buckhaven, stone by stone, and erected again in 1872. It was later extended, the congregation eventually amalgamating with St David's, and it is now a theatre and community centre, and has a café which might be welcome. Return to the crossroads and turn left along College Street. Opposite is a garden which is on the site of Braehead School (1957–71), the first to have Outdoor Activities as part of its curriculum. I wonder if pupils from any other school have climbed all the Munros?

Further along, on the right, is the Buckhaven Library, which contains a small local museum upstairs, giving something of the fishing and mining background of the town. There are many boat models and a local man's match-models of Wemyss Castle, the White Swan, etc. One room is laid out as a pre-war kitchen. There is a small shop selling excellent souvenirs, including the Leven-made Methil Moggies and plates commemorating the various pits along the coast. Open Tues, Thurs, Sat 10 a.m.-1 p.m., and Mon–Fri 2-5 p.m. Telephone (0592) 712192.

Continue along College Street. Buckhaven Primary School is passed (facing Rising Sun Road) and then the road swings left. There is a view to the fabrication yard whose spidery construction work has been silhouetted against the sky from viewpoints along our day's walk. It occupies the site of the Wellesley Colliery which closed in 1967. From there along the seafront westwards is covered with redd, even to burying the hamlet of the Links of Buckhaven (the Wemyss estate had to build new houses along the Wellesley Road for the Links occupants). When space ran out the redd was simply dumped in the sea, ruining the sands and silting up the harbour. In 1938 a big storm made a 35ft break in the east harbour arm. In the 1960s when I knew the area, one could well have asked, 'What harbour arm?'

Turn right at the junction, along the long straight Wellesley Road. The pre-war houses with their red roofs, on the right, and red-roofed cottages beyond the green, on the left, make this a gentler spot. At the far end the Randolph-Wemyss Hospital is an old building with modern extensions which has actually had thought given to the changes. There's a porticoed entrance, a clock tower and, on a gable, a coat-of-arms with a swan and the date 1908. The swan, of course, is the Wemyss family emblem – a certain paternal philanthropy went with their exploita-tion of the local people.

This is really no longer Buckhaven, nor yet Methil, but Denbeath, a hamlet in its own right, lying inland from Wellesley Road. The Wellesley Colliery was originally Denbeath Colliery (started 1875 by Bowan and Co, lease expired 1905, and reopened by Wemyss Coal Co as the Wellesley). The Wellesley name is from Lady Eva Wellesley Wemyss, the second wife of Randolph Erskine Wemyss. When the new housing was built along Wellesley Road and College Street, Denbeath was laid out as something of a garden city. The Wemyss architecture is dominant throughout the area. Having had some years of neglect, many of the buildings are now being restored and made more cheerful.

When Wellesley Road bends we are right above the RGC (Redpath De-Groot Caledonian) Methil works where many a North Sea oil platform has been constructed. The interest in the view increases as an order nears completion. You may notice the platforms are built on their sides and are launched like that before being turned upright. The scale is huge, and there's something like 200,000 tonnes of Methil workmanship out in the North Sea. The huge assembly hall allows topside modules to be constructed and fitted-out under cover. There's a workforce of 600, a vital factor in the local economy.

Walking on, on the left there is an attractive 'row' of flats with forestairs (St David's, B&B, on right). Just past the row a road breaks off right, in front of the listed White Swan Hotel to drop down to Lower Methil. This is signposted as TOURIST ROUTE, a somewhat

The construction yard at Methil with an oil rig under way – built lying on its side

fanciful indication as is SHEPHERD'S PARK for the area of 1960s concrete tower blocks with their views straight into the offshore construction yard. Rather than turn down here, continue along till you reach the Memorial Park, which has the local war memorial in the middle. The last house before the Memorial Park (Aldersyde) does B&B so this little cluster on Wellesley Road offers an alternative to staying in Leven.

The war memorial lists 337 names from the World Wars. Above a base of Arbroath stone rises a thick column which is surmounted by the figure of a kilted soldier. Ex-servicemen raised funds to stock the library opposite, opened in 1935. The parish church lies at the other end of the Memorial Park and dates to 1926. Of monastic cruciform shape, the interior is even more historically influenced, with features reflecting all periods back to the original Gueldres Church. Wood carvings of the Bestiary motives are unusual.

Turn into the Memorial Park, passing a shelter with seating, and follow along above the fence. (On the downward slope there are goats and Shetland ponies.) There's a clear view into the construction yard and along to the docks. If not looking at the war memorial and church, just follow the path down and turn right to pass the second concrete tower block and out onto the start of Methil High Street.

Turn left and walk past the Wonder Store to a junction. Straight ahead is signposted for the town centre but we swing right (TOURIST ROUTE) on to Station Road (though the sign is not obvious) which then becomes South Street as it runs along outside Methil

Docks, still a working port though some of it has been filled in and the great days have passed. It's worth mentioning a few things which have come and gone.

The Wonder Store used to have shops all over the town. Its creator began in 1925 by peddling drapery door to door. He then opened shops, went into army surplus after the war, and had big premises in the High Street by 1971. A fire a few years later was a disaster and now only this furniture store remains, in what was built as the Cairn Greg Mansions. The names are those of the occupants of houses facing what was originally built as a lodging-house. They objected to the plans and the developer retaliated by naming the building after them! The station stood next door and existed from 1881 to 1955. Built on part of the Wemyss and Buckhaven line from Thornton, its history was tied to that of mining and the docks – 'Carbon carbasque', as the motto on the Bawbee Bridge says: 'by coal and sea'. The Wemysses were also responsible for the tramway along the coast, 1904–31.

As we walk past the docks there is no sign of the big archway that once marked the entrance. Half the docks have been filled in. (Inland, a picture-house, a school, the old parish church, the Free church, the Miners' Institute and a German Seaman's Mission have all disappeared, though in some cases the buildings have been recycled.) I wonder if people a century ago could have envisaged this startling change. In 1904 the coal output was 6,586,154 tons. Randolph Wemyss in 1883 had bought the harbour at Leven (he already had West Wemyss) and began the construction of Methil Docks. It is a very *modern* story! This monopoly lasted till after the Second World War but the decline in mining was fatal. About the only export now, as at Kirkcaldy, is scrap. Quite a change to the thousand ships (steam and sail) of a hundred years ago. The master of the *Cutty Sark* was born in East Wemyss and retired to Methil. The harbour head had its ghost last century, a Dutch merchant called Thrummy Cap. He haunted the Salt Girnel in a vain effort to have an unsettled account paid. He finally gave up when the building was taken over by the Free Church.

LEVEN

The road eventually swings left (inland) as we have come to the mouth of the River Leven, landmarked by the big Methil power station. At the roundabout turn right over the Ba'bee Bridge (a bawbee is an old Scots halfpenny and this was the pedestrian toll). Buckhaven and Methil are now behind and we are entering Leven. The provosts of these towns met and shook hands in the middle of the new Ba'bee Bridge when it opened in 1957. The largest bridge built since the war, it had cost £200,000, a figure soon dwarfed by the Forth Road Bridge. Upstream, you can see an old iron bridge, the Kirkland Bridge, which had to take all the traffic while the Ba'bee was being rebuilt. For centuries the nearest bridge was at Cameron, 3km upstream. Coaches could sometimes ford the River Leven and pedestrians were ferried across. Seawards, you may see the moving gantry at the power station sliding back

and forth.

The power station may not be beautiful but it is interesting: for a start, it is not conventionally coal-fired but is, rather, fuelled by slurry (the residue left from the mining process) of which it gobbles up 1,000 tons a day. Fife had several million tons of this ugly waste and, in 1960, was creating plenty more as the Denbeath washery was producing 4,000 tons a week (the Wellesley and Michael were in production and the Seafield was being sunk). A power station able to use slurry was ingenious. The site was chosen because 3 million gallons of water an hour are needed and the Firth of Forth obliges.

The slurry arrives, looking like lumpy black pudding, and is handled by overhead cranes onto stockpiles or into bunkers whence it goes into beating mills to be pulverised, fine as face powder, before being blown into the furnaces. The ash residue is caught by electrostatic precipitation and even this waste of a waste has value today, being mixed with cement or used in bricks and foundation works.

Edinburgh's sewage is processed at Leith: sand and gravel is recycled, scrap metal extracted (whole bicycles turn up in the sewers!) and the resultant sludge is shipped out by the *Gardyloo* and dumped at sea, a process which is to be stopped under EC regulations. Experiments are being made to see if this household slurry can be used in the power station.

It is hard to imagine this area being a busy harbour at one time, exporting coal, linen, whisky, iron, potatoes and bone dust. Boats just used the creek originally until a quay was built and in 1880 a proper harbour for sailing ships.

Methil Docks later stole the trade and eventually the area was simply filled in.

Keep right at a roundabout and on to the pink (yes, pink!) building which is the modern-style, luxurious Levenmouth swimming pool, sauna, and sports complex. (Open till 10 p.m., so it may tempt after the day's walking.)

A pedestrian crossing opposite the pool's entrance takes us over to the Shore Head. On what was the harbour 100 years ago we now have a busy bus station (no office, but timetables are on display) and taxi rank with the pedestrianised High Street leading off beyond. Leven is a busy place, being the main shopping area of this part of Fife. As most of the accommodation is conveniently located on the Promenade, you may like to walk along it to settle in before any further explorations (if any) but I'll mention a few of the curiosities now. The town itself is unpretentious, apart from the churches all aspiring to outdo each other.

At the far end of the High Street, left, is an older brick Co-op building with a plaque showing a skep and bees flying about it. The big 1930s' Co-op building 100m further on has skeps flanking the clock – but no bees. Further along (Durie Street) there's a cluster of churches. A few minutes further on, right, is the entrance to Carberry House where there's a partially restored, multifaceted, red sandstone sundial which was once Leven's mercat cross. It was dismantled in 1767 to ease congestion at the funeral procession of a local laird. It then disappeared and was found again in 1889 as part of a wall, and was restored and re-erected near the Greig Institute. Traffic demands led to its moving to Carberry House. The only comparable sundial is at Drummond Castle, near Crieff.

Durie Street becomes Scoonie Road and leads to a roundabout and the Scoonie Brae where the cemetery is found. It is quite a long way out but the enthusiast will enjoy its treasures. Quite how much of Leven you see will depend on when you reach the town. The area between the High Street and the seaside Promenade is mostly taken up by a large carpark and at the eastern end of this is the attractive Greig Institute and its guardian tree. The Tourist Office is now in the Beehive building at the end of the High Street.

PRACTICAL INFORMATION / ACCOMMODATION

Telephone code (0333)		Forth Bay, Promenade (east)	423009
		Inchkeith, Promenade (east)	426508
Leven Tourist Information Office	429464	Almora, Church Road	
		(off east Promenade)	423743
Leven		Burnlea, Balfour Street	
Westora, Promenade	426164	(next golf club house)	426291
Mont Clair, Promenade		Morven, East Links	
(evening meals)	426215	(overlooking golf course)	426075
Beachmount, Promenade	425491	4 Bayview Terr, Links Rd	
Braeriach, Promenade	423989	(one in from east Promenade)	426977

Janeda, Linksfield Street   428080
32 Glenlyon Rd (on B933, N from
bus station)   429570
9 Kinnarchie Crescent, Aberhill
(back over Bawbee Bridge)   426435
St Ayles, Sillerhole Rd (off A915,
north side)   426738
New Caledonian Hotel, High Street
(expensive)   4424101
Hawkshill Horel, Hanslow Street
(at the centre)   426056

Methil back a bit (bus/taxi)
Aldersyde, Wellesley Road,
Methil   (0592) 713486
St David's, 626 Wellesley Road,

Methil   (0592) 712942
White Swan Hotel, 552 Wellesley Rd,
Methil   (0592) 713346

Camping: Leven Beach Holiday Park (0333)
426008
Swimming Pool and Sports Centre
Levenmouth   429866
Taxis: Leven 426486, 427222, 4
                                             428595
                 425444, 426601, 423139, 428899
Methil   (0592) 429934
Buckhaven   (0592) 715000, 713551, 716000
Tide Times: Tel. (0333) 426725 (Methil
Docks)

THE EAST NEUK

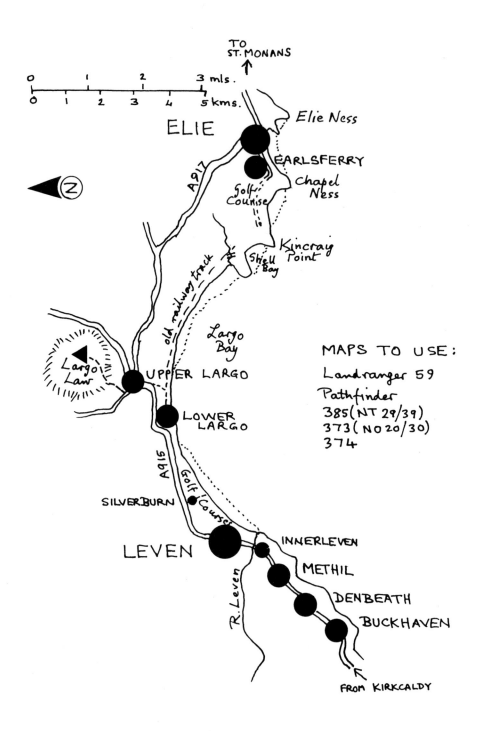

TO
ST. MONANS

0   1   2   3 mls.

0   1   2   3   4   5 kms.

N

ELIE

Elie Ness

A917

EARLSFERRY

Golf
Course

Chapel
Ness

Kincraig
Point

Shell
Bay

old railway track

Largo
Bay

Largo
Law

UPPER LARGO

MAPS TO USE:

Landranger 59
Pathfinder
385 (NT 29/39)
373 (NO 20/30)
374

LOWER
LARGO

A915

Golf Course

SILVERBURN

LEVEN

INNERLEVEN

METHIL

R. Leven

DENBEATH

BUCKHAVEN

FROM KIRKCALDY

DAY 6 *Fair Largo Bay*

Lower and Upper Largo–Largo Law–Elie

Maps to use: Bart 49, OSLR 59, OSPF 373 (NO 20/30)/ 374 (NO 40/50)
Walking distance: 19 km (72 km)

Having had the most built-up stretch of the walk yesterday, today offers one of the two most constantly rural walking days, picturesque Lower Largo being the only town on the way to Elie. It is a fine introduction to the fresh world of the East Neuk.

Today's walk can be inconvenienced at one stage by a high tide. High tide can also stop the adventurous rounding of Kincraig Point, so it is best to be leaving Lower Largo with the tide falling, or out. The Cocklemill Burn which braids and is passable on the sands at low tide can prove an annoying barrier when the tide is in and will entail a diversion to a bridge inland. The famous Chain Walk round Kincraig Point is not practicable at high tide either, though there is a nearby alternative. Maybe we should say that is the normal route and the Chain Walk is the alternative – for those with a liking for the unusual. Greater details are given later, but plan the day to suit the tides if you can.

LEVEN TO LOWER LARGO

If not already on the Promenade from your B&B choice, walk through to it and head off eastwards along the coast, passing a roundabout which takes the A915 through traffic off the Prom. The power station bulks large behind us and ahead is the huge sweep of Largo Bay leading to Kincraig Point with a radio mast on it. One can either walk along a path right by the shore or just follow the road. On the left, between a bingo hall and amusements and a group of new houses, there is a garden. A plaque on a granite monolith commemorates the Polish First Independent Parachute Brigade who were based and trained locally during the war. On the corner of Church Street (B&Bs) is a coastguard building, dated 1904.

The last buildings, in bold red brick, belong to the Leven Golfing Society, (1894 on the gully boxes). A crest on the gable has the date of their founding: 1820. Golf clubs seem to breed here. Inland, beyond the 150-year-old walled bowling green, is the clubhouse of the Leven Thistle golf club. These share the Links. Further inland again is the municipal Scoonie golf course. The Scoonie Burn wends across all the courses and we cross it as we walk along past another red mine and a children's play area, the road finishing at a parking area outside the wired-off Leven Beach Caravan Park (telephone (0333) 26008; camping is possible and there are snacks/meals available). A path leads along outside the site on the golf course side, an easier alternative than the dry white sands of the bay.

The walk along beside the golf course is pleasant. There are wartime defensive concrete blocks most of the way and an odd burn or two. The first burn, well bridged, marks the boundary between Leven golf course and Lundin Links golf course (and Kirkcaldy and NE Fife districts). More precisely the wall, the Mile Dyke, running inland is the boundary, as the burn wriggles its way on both sides of the wall. A five-minute walk up the Mile Dyke leads to the smart Silverburn policies which are worth a visit (open office hours, weekdays and afternoons at weekends, telephone (0333) 427568).

Various estates were bought and brought together under the Silverburn label in 1854 when a flax industry was established by David Russell. He planted many exotic trees which are now superb, mature specimens, and laid out the walled garden. The estate passed to the local authority who have turned it into a many-faceted centre using the old flax-mill buildings and turning cottages into good housing. The big house offers residential facilities but, for us, the main interest is a walk round the Tree Trail (giant redwoods on the Fife coast!) and a look at the mini-farm with its collection of old machinery, displays on many aspects of farming, angora goats, pigs, ponies and rare poultry breeds. You may come away knowing the difference between a Scots Dumpy and an Indian Runner.

Return to the Mile Dyke. Note the iron 'steps to nowhere', a viewing point for golfers. Back at the sea, continue eastwards. Once a year there is an unusual golf match whereby teams play half of both courses so they head from Leven to Lundin Links and back, or vice versa, with a good social interval in the appropriate clubhouse at the halfway stage.

Largo Law (law is often used for hill) now looks quite impressive and you may like to climb it once at Lower Largo. I hope you don't test the reality of a local weather rhyme, as I did one day:

When Largo Law puts on its cowl
Look out for wind and weather foul.

The coast is more often windy than wet. And the links in spring reel with larksong, 'black stars in sunny skies' (W.H. Davies). The golf course was originally designed by James Braid, and as well as the wind has tree and water hazards. If the Open is at St Andrews it is used as a qualifying course. Maybe we should be calling this the Golf Course Coast.

Nearing the end of the bay, after a second burn is crossed, the golf course is protected from tidal erosion by a wall of railway sleepers. Where these stop there are concrete steps down onto the sands, the best continuation for us. If the tide is high, however, walk on to the golf shop (white mast) and clubhouse, cross the carpark area and go round the seaward end of a fence and drop down to paths through the marram dunes. If keeping to the shore, the traveller joins these paths as the shore becomes too rocky for easy walking. (Note the pillboxes set below the golf shop.)

The shore rocks become a crazy mixture, the 100m beyond some swings showing multi-hued slabs slicing into the sea. On a winter ebb tide these nooks of sea offer a hunting ground for ducks and waders in great number. Keep along behind the first row of houses overlooking the sea which leads out onto the main road into Lower Largo. Turn right but after only 40m turn right again (Drum Park) to walk down to the sea. An old house (it calls itself the Old Net House) was once used by the fishermen of Lower Largo. In 1855 there were 36 herring boats based here, employing 80 people; now there are none, though something of the flavour of the fishing days lingers on. This is the first of the succession of such ports which we will be seeing on our way out to Crail in the extreme East Neuk.

Take the footpath behind the Old Net House; this leads out to the delightful setting of the old harbour/river-mouth of Lower Largo. Crusoe Hotel, Railway Inn and Harbour Café and Fish Bar ensure some refreshments. The viaduct acting as a backcloth to Largo's stage-set scene is that of the defunct coast railway line.

The Crusoe Hotel was once a granary. A comparable granary at a harbour will be seen at Elie. Hutchisons at Kirkcaldy Harbour must have started like this. Cross the Keil Burn to follow the twisting Main Street through the straggly village, another feature common to East Neuk harbour towns. All are architecturally delightful. Don't think the towns are twee, however; East Neuk folk can be very down to earth.

The village road wiggles on, passing St David's parish church, left, and the post office, right. Just beyond, on the right by the Baptist church, is a break down to the sea (The Orra) with carparking spaces, telephone kiosk and letter box. Small yachts stand parked by the sea, and if you go down to them you'll see an area of extra-red sandstone on the shore.

Keep on along the Main Street (a road heads off up to the A915) and beyond the first houses, left, set back a bit, is the main tourist attraction of Lower Largo: the statue of Robinson Crusoe or, to be precise, of Alexander Selkirk, the local lad who was Defoe's model for his castaway. Selkirk was born here (in an earlier house) in 1676 and was forced to become a shoemaker like his father, rather than go to sea. However, a family quarrel and a public rebuke in church convinced everyone he was best away. He proved a capable

The Robinson Crusoe statue marking the birthplace of Alexander Selkirk at Lower Largo

four months (1704–09) he was alone were probably more than he'd bargained for. An English privateer rescued Selkirk who made good in this trade before heading back to England where Defoe interviewed him and later wrote his bestseller. By then Selkirk had returned to sea but died of yellow fever off the West African coast in 1721.

Continue heading eastwards. Note the old, sett-surfaced lane going off left. Soon afterwards the road makes a right-angled bend seawards as buildings block the natural continuation line. Cardy Works is mentioned on a gate and this was a Victorian net factory. A white mast in the walled grounds is topped with a weather-vane in the shape of a fish. A footpath runs through behind the works, with Cardy House above it, another gillie's house with plasterwork by Italian artists and plenty of rooftop adornment.

Keep to the road rather than this footpath which simply lands one in a carpark. We pass the carpark anyway as we follow the road – with another right-angled bend. There is a toilet block and the carpark is on the site of the old railway station. We are now in the village of Temple, as the east end of Lower Largo is called. The houses beyond are separated from their gardens (and cars) by the road. Space is at a premium in all these villages, something which has helped prevent obtrusive new developments.

seaman and eventually rose to be sailing master on the ill-fated *Cinque Ports*, a ship where captain and crew (particularly the sailing master) were at daggers-drawn. Selkirk resolved to get off the old, leaky, overcrowded death-trap as soon as possible – which turned out to be the islands of Juan Fernandez, off the South American Pacific coast. The captain was only too glad to have him rowed ashore and left with a few supplies. The *Cinque Ports* sank soon afterwards! There was no shortage of meat, fish and fruit but the four years and

UPPER LARGO AND THE LAW

After a few minutes' walking you'll see that a small lane forks off and there is a sign, SERPENTINE WALK TO UPPER LARGO. Those wishing to climb Largo Law, or see Upper Largo, turn off on this track, a side trip which will take two to three hours, and is now described.

The path angles across another track, which is the line of the old NB coastal railway, and this can be followed on rejoining the walk. There is a Woodlands Trust sign and, on the left, you can see new plantings before a stand of beech trees in a den (dell). Note how the beech trees are planed by the wind. The path crosses a small stream (Largo Burn) and swings right to go along beside it. If you look eastwards across the fields when the path re-crosses the burn there is another example of trees contoured by gales. Trees, east of here, are going to become rarer and smaller, only surviving in sheltered spots.

As we walk up the path, Largo Law looms ahead behind the houses of the Kirkton's South Feus. Some buildings are painted black, with the rusticated quoins picked out in white, a striking effect quite common in the East Neuk. We come out onto the A915 main coast road at a nasty bend. Across the road you can see the eagle-topped pillars of a gateway once leading to Largo House, a 1750 John Adam mansion which was allowed to go to rack and ruin, the pre-war owner doing nothing though refusing to sell; then Polish refugees were there during the war, and finally the roof came off to avoid

taxes. We turn right and puff up to Kirkton of Largo/Upper Largo (it answers to both names).

The road swings right past the hotel (note the painted inn sign showing the *Yellow Carvel*, named after one of Sir Andrew Wood's ships) and on the left is a garage, then Path House (with a thermometer on its house sign!), then a minor road, which we take. The road is not signposted and twists down and then up and over the west shoulder of Largo Law.

In the dip we can turn left to explore the old church on its walled-off knoll. The church is mostly early nineteenth century, though the tower and chancel date from the early seventeenth century. The interior is bright and, not unusual in Scotland, the minister is female. Beside the churchyard entrance is a Pictish symbol stone, much weathered and now roofed over, but you can just make out the cross on one side and, on the reverse, a hunting scene with several mounted figures and one of the puzzling 'swimming elephant' beasts which appear on symbol stones.

Turn right on leaving to follow the road round, and take the first road on the left (just before it says PRIVATE ROAD). Follow this up to a junction and turn left, back on the road that leads off inland. There are a couple of piebald cottages. Almost at once climb up the bank on the left and peer over the wall. You will notice a hollow running away across the field and bending round towards a pepper-pot tower at the far end. This is the remains of the first canal ever to be cut in Scotland, back in the fifteenth century, for Sir Andrew Wood, local lad and national hero, a sort

127

of oceanic Montrose, except he died in his bed and not on a scaffold.

Wood was born in the Kirkton and became a successful merchant trading with the continent, part of that success being his ability to deal with the dangers of piracy and enemy shipping. This led to his being appointed admiral by James III, though he had largely to find his own navy. He also served the more brilliant James IV. Early in his reign five armed merchantmen entered the Forth and, though Scotland and England were not at war, began to attack shipping. Wood, with just two ships, captured them all. Henry VIII was not pleased and sent his best captain, Stephen Bull, with three ships of war to capture Wood, dead or alive. Wood was in Flanders with two ships, the *Yellow Carvel* and the *Flower*, which were attacked off the May as they sailed in. The fight went on all day and night and ended off Fife Ness with Bull's surrender. They were sent home honourably; after all, the Scottish king was married to Henry's sister, Margaret. Wood, however, first used the lower deck prisoners to dig his canal. He also oversaw the building of the *Great Michael* (far bigger than the *Mary Rose*), whose construction devastated Fife's woods.

Wood was awarded lands at Largo and built a castle where he retired. The single tower (once used as a doocot) is all that remains – plus that hollow indicating the line of the canal along which he was rowed to church each Sunday in his admiral's barge. He is buried in the kirk.

Continuing up our country road we pass the Kirkton of Largo primary school. There is a gap, with the modern churchyard beyond, and we turn off at this gap to a kissing gate by the churchyard wall which leads to a path up beside the field. Chesterstone Farm, clearly seen ahead, is our objective. Our path becomes a track leading to the farm and passes a restored row of old farm cottages. Part of Chesterstone may date back to the 1700s but the farmhouse is late nineteenth century, built of dark whinstone. The track goes into and out of a farmyard and passes round the back of the farm to turn sharp left, uphill, as a green track aiming straight at Largo Law.

The path leads directly up between fields to a kissing gate and the rough pasture of the Law itself. Cattle graze even at this altitude, so keep an eye open for the cow that may be a bull: there aren't many trees to climb! There is plenty of gorse, rather reminiscent of the Eildons.

Our view across the estuary has changed, as ever, and now we are seeing the eastern extremities: North Berwick Law and the Bass Rock, Fidra, the Cockenzie power station chimneys, the Lammermuirs and Edinburgh itself (well upstream now) with its backing of hills. Methil power station chimney balances the view on this side. The May Island now replaces Inchkeith as the offshore island and, hopefully, can be visited in a couple of days' time.

We reach a summit but not *the* summit, so dip down beyond to cross a stile in the fence and on up to the highest point where there is a trig point at 290m (952ft), as high as we can be on our walk.

Retrace the ascent route by the farm and primary school but thereafter walk down the road directly into the village and the A915. The big building, marked 'hospital' on maps, was a seventeenth-century charity endowed by a John Wood of Orky to maintain 13 ancient men, all named Wood, with chaplain, gardener and porter. The original 1665 building was washed away in a flood rushing off Largo Law: furniture was swept down to the sea along the line of the Serpentine Walk, which seems impossible when we see the tiny stream there. In 1932 no suitable Woods were found so people with other names were admitted as well. It is still a series of flats and houses for elderly people.

Having quoted rude comments about Kinghorn I'm glad this part comes under fire too:

> Lundie Mill and Largo,
> The Kirkton and the Keirs,
> Pittenweem and Anster,
> Are all big leears.

Take the Serpentine Path back to Temple. When the old railway track is reached turn left (east) along this; it gives easier walking than the sands, a glorious sweep when the tide is out. There are steps leading down to the turning spot where the tarred road ends. The posts beyond are for hanging nets to dry and the wooden building is a salmon fishermen's bothy. If you have simply walked along through Temple, walk past the bothy and angle up to join the railway line at a stile.

The name Temple is thought to have associations with the Knights Templar order which dates back to the twelfth century, when knights took on the duty of guiding pilgrims to the holy sites in Jerusalem. David I brought the order to Scotland. In 1314 the Pope banned the order as it was becoming too powerful and wealthy. One of their temples may have stood here.

THE COAST TO ELIE

Walk along the line of the old railway, passing the ruin of a house (Viewforth), left, to reach an area where a burn comes down by a bigger house, Carrick Villa, and a road has cut the railway's line. Abandon the railway walkway here as it swings well inland, and follow paths along the dunes, very enjoyable going with a feeling of great spaciousness and summer skylarks singing overhead. The Lammermuirs rather than Pentlands now face us across the firth. All that mars this stretch is the huge accumulation of plastic junk which wind and tide collect at the back of the bay. There are some anti-tank blocks and pillboxes across our route at one stage and, nearing the end of the sands, there are lines of salmon-fishing poles. I noticed one half-buried bottle in the dunes had become an 'anvil' for thrushes and was surrounded by heaps of broken land snail shells. There are plenty of rabbits too, with their burrows in the dunes.

Cocklemill Burn may come as a shock. If the tide is well out one can cross where it braids out on the sands, but not otherwise. It flows through the whole inland salt-marsh area in a tortuous series of loops, too wide to leap and too deep and muddy to wade. There is a derelict salmon-fishing station across the burn and plenty of tidal litter.

If the burn is not easily crossable,

129

walk upstream (cutting corners) to find a well-hidden bridge just below the corner of the St Ford Links wood (GR 463009). Giant hogweed grows nearby. Walk down the other bank, joining a track outside the caravan park's shelter belt boundary of conifers, to reach Ruddons Point, a good viewpoint, sometimes called Shooting Ho Point though the rifle-range has long gone.

Eventually walk round the edge of Shell Bay which has some big dunes and is backed by a large caravan site. Camping is possible and if this option is taken it would be best to set up camp before going on to do the energetic Chain Walk, returning over the top of Kincraig Hill thereafter. Shell Bay not only has shells in plenty but the sand has a high proportion of pulverised shell in it as, indeed, do the rich black soils of the fields along the raised beaches.

A couple out walking at the back of Shell Bay at the start of the century noticed some bones lying in the dunes. The quick-eyed wife then found a bone pin and, after poking about, they realised they'd found a prehistoric midden. When excavated, the site produced decorated combs, a spindle whorl, pins, a cup made of bone and bones of a range of animals like ox, sheep, pig, rabbit, red and roe deer, dog and fox. There was also a pile of stones used, once heated on a fire, for dropping into water for cooking purposes.

Cultivation frequently comes right down to sea-level along the East Neuk, which was famous for its cereal crops back to medieval times. (Kingsbarns, in the East Neuk, was just that: the place where the king's grain was stored.) A local saying about sowing goes:

> Ane for the cushie-doo,
> Ane for the craw,
> Ane that will rot
> For the ane that will graw.

Heading round the east side of Shell Bay the distinctive terraces of three raised beaches will be noticed. These indicate former sea-levels above that of the present, and have provided the geologists with endless fun trying to date them. They are a feature all coastal walkers will come to recognise and often appreciate for the easy, horizontal walking they give. They frequently provide a useful platform for siting farms, castles and even villages. Walk right out to the grassy point; the path runs along between fields and shore in a leisurely fashion – quite a contrast to what lies ahead. Rock rose, agrimony, cranesbill and bugloss indicate the lime-rich soil of the point.

Turning the point the path climbs the first raised beach; for the second it breaks into steps, and just as it swings left for the third rise, a small path breaks off right. This is the route for the more interesting but serious Chain Walk alternative (see p.131). Those of a timid disposition or who don't fancy dangling across cliffs on chains above the sea can keep to the path along the cliff-top. There are steps again for the last pull up onto the third raised beach and we then wander into some wartime defensive remains.

Shortly afterwards leave the main path to wander a lesser path on the cliff edge. This will give you the widest

The Burry Man, Queensferry

St Bridget's churchyard

North Overgate, Kinghorn

Back stairs, West Wemyss, as they were in 1969

Opposite: Climbing on Hawkcraig, Aberdour

The Beehive house (now the Tourist Office), Leven

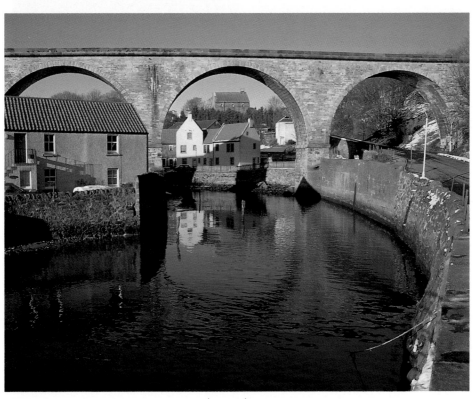

Lower Largo

Storm over Largo Bay

Elie Church

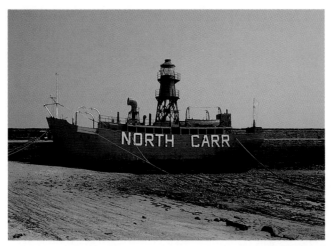

The North Carr Lightship, Anstruther

Anstruther Harbour

Opposite: Basalt columns, Kincraig Point

The Maiden Rock and St Andrews

Old grocery shop, St Andrews Preservation Trust Museum

views and you'll see a flight of steps descending to an observation-post. If the tide is out, note the strangely flat areas below and the sea-worn dykes. The observation-post on the cliff-top has a collapsed roof. From it we look along the sandy bay to Earlsferry. The view down will probably convince you that *not* taking the Chain Walk was a wise decision!

The path joins a track up to the communications mast. There is a trig point just before it. Kincraig Hill, 63m, feels much higher. Take the path on from the mast to pass one of the many hill-top gun emplacements and then on along the crest of the hill to just beyond another lookout-post, which also has had its visor pulled down on its nose. There is no way down before this. The path angles down to cross the end of the golf course and runs along the dunes edging the bay.

The Chain Walk alternative offers a unique experience, but I'd only recommend it to the fit and hardy or those with mountaineering experience and a head for heights. It is, in Alpine terms, a *via ferrata*, progress being determined by using chains draped across cliff-faces or over necks of crag, often with footsteps cut in the rock as well. There is a great deal of geological interest, too, so, while stressing its serious nature, I'd also say it is not to be missed if possible. Ability will not count at all if the tide is fully in, as much of it will be under water. At least two hours off high tide would be wise, more with the tide coming in. The crux is at the east end and if courage fails there then everything else has to be repeated in reverse. There are no escape routes. So watch the tide and if

you don't like the first chains, retreat then. It can take up to an hour to win round Kincraig Point. At low tide one can scramble and slither past the prows, avoiding the chains in most cases.

When leaving the grassy point after Shell Bay, if you look along, beyond a couple of coves, you will see a path zigzagging down. That is the start of the Chain Walk. Now carry on up and round the rim onto the level of raised beach; then, when the path swings left to go up and over a steepening out of sight, turn off on a smaller path, right, which is the one wiggling down to the Chain Walk. Once down to a green patch you'll see a rectangular cave set in the back of the cove. The Devil's Cave is worth a visit at low tide, the route down being a shallow gully seawards rather than any direct descent. The trench running into the cave gives an awkward 3m wall to climb down. The cave runs in for an impressive distance. Return to the foot of the zigzag path again.

Head off east from the green patch – the last grass for some time – and wend up and down over a series of rock ribs running seawards. (Breccias and basalt are the main rocks on the point.) There's a short chain down, leading into a cove with one shallow and one deeper cave, then a traverse of cliff with horizontal chains for security. This leads to a vertical chain in a corner which will give the longest haul up, made easy by steps, big as buckets in the top half, leading to an iron post on the neck.

Beyond is a beach with a huge flat area (between the tidelines) marked with straight lines which look man-made but which are natural. The flat area ends at Kincraig Point itself, an area of jagged spikes of erosion-defying rock. Many of the dykes have weathered out in long slots in which the seas suck and surge noisily, other dykes and veins have been harder and stand up in lines: a fascinating area. A wartime observation-post perches halfway up the cliff.

A wall of organ-pipes (columnar basalt) will entertain, then there is another vertical chain to climb up, then down, into a wee bay where we swing left to a marked neck in another lava flow. A short chain takes one down onto the major area of geological interest, a big spread of 'organ-pipes', lying across a scree of the hexagonal blocks from past disintegration. A huge detached bunch of pillars leans against the main area.

In the bay beyond, the weathered stumps of long-gone pillars have weathered into what looks like a lime-stone pavement formation. The shingle here is dark grey, rounded and sized by the sea in an attractive way. From the top end of the shingle, steps lead up to traverse along the rocks and round a point. Large steps lead down to one of those strange flat areas. Head up left of a natural arch. The cliffs above are at their most impressive now, beetling out, great bellyfolds of rock, noisy with fulmars from January on into summer.

The next (last) cove is the most serious so have a look across to the continuation. There's a horizontal chain leading to a broad ledge which peters out and one descends by small steps onto a tidal ledge. This tidal ledge can be gained direct by big steps off the beach if the tide is right out.

The immediate route on down into the cove can't be so studied and can be intimidating. I suspect there was a chain here at one time for it is quite an exposed descending traverse into the narrow cove (in the north it would be a geo), ending with a step across to a detached fin of rock in the cove itself. Take it easy and don't lean in, as this only constricts movement and visibility.

The great sweep of cliff at the back of the cove doesn't have a cave and is best left unvisited. (There's a great deal of recently fallen rock.) Escape along the horizontal chain, with big carved steps, to the broad ledge. When it fizzles out, the route is *down*, on rather shallow steps. Descend, facing in the way. The lower ledge is a bit slippery, being tidal. If the tide is well out steps lead onto the lower ledge direct, as you'll have seen from the other side. After that you swing left, and *Eureka!*, you've completed the Chain Walk.

After one visit I had complaints from a friend that she spent all night doing it over again in her dreams, but I suspect overindulging at the supper-table was involved. I'd always thought the Chain Walk was Victorian, and had visions of Amazons in long dresses tackling it, but when I eventually found information on its building the date proved to be 1929.

Follow the path, partly on the shore, partly on the grass slopes, then wholly on the grass till the golf course is reached and we join those who went over Kincraig Hill instead. Golf has been played here since the sixteenth century and is really Scotland's national game.

Nearing the end of the Chain Walk, Kincraig Point

The beacon out to sea marks the East Vows reef, off Chapel Ness, a vital navigation aid for approaching Elie Harbour from the west. Locally, the beacon is known as the 'Chair of Refuge'. Look back to Kincraig Point, 'the most conspicuous as well as the most interesting and picturesque on the Fife coast' (Steers). Keep along the edge of the golf course till you come to an obvious sunken track running down to the shore. Walk up this (watching out for flying golf balls) then turn off, right, on the edge of the fairway to walk along by the high wall of the big villas (an area favoured by cowslips, by no means a rarity on our walk), to reach a stark, ruined gable. This is all that remains of an eleventh-century chapel, where pilgrims heading to St Andrews could rest after their often overexciting crossing of the Forth Estuary. Macduff, Thane of Fife, is thought to have built the chapel in 1093 as an offering to the Earlsferry ferrymen who rowed him over to Dunbar and safety in England after Macbeth had slaughtered his family at his castle at East Wemyss in 1054. The name Earlsferry is thought to have originated from this event. The long, narrow cave on the Chain Walk is Macduff's cave where he hid out while waiting to be ferried over the firth. The Earls of Fife, having lands in North Berwick as well as in Fife, frequently used this ferry and the name probably came from this more prosaic origin. As many as 10,000 pilgrims may have crossed in a year. Robert II made it a royal burgh in 1373. Elie followed. Pilgrimages had died out by the time of the Reformation and thereafter people preferred to use the ferries further up the Forth, at Pettycur, Burntisland or Queensferry. There were steamers operating Leith–Elie–North Berwick in Victorian times but the First World War put an end to those cruises.

Aim to pass inland of the houses, joining Chapel Green (the tarred road) at a car turning area, marked with white posts. At once you will feel transported back a few hundred years for Earlsferry has a genuine olde worlde feel to its architecture. Note the cottage on the right with its fancy iron brackets supporting the gutters and the graceful doorway beyond. Chapel Green leads to Earlsferry's High Street (Earlsferry leads on into Elie without any noticeable break, but they were separate burghs till 1929) with a 'No entry' sign for cars. The clock tower pinpoints the town hall (dated 1872) and the weather-vane is a sailing-ship. The house opposite has a sundial with several faces perched on its west skew putt.

By the door of the town hall is a plaque to James Braid, a local golfer, five times Open Champion in the years 1901–10. Polish soldiers are commemorated on a wall plaque at the east end of the building. Many stayed on after the war, as in Leven, and you have broad Fife accents belonging to people with names like Peplinska and Matyssek.

Cross Wynd next door presumably indicates a cross here at one time. On the way we've passed Glovers Wynd and Cadger's (Carrier's) Wynd. Once past Ferry Road two-way traffic resumes. St Margaret's Nursing Home lies right and on the left is an ugly brick barn of a building, about the only eye-

sore in the joined towns of Earlsferry, Williamsburgh, Liberty and Elie.

Continue along the road, signed LIBERTY, but turn left up the next road, Golf Club Lane, to see a curiosity at the Elie Sports Club complex. Walk along to the clubhouse and round it, left, to reach the far end where you'll see a hut with a tall, narrow tube rising from it. This is the starter's hut for Elie golf course, and because the first drive is made blind over a bank, in 1966 they installed the periscope from a 1954 submarine, *Excalibur*, to see over the obstacle! (*Excalibur* was an experimental submarine powered by hydrogen peroxide, an idea soon superseded by nuclear power.) There are actually two golf courses, one 18-hole the other 9-hole. Treeless, undulating and windy, Elie offers a fine challenge to players.

Return to the original route, turning onto what is now Links Place. A new housing development on the right has been tastefully made to blend in. The site was a carpark for the Marine Hotel across the road which burned down some years ago. Note the mural carving of a boat. The name Sahara Park is older and may have been given by cynical locals who were always having dunes building up on their doorsteps or gardens. The painted sign at the post office is attractive. Just beyond, turn right down Fountain Road which brings us to South Street, the original High Street of the old royal burgh, where several ancient buildings survive. In summer you may notice the wooden huts on the sands, a tradition largely gone from seaside resorts elsewhere but which is kept alive here by the local joiner.

Gillespie House on the left is obviously old. The 1682 marriage lintel is for Alex Gillespie and Christina Small (their family grave is in the churchyard against the wall, just left of the entrance). There's the remains of a complex sundial over the door. This doorway is all that remains of the Gillespie's Muckle Yett, where they had a sawpit for timber imported from the Baltic.

A ram's head (modern) adorns a house more or less opposite, while on a bit is the big, sturdy harled house known as The Castle. This dates back to the fifteenth century and was the town house of the Gourlays, who were related to the Sharp family, one of whom, the archbishop, was to be murdered on Magus Muir as he rode in his carriage to St Andrews. This led to the judicial slaughter of the murderers – not a very restful period in religious history.

Turn left up School Wynd to reach the main crossroads of Elie itself, as one could gather from the names: School Wynd, High Street, Park Place and Bank Street. The Victoria Hotel occupies one corner, while opposite is a war memorial which has pillars so it looks like another gateway site. The churchyard beyond is entered from further along the High Street where the old session-house, with its odd finial, has been turned into a bus shelter. Diagonally across from the Victoria is a really good baker's shop, Adamson (they have several shops in the East Neuk), so do go in and buy a sair heid or twa! Further along Bank Street, on ·the right, is the baronial red sandstone pile of the Golf Hotel. Elie Primary School, a few minutes up Park Place (which has a couple of B&Bs), is a

pleasant Victorian building with an array of Jacobean gables.

The attractive church is worth a quick visit. It dates to the early seventeenth century though the well-integrated tower (with a cockerel vane) was only added in 1726. It was not a good time to be building a new church. When the Civil War broke out in England, Scott of Ardross, the laird/heritor, went south to support King Charles, while the Scots supported parliament and the minister of Elie went south to attend a regiment, thus finding himself opposing his own patron. The church later supported the king, against Cromwell. Scott was captured at the Battle of Worcester and his estate sequestrated. The impoverished family had to sell out in the end and the Anstruther family became the owner of the Elie estate. The Anstruthers had survived the wars rather more successfully and bought up quite a few local properties. It was one Sir John who removed a whole village (Balclevie) because it was situated too close to his big house. One of the old wives predicted the family would not flourish through seven generations; the sixth proprietor in fact sold up after his predecessor had been shot dead at the age of 13 in an accident at Eton. It was the same Sir John who built the steeple, and as Adam was working on Elie House, he may have had a hand in its design. He certainly *didn't* plan the laird's wife's tower, of which more later on. (Balcaskie House, several miles inland, is still home to the Anstruther family and is open to the public.)

The church is a typical T-shape with the pulpit central and facing the laird's loft opposite, but there have been many alterations since with outside stairs and doors removed or added and, when the church joined with the Wood Memorial (Free) Church, the stained-glass windows from there were added – two of which were by Edward Burne-Jones. One strange connection: the clock mechanism that drives the famous floral clock in Edinburgh's Princes Street Gardens came from the tower of Elie Church after the clock in the church was renewed. There are only three faces because, when originally installed (1900), there were no buildings north of the church.

The graveyard is mostly Victorian but some of the best earlier stones have been placed at the east end of the church. Most noteworthy is a skeleton which seems to be 'rolled up in a carpet', so all that shows is the skull and stark ribs, and the feet. This is the memorial of Elizabeth Turnbull, a daughter of Turnbull of Bogmill (*d.*1650) whose large decorative slab with a vine border stands against the church wall. The bull's head, turned aside, is a pun on the family name. There's a black stone inserted by the masons when building the kirk as a guard against witches, a topic we keep coming back to in Fife. Between 1590 and 1680 it is estimated that 4,400 women were burnt as witches and it was 1736 before the Act of 1563 allowing such, was repealed.

To revert to the graveyard again. At the meeting of paths by the east porch is a stone inscribed to 'Charles Fox Cattanach, wife *(sic)* of James Smith, Ship Master, Elie . . . and James Smith, her husband'. Apparently, the minister at the christening mixed the names of two infants and the superstitious family insisted she was called as baptised! There is no sign now of the 'lang grave', that of a drowned sailor found with arms outstretched (as if swimming) and who was so buried rather than break the arms to fit a conventional space. There are a score of stones testifying to the dangers of the sea. One accident occurred in full view of friends and families when a boat was fishing offshore between the harbour and the Ferry Chapel on a calm day. It was overturned by a sudden squall and several young men drowned. One widow gave birth to a daughter six days later and, in memory, the child was named Andrew. One woman in the town lost husband, brother and brother-in-law in this tragedy.

PRACTICAL INFORMATION / ACCOMMODATION

Telephone Code: (0333)

Accommodation is fairly limited so book ahead, or be prepared to find digs elsewhere for the night. There's a good coastal bus service so this is not a real problem.

Elie
Mount Stuart, Liberty

(Earlsferry end)	330653
Rosebank, High Street	330207
The Elms, 14 Park Place	
(A917 Largo Road)	330404
33 Park Place	330391
39 Park Place	330418
43 High Street	330412
57 Woodside Road (NE)	330608
5 Baird Place (off A917	

St Monans Road)   330662
Victoria Hotel   330305
Golf Hotel   330209

Others, within bus distance:
St Monans: Telephone code   (033-37)
Mayview Hotel, 40 Station Road 564
52 Station Road   668
20 Braehead   0333-73 0205
Newark Farm (1km west)   357
20 West End   617

Pittenweem: Telephone code (0333)
29 Viewforth Place   311405
19 Viewforth Place   311304

11 Viewforth Place   311998

Anstruther: see under tomorrow

Evening meals:
Giovanni's Brasserie, 41 High Street
(Italian)   330117
Bouquet Garni, 51 High Street (good
evening meals, book earlier at busy times).
Cheaper bar meals in hotels and pubs.

Camping: Elie Shell Bay
caravan park   (0333) 330283

Taxi: St Monans   (033-37) 611

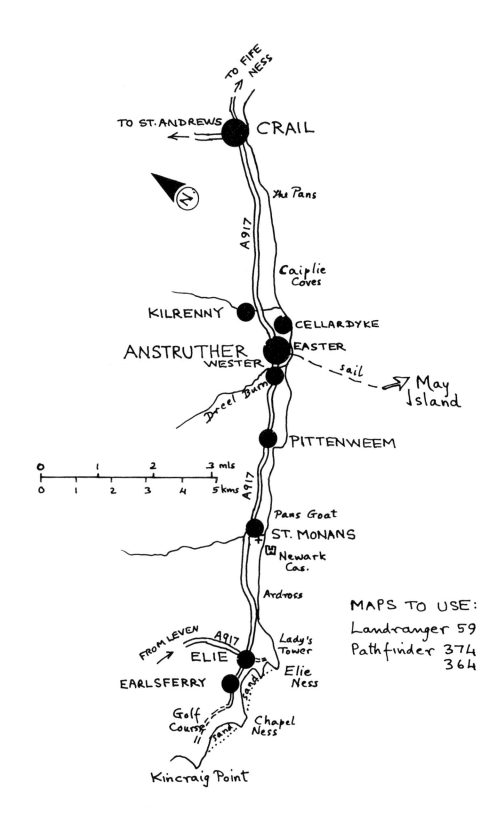

DAY 7 *The Siller Ports*

St Monans–Pittenweem–Anstruther

Maps to use: Bart 49, OSLR 59 OSPF 374 (NO 40/50)
Walking distance: 9 km (81 km)

After an initial solid tramp from Elie to St Monans, this day switches repeatedly from coast to town. One is apt to end in a daze of delight over the diet of East Neuk domestic architecture, trying desperately to recall what was where and no doubt wishing extra film had been available. Keep 'leaning on the day' or you'll be apt to run out of time as well as film.

TO AND THROUGH ST MONANS

We really complete exploring Elie this morning. Elie Point (Elie Ness) with its lighthouse is the most southerly point we will be on for the rest of the walk. From Pettycur to Elie Ness we have followed one huge bay made up of many smaller bays. Stenton Row takes us down from the High Street to the shore at the Toft. Admiralty Lane, left, is our continuation but it is worth walking out the 1586 harbour arm first. The big building is the Granary, now used for drying nets and storing sailing gear. There are plans for its development. The local sailing club was founded in 1964, with Admiral Sir William James as Hon Commodore – remembered as the boy in the painting, 'Bubbles', used by Pears Soap advertising. The club's first boat was also called *Bubbles*. The town still maintains the harbour, which dries out, leaving sands of a delightful rich hue. I think you'll have liked Elie.

If the 1715 Jacobite Rebellion officially began with the raising of the standard at Braemar, Elie had its part, for the fated Earl of Mar landed here to initiate proceedings.

Return and turn up Admiralty Lane, then turn right again to reach the carpark/picnic area above Wood Haven, as the bay is called. Gabions have been stacked at the back of the bay to counter erosion. At the far end of the park, right, there is a gate and a sign indicating the coastal path to St Monans.

Walk round Wood Haven (or Ruby Bay – but the rubies are only garnets), passing some concrete blocks on the way and reaching a prow overlooking the lighthouse, a pair of battlemented towers, one square, one round, which are actually on a small island reached by a concrete footbridge. The light-house was built in 1908 under the supervision of David Stevenson and originally lit by carbide gas. It is now automatic.

The grassy path swings east towards an obvious tower. The shore rocks are spotted with lighter material and just before the bay at the Lady Tower the strata curve out to seaward. The East Neuk is full of geological features. In the corner of the bay you can see an arched grotto. The Lady Tower was built c.1760 as a summer house and is named after Lady Janet Anstruther, 'a coquette and a beauty', according to Carlyle. She liked to bathe in the sea so built this folly and the grotto below, where she could change, a bellman meanwhile being sent round Elie to give warning for the plebs to keep away. Presumably the tower was roofed for there is a fireplace and evidence of a floor. It makes a good viewpoint still.

As we walk on, the bay has some lumps of lawn sticking up and then it becomes sandy along the East Links. The path heads along the marram-clad dunes above the warm-coloured sands, a feature of the coast. Inland, we can pick out Elie House. Note how tree clumps grow in height, west to east, as they are battered by the prevailing winds. The dismantled coastal railway lies across the field and by Ardross there is only just room to squeeze road, railway and path in beside the cliffs.

As we near some cottages (Ardross Cottages) there's a basalt dyke running down the shore like a man-made wall. The path wiggles down to the shore edge and runs tight below the railway, the walls and embankment of which are being eroded by the sea. There's a bridge under the railway leading up to the cottages and the A917. The rock is suddenly a tawny sandstone so the next bit of bay has 'silver' sands, a con-trast for, if you look back along the East Links, the 'golden' sand colour pre-dominates. We walk on to a small point and it is worth going to the edge, first, to see the pleasant view along the coast past Newark Castle and St Monans Kirk to Pittenweem and, immediately below us, to see slabs bearing fossilised wave marks. A few feet above them a coal seam is visible.

A short pull up leads to Ardross Castle which is in a very ruinous state. The path wends through the middle of it and on the right-hand side some vaulting has survived, possibly belong-ing to the castle kitchen. Sir William Dishington (who built St Monans Church) erected the castle in 1370 when sheriff of Fife. He had married a sister of Robert the Bruce.

From the castle there is a good view to an eighteenth-century rectangular lectern-type doocot beside the main road. Prosperous-looking Ardross Farm has commandeered the railway. The line closed as recently as 1969, illustrating how quickly a change of

Fossil ripple marks and coal seams, on the coast of Ardross

use can obliterate past history. Our path leads down, passing a filled-in railway bridge, to a bay where proper embanking has had to be made to protect the line. Ahead, at high tide, a spindle of rock jags out the sea, and if you look back there is a good view of the Lady Tower and Ardross Castle on its cliff. The spindle rock you'll see is made up of two quite distinctive rock types. The geological shambles ensures the coast along to Newark Castle (now clearly in view) is very broken. At one part steps lead down onto a shingle beach with a clay bank beside it and another cross-section of the land where the sea has cut it cleanly.

A rich green field leads to Newark Castle on its jutting prow of sandstone; steps up pass through remnants of outer works with a vault visible, left, and even signs of masonry works on the cliff itself. The castle is a spectacular ruin and, being built with the local sandstone, has weathered badly (harling is popular in the East Neuk as a practical defence against the elements). The lintel on the right of two big doors marooned on the west-facing wall is worn to a sliver, and the grey sandstone outside the impressive vaulted range is attractively striated by the elements.

Fifer David Leslie bought Newark in 1649 and it was from this building (and not the one where his godly arm

massacred the prisoners after the Battle of Philiphaugh) that he took his title, Earl of Newark – his reward for finally defeating 'the great Montrose'. He was an elder at St Monans Kirk for the rest of his life.

The castle is impressive for its setting rather than in itself, for little remains apart from four walls and a row of vaulted cells. Last century the architect Sir Robert Lorimer produced a grand scheme for restoring the castle for Sir William Burrell, the shipping magnate. Had their plans been carried out, Glasgow's Burrell Collection could well have been housed here.

Just beyond the castle is a sixteenth-century beehive doocot, weathered but near-complete, perched on a prow above the sea with the Isle of May in the background. Descend between castle and doocot to follow the shoreland path. St Monans Church soon appears, the most sea-set of the churches of our walk, and one not to be missed. It dates back to c.1265. Approaching the churchyard wall the path turns down a flight of steps to the shore rocks (note how a trap dyke heads over the rocks in the same direction) to follow round under the wall and up again to the entrance beside the Inweary (St Monans) Burn.

From the steps/gate walk ahead to what appears to be a side door but is in fact the main entrance to the church. Beside it is the Honest Man grave, a flat slab dated 1605 and appropriately inscribed round the edge.

The interior of the church is whitewashed and, against this stark simplicity, the furnishings, hangings, etc., are seen to advantage. We have actually entered by the south transept and the communion table and pulpit stand at the crossing, facing the chancel. There is no nave. In pre-Reformation days the altar would be at the far end and sacramental niches, piscina and sedilia have, surprisingly, survived.

Several display boards tell of the more interesting people and events connected with the church. You'll notice a model ship (eighteenth century) hanging in the church, as one does in nearly all the fishing port churches of Fife, and there are many mariners' stones in the graveyard.

David II was largely responsible for the church's rebuilding in 1346. Sir William Dishington, the local laird, picked up the bill. Conflicting legends give the reason for this royal commission: one says the king was crossing the Forth to Ardross Castle and was caught in a storm and vowed he'd build a church if he landed safely; the other says that he'd been hit by two arrows at the Battle of Neville's Cross and at St Monans Shrine one of the shafts 'leapt out of the wound'. The English burnt the church in 1544 but in 1646 it became the parish church. The twentieth century saw it falling into disrepair and in the late 1950s it had to be rescued from decay and heavy-handed Victorian alterations. Oddly, there is no weathercock.

Looking out from the wall seaward you'll see another ragged lava formation, called the Boiling Cauldron; it is hollow in the centre and has a passage on the seaward side so it thunders and echoes under the assault of wind and

The stark ruins of Newark Castle

St Monans and its landmark (seamark) parish church

tide. Legend reports that witches were thrown into the sea to ensure a good catch of fish. By tradition fishermen were both godly and superstitious and nowhere more so than in the East Neuk. A boat would not go to sea if a pig, a cat, a minister or a female was encountered before putting to sea. Certain words were taboo including personal names with double consonants – for instance, Watt, Ross, Marr – and if anything mischanced it was vital to touch iron (not wood).

When John Paul Jones, the American hero, made his raid on the Forth he kidnapped a St Monans man as pilot but he was so bad Jones had to find another victim. John Paul was a Kirkcudbright lad and a brilliant seaman who became one of the new United States' first heroes – a very different reality from what we are told in British history books.

Leaving St Monans churchyard, cross the burn and go right of the house opposite. A footpath climbs up through several gardens to come out on a road which forks; we take the right fork, down again. As the road swings left there is a view of the harbour and the huge shed of what was Miller's boatyard. The firm had been building boats, mostly fishing vessels, at St Monans for 250 years and it was only during the research on this book that redundancy notices were given to the 46 workers at the yard – a few days after completing their biggest-ever fishing vessel.

We wend along the attractive West Shore to reach the harbour at a big slip. The central pier is the oldest, built by national donations to help local poverty, while the other two arms were built by the Stevenson family.

Mid Shore leads to the eastern half of the harbour. Several wynds lead off it and inland there is quite a maze, with the typical architecture of forestairs and harling, crowstep gables and pantiles. St Monans is a delightful place. (St Monance is an alternative but less-favoured spelling, being the possessive of the name. Before the saint's cult it was Inverie of Inweary.) The post office and several other buildings along from it are all careful NTS restorations: no. 4 has a fine, weathered forestair, net loft and hoist; no. 2 has a nice new plaque. Just beyond, opposite the Shipwrecked Mariners Society mine, we can turn up Station Road, then first right, East Street, to see more recent housing, either restorations or new houses made to blend in tastefully – 'imitation vernacular' sounding a bit rude. East Street swings right and brings us out to Virgin Square with the Miller shipbuilding shed opposite. (It may have disappeared, of course.)

This was the oldest boat-building yard in the country, famed for its fishing boats. The work was originally undertaken by local joiners and undertakers. The last wooden-hulled boat was built in 1984. High-tech studies here produced a new stabilising system (my stomach turns over just watching the fishing boats wallowing into harbour) and orders came from as far away as America and Australia, besides the ever-changing, upgrading local fishing boat demand. In 1991 they took an order for building a new, larger ferry to operate from Fionnphort on Mull to Iona. And now the yard has closed.

Don't head off along East Shore (which looks the obvious route) but head up and then right at the next street, Rose Street, which is really a narrow lane. It ends at a car turning place and we are back to rural/seaside walking again. A path of red chips will take us through to Pittenweem. Beyond the green area we can see the tower of a windmill; to reach it, walk along by the grassy recreational area. The row of houses above is on a very clear raised beach. There is a large tidal bathing pool which opened in 1937 but is no longer maintained. The landward end is built up with cement bags. A path breaks off to the windmill tower.

The windmill was used for pumping sea-water up to salt-pans, the site of which is fenced off. There are plans for some restoration work to show just what was involved in a process once so important on both the Castles Coast and the East Neuk. To make one ton of salt required 32 tons of water and 16 tons of coal, which is why places such as Dysart were sites for the industry. The farm just inland is still called Coal Farm. Coal had been mined here for centuries but Sir John Anstruther in the eighteenth century created new pits, opened the salt-pans and connected both with Pittenweem Harbour by a waggonway. This operated till 1794 when a major underground fire caused coal production to slump. The salt-pans were abandoned by 1823. You can still see the holding tank between the tidelines and the cut of the pipeline from it to the windmill. Display-boards now describe the setting.

The stream rushing out down onto the shore is the old chalybeate well of

St Monans. Being so impregnated with iron (as the rust colour indicates) the local fishermen used to wash their nets in this water to make them more durable. Old maps point out many other wells along the Fife coast but most have disappeared. A long reef runs out again and below the path, on the modest cliff, there are distinctive shale bands. The sea is nibbling at the path in places. We pass a natural outcrop of grey sandstone, left, which is weathering just like the same stone back at Newark Castle. We come on a grassy area again, with three benches and a well at the west end (remember 'well' in Scotland means *any* gush of water, from spring to bathroom tap).

There are several concrete foundations, steps and railings, all part of the bathing area below where two long concrete arms run out to sea. This one pre-dates the First World War. (Earlier there were salt-pans.) There is a pristine sandy beach and at high tide a dip here would be an enjoyable distraction.

PITTENWEEM

Steps lead up to a children's play area. Turn right to walk along outside this – and suddenly Pittenweem is in sight.

> Largo, Blebo, Dunino
> Into Europe seem to go,
> But plainly Scottish we may deem
> Auchtermuchty, Pittenweem.

> *Anon*

Our first view of Pittenweem is of an utterly captivating row of houses, clean-gleaming, rimming a quiet bay. As there is no car access most tourists never see this delightful corner. A gasworks at one time must have been an eyesore. The hollow, backed by a wall, just before reaching the first house, was its site and the slip probably allowed coal to be brought by sea.

Many of these West Shore houses have forestairs and the sea-wall at times must have given minimal defence against big storms. The wall was once tarred to protect it. At the end house there are spur stones on both sides of an opening. Beyond we come on the wider area of Mid Shore. There is a slip on the right, and a house with a pend called The Cooperage to the left, which points to a one-time trade carried on there.

If all these towns look delightful now, there are stories enough of past troubles. They suffered badly from English attacks and in the wars of the intolerant seventeenth century. Witchcraft was a very real horror, and in 1705 three women died and many others were tortured in Pittenweem following the accusations of a teenager. One of the three died as a result of her five-month incarceration and torture in a dark, dank cell; another was starved to death in her cell; and the third escaped only to be caught and lynched by a mob who dragged her by the ankles to the harbour and swung her up over the water to be stoned. She was then crushed below a door heaped with boulders and a horse and cart repeatedly driven over her body.

The first mention of a port here was in 1228, and this is now the main harbour in the East Neuk for landing fish. The KY registration stands for

Kirkcaldy but the whole system of registration of vessels is being altered, I believe. The fishmarket is due a facelift, too, and is going to be completely rebuilt. One new feature will be a viewing facility. The breakwater is also to be extended to make the entrance less demanding, and there will be some tidying up generally.

One should really explore all the wynds between the harbour area and the old town up the hill based on the High Street, but time is short and we must be selective. Cove Wynd (it should be Cave Wynd) opposite the red mine collecting-box leads up to the most historically interesting feature: St Fillan's Cave. It is locked because of the risk of vandalism but at the top of Cove Wynd you'll see a notice about obtaining the key from the Gingerbread House just 50m along the High Street. The town hall and the priory also lay on Cove Wynd and at the top, facing along the High Street, is the historic parish church. A note by the

A delightful old house at the Gyles end of Pittenweem Harbour

church entrance indicates the key can be found at the butcher's shop in Market Place, further along the High Street. (Keys are available during shop hours only; check the notices in case there has been a change.) The Gingerbread House has a café and there's another almost next door. The High Street is still the local shopping street.

Halfway along the High Street is the Kelly Lodging, the town house of the Earls of Kellie, with a corbelled turret and other neat sixteenth-century features. Even the wealthy had surprisingly small dwellings.

Walking back one sees the 1588 church to advantage. There is a strong look of a tolbooth about the tower and that is what it was; sixteenth/seventeenth-century work. Records mention it being used as a gaol. The Swedish bell in the tower was cast in 1663 by 'Joran Puttensen's widow'. Set against the wall of the tower is the shaft of the old mercat cross, placed here for safety. A horizontal table-stone grave just left when you go into the churchyard has a rather immodest inscription! There's quite a collection of table-stones from the seventeenth century. At the far side of the graveyard is the Episcopal church and, seaward, the Augustinian Priory ruins, where the monks of the May had been granted a site near the already established cave by David I. *Pit-ne-weme* is the charter's spelling, 'the place of the cave'. What little is left has been restored and faces Cove Wynd.

St Fillan's Cave almost certainly began as one of the raised beach series but religious and smuggling activities have probably much changed it. Walls have been built to form inner and outer chambers and a genuine stair has been cut in the rock up to a chamber 10m overhead, sunk in the priory garden. A well is found in the left inner chamber and the right chamber has been reinstated as a small chapel. St Fillan was a seventh-century missionary saint so this is one of Scotland's oldest religious sites.

Having returned the keys, descend School Wynd back to the harbour and walk along this to its eastern end where the much photographed houses of the Gyles, restored by the NTS, look on the outer harbour. The three-storey house is a sea-captain's home of 1626. A walk out to the entrance light is worth while as there are views along the coast, both east and west, and a fine panorama of the town.

Now we must push on for Anstruther. Return to the Gyles then head up Abbey Wall Road and when the brae swings left, take an opening in the wall, right, to walk through a play area and on along the cliff-top behind a housing scheme. The marked diagonal lie of the rock strata is well seen from up here. One advantage of the Pathfinder map is its delineation of shore features. These reefs are, ominously, called the Break Boats.

Just beyond the houses part of the cliff has collapsed. Not far beyond, take the path that leads down to the shore again and the edge of Anstruther golf course. Without the golf course one feels Pittenweem could well have joined up with Anstruther, just as Anstruther is an incorporation of four ancient royal burghs: Anstruther Wester, Anstruther Easter, Cellardyke and Kilrenny, an urban union which has something of an aesthetic edge on the Buckhaven, Denbeath, Methil, Leven combination.

The square concrete 'box' on the shore is apparently an anti-aircraft gun emplacement from the last war. Just walk along the edge of the shore, ignoring any diverging paths, passing below a lookout-post (closed) and another rock bathing pool which, I suspect, gains few customers, such is the lure of the costas.

THE AINSTERS

At a grassy point, Billow Ness, we have a good view to the Anstruthers. (Anstruther is pronounced 'Ainster' locally.) The jut of rock offshore (marked by a post on top) is Johnny Doo's Pulpit but it has other ecclesiastical connections for it was here that the young local lad, Thomas Chalmers (1780–1847), came to practise his sermons. He was licensed to preach by the St Andrews Presbytery at the early age of 19, but then studied mathematics at Edinburgh before an appointment at St Andrews. He later became minister of Kilmany, in Fife, before moving on to Glasgow, successively at the Tron and St John's, where his ideas on helping the poor and his preaching were both noteworthy. The hundred-year-old fight against patronage was coming to its head, and in 1843 Chalmers was a leader of the Disruption when nearly half the ministers of the Church walked out, rather than tolerate the undemocratic system any longer – an incredible act of faith and defiance, for the ministers lost church, manse, and income and often faced great problems in establishing new churches, landowners being anything but helpful. Congregations sometimes met between the tidelines and in the west used a floating church.

Continue round a last small bay of golden sand beside the attractive 9-hole golf course. (Walkers are given the protection of nets, though I suspect these are there primarily to stop drives being pulled into the sea!) The battlement tower on the course is the local war memorial. Continue on by the clubhouse to reach a curve of street, Shore Road. Turn right along this as far as the primary school, then turn left up to the main road on Crichton Street. Pittenweem Road lies left, with the Craw's Nest Hotel and other accommodation options (see list), and, if booked here, you could check in and leave your pack before going on to explore the town.

We turn right on the start of the High Street and pass the Dreel Tavern (and a B&B next door), left. The tavern has a plaque mentioning one of the stories of the Guid Man o' Ballengeich, as James V was called on his anonymous wanderings among his people. There was no bridge over the Dreel Burn then, and he was quite happy to be carried over by a tough gaberlunzie (beggar) woman who was rewarded, not with the usual pittance, but with a purse of gold!

Continuing along the High Street, we come to an interesting area beside the Dreel Burn. The road turns sharply left to cross this quite big stream, with the Esplanade leading off, right, down to the sea. The seventeenth-century house on the corner was decorated with shells by one Alex Batchelor last century, and is called Buckie House. (A

The Buckie House, Wester Anstruther

buckie is sometimes specifically a top shell but often used just to mean shell in general.) Part of the house has a shell harling but the main front is patterned with a variety of shells. He used to charge the public a penny a time to see his coffin which was also decorated with shells.

Across the road is an obviously old church, now the parish church hall, and beside it, on the Esplanade, is the old eighteenth-century town hall. The church tower is said to have had an iron basket fitted in the thirteenth century to light a beacon to guide shipping to the harbour. The weather-vane is a salmon. The church was dedicated in 1243 to St Nicholas, patron saint of the sea.

If the tide is well out, just cross the bridge to glimpse the Smugglers Inn,

then return to go down the Esplanade. If the tide is well in, go down the Esplanade first, then back and on into town over the bridge. At low tide historic stepping-stones cross the burn on the shore – hence the options. At one time the Dreel Burn was a very real boundary between the two burghs. I'll comment on these options in turn.

The plaque on the bridge marks a rebuilding of the 1630 bridge in 1795 but is sited on the last remodelling, of 1831. Looking upstream you can see where the old route came down to the ford below the Dreel Tavern. A wooden footbridge was built over the Dreel in 1630. At one time there were six mills getting their power from its water. The white building down behind the bridge was a corn-mill till c.1880. The Smugglers Inn is an old

Steam drifters in Anstruther Harbour in the 1930s

coaching inn, dating back several centuries; even if the name is modern, there was good enough justification for its use. This was very much a smugglers' coast.

Beyond the inn the High Street is the smaller right-hand road, with the Royal Hotel visible at the end. Off it is the house where Chalmers was born. It was old when bought in 1707 by a skipper burgess, Philip Brown. Old ships' masts and timbers have been used as roof beams.

There are some interesting stones in the old graveyard with its superb sea view. A re-sited stone on the wall has the very early date of 1598. The spelling on the tablet before it needs a bit of translating, being Biblical Scots. Yat (yett) is gate.

At the start of the Esplanade there is a plaque on the wall indicating that this was the home of another local lad made good, John Keay (1828–1918), who was captain of the *Ariel* and other clipper ships. The *Ariel* and the *Taeping* (built for Captain Rodger of Cellardyke) raced from Foochow in 1866 to try and be first back with the year's new tea supply. Both came in on the same tide.

All the houses here were built several centuries ago: the old manse is dated 1703; no. 4 has a 1718 marriage lintel; and, opposite, an older cottage has a wheatsheaf symbol which may have been an inn sign. The mouth of the Dreel itself was the original 'harbour' of this area, Wester Anstruther.

Steps lead down to the large blocks of the stepping-stones across the Dreel Burn, usable at low tide when the burn is not in spate. The leftmost house across the river stands on the site of Dreel Castle, once quite a fortress. Mary Queen of Scots slept there, as did Charles II – who reputedly gave his hosts the back-handed compliment of 'Aye, no' a bad supper for a craw's nest'. The row of houses (Castle Street) leads us to Shore Street, the heart of both Anstruther Easter and the combined burghs. If the tide is in, then the High Street is followed past the Smugglers Inn to the Royal Hotel on Roger Street, which descends to the end of Shore Street.

The first wynd, left, is Tolbooth Wynd, but the tolbooth was demolished in 1871 and only its iron yett survives – now sited at the Fisheries Museum. Note the colourful 1885 masonic crest on the gable. (Café in this wynd.) The 1908 Murray Library is a red sandstone building ('fussy Renaissance'), named after a local lad who made good trading with Australia; across from it, sited rather unhappily by the bus stop, is the old mercat cross of 1677.

Walk out the harbour arm to the entrance light; as with Pittenweem, it will give a useful panoramic view of the town. The light itself is the Chalmers Memorial Lighthouse, the 1880 gift of a Cheltenham lady who never visited the town yet donated the

first lifeboat in 1865. The Chalmers Memorial Church for long dominated the town and acted as meads (a seamark for taking bearings, the low land of the East Neuk being featureless from the sea) but in 1991 vandals fired the unused church and, for safety, it had to be demolished. The spire dominated the town and I must have taken some of the last pictures of this landmark. The buildings facing the harbour still retain some old features and make a handsome front.

Berthed in the eastern outer harbour is the North Carr Lightship, Scotland's only surviving lightship. It was stationed off Fife Ness, marking the North Carr Rocks from 1933 to 1975. It can be visited Easter–October, 11 a.m.-5 p.m.; winter, Sunday noon-4 p.m. The Fisheries Museum, a major attraction, is opposite. The slip from a big shed is the lifeboat station. Though bigger than Pittenweem, you'll notice Anstruther is a quieter harbour. At one time it was packed with herring fishing boats but, after the war, when the herring started to disappear, the fishermen were loath to change to another fish and lost out to Pittenweem and elsewhere.

Robert Louis Stevenson stayed in Anstruther while his father was enlarging the harbour in 1860. (It was built in the eighteenth century.) R.L.S. was very much the odd man out in this family of practical engineers. At that time he was expected to follow the family tradition and was in Anstruther assisting his father, not yet having made his break for literature. He wrote later:

> I came as a young man to glean
> engineering experience from

the building of the breakwater but indeed I had already my own private determination to be an author. Though I haunted the breakwater by day and even loved the place for the sake of the sunshine, the thrilling seaside air, the wash of the waves on the sea-face, the green glimmer of the divers' helmets far below, and the musical clinking of the masons, my one genuine pre-occupation lay elsewhere, and my only industry was in the hours when I was not on duty.

He lodged with a carpenter, Bailie Brown, at Cunzie House on the Crail Road and a plaque on the house commemorates his stay.

The Scottish Fisheries Museum building is as historic as it looks. The buildings are on St Ayles Land, which has recorded connections with the fishing industry in 1318. The laird of 'Anstroyir' made over rights to Balmerino Abbey, including the erection of fishing booths and permission to dry nets. A chapel was built in the fifteenth century but the site has been recycled frequently. A brewer, William Lumsden, lived on the site and his is the 1721 marriage lintel in Haddfoot Wynd. A ship's chandlers closed in the early 1960s and the museum was opened in 1969. Now it is probably the finest fisheries museum in Britain, with an incredible range of exhibits, recreations with life-size figures, a working wheelhouse, and a varied collection of boats. Allow plenty of time for the museum. There is also a shop and tea-room. Open: April–Oct,

10 a.m.–5.30 p.m., Sun, 11 a.m.; Nov–Mar, 10 a.m.–4.30 p.m., Sun 2–4.30 p.m. Telephone (0333) 310628.

The Battle of Kilsyth in 1645 is blamed for the decay of the East Neuk towns. Many local men never returned from that disaster. In 1670 a huge storm wrought havoc on several ports, destroying harbours and houses. The 1707 Union was hardly welcomed. In that year there were 30 fishing boats in the Ainsters; by 1764 there were just five. The minister of Ainster drew his teinds (tythes) of fish and this could be up to £15 a year; but by the end of the eighteenth century it was a mere 13 shillings. The herring declined throughout the second half of this century largely as a result of over-fishing locally and by Dutch and Scandinavian encroachment. At one time you could walk from one end of the harbour to the other on the boats' decks.

Just east of the museum is Whale Close. If you walk through you come out on East Green and almost opposite is The Tea Clipper café and B&B, well named as a plaque indicates the one-time home of Captain John Smith (b.1823), skipper of *Min* and *Lahloo* in the tea-clipper days. He died when his ship was lost with all hands off the Hebrides in 1874. Waid Academy (1886) the town's famous school, was endowed by Andrew Waid (1736–1803), a Royal Navy officer. You cannot escape the sea in Anstruther. The original school was nineteenth century but was extended 'in polite harl and red brick' in 1930 and again in 1956 with Fife County Council's 'aggressive concrete' (Gifford).

If you walk back westwards East Green meets Haddfoot, a steep brae to which it owes its name, *hadd-the-feet* (watch your feet!), and over on the other side is some concrete decoration which relied on egg-box moulds. Behind gates lies one of the posher merchant memories of the prosperous early nineteenth century, Johnston House. At one time it was the home of a Tahitian princess. She had been married to a Scots merchant for whom one George Dairsie worked. When his boss died Dairsie married the widow and they returned to the family home of Johnston House. A solicitor who'd married one of their daughters bought the house and had a ballroom added for his fun-loving wife. Widowed and in debt she had to sell to a half-sister, who had married a local minister who studied the *Financial Times* as much as the Bible and made a pile. Later the house fell into disrepair, was bought by the National Trust for Scotland and turned into flats.

When the Spanish Armada came to grief round the Scottish coast a party of 260 Spaniards made their way from the Northern Isles and turned up at Ainster, much to the consternation of the populace. The minister, James Melville, could speak Spanish, however, and left the visitors in no doubt about his considered opinion of Protestant superiority. Scottish merchants in those days were often imprisoned or burnt as heretics in Spain but, let them take note, Scottish hospitality was altogether different. The Spaniards were taken in and looked after till repatriated. Later an Anstruther ship was seized in Spain but the incident came to the notice of Medina who rescued both ship and men and entertained them in return for their earlier favours at Ainster. Melville was a keen golfer, having been a boy at Montrose and then going as a student to St Andrews in 1571.

Melville's Manse, the site of the Chalmers Memorial Church and several B&Bs on the Back Dykes lie up Haddfoot, but at this point we will leave off exploring the town. (There are local booklets in the museum if anyone wants fuller details.)

PRACTICAL INFORMATION / ACCOMMODATION

Telephone code: (0333)

Tourist Information Office, Scottish Fisheries Museum 311073 (seasonal)

Anstruther

8 Melville Terrace	310453
2 Union Place	310042
13 East Green	312260
15 East Green (café as well, walkers welcomed)	310377
2 St Ayles Crescent	312248
32 Glenogil Gardens	310697
14 St Adrian's Place	312005
Elm Lodge, Union Place (walkers welcomed)	310313
Spindrift Guest House, Pittenweem Road	310573
The Dykes, 69 Pittenweem Road (Wester)	310537
Beaumont Lodge Guest House, Pittenweem Road	310315
St Helens, St Andrews Road (A9131)	310309
Mayview, Crail Road (A917)	310677
18 High Street	310902

Royal Hotel, Roger Street	310581
Smugglers Inn, High Street	
(more expensive)	310506
Craw's Nest Hotel, Pittenweem Rd	
(more expensive but worth it)	310691
16 Roger Street	311712

Cellardyke

St Leonard's, Toll Road	310041
Marchmont, Toll Road	310203
28 James Street	312029
55 George Street	310742
57 George Street	312037

34 Shore Street   310643

Kilrenny
(1 mile east, on A917 – can walk on through
Cellardyke, then track up to Kilrenny)
Rennyhill House   312234
Other accommodation at Crail (see
tomorrow) or towns to west (see yesterday's
listings).

Camping: Anstruther Holiday Village 310484
Taxis: Anstruther/Cellardyke: 310489,
                                  312181, 310972

DAY 8 *The Bracing East*

May Island–Crail

Maps to use: Bart 49, OSLR 59, OSPF 374 (NO 40/50)/ OSPF 364 (NO 60/61)
Walking distance: 10 km (91 km)

The Island of May is well worth a visit and there are daily sailings from Anstruther in the summer months, though obviously these are 'weather permitting' and the actual times may vary depending on the state of the tides. Allow five hours (three hours ashore). Check the night before and book a place if possible, as sailings are often over-subscribed. Contact Jim Raeper (0333) 310103 for sailings on the *Sapphire* and the *Serenity*. Our walking distance today is less than usual as half the day will be taken up with visiting the May but it is in character with the last day or two, a mix of village worlds at start and finish (Cellardyke and Crail) open coastal tramping between. If the short coastal walk onwards is largely unspectacular, Crail is regarded by many visitors as the most picturesque of all Fife's coastal towns. An easy day before the hard one on the morrow.

THE MAY ISLAND

The Island of May is a renowned nature reserve and has a residential bird observatory. The Scottish National Heritage warden meets boats and there are descriptive leaflets and booklets available at the Fisheries Museum. The island lies 56km (35 miles) east of the Forth Bridges, happily emphasising the distance we have travelled. The basalt rock gives it a rather dark appearance in approaching from the sea. We land in Kirkhaven, just one of the many names pointing to past ecclasiastical use.

The main observatory (established in 1934) is in the Low Light building, and in the spring and autumn migration periods much ringing of birds is carried out. The May is often the first landfall for birds driven across from Scandinavia or commuting from Arctic breeding-grounds. Well over 200

Looking along the May Island from the south end (© Cambridge University Collection of Air Photographs)

The *Mars* aground on the May Island (© St Andrews University (Cowie) Photography Collection)

species have been recorded on the May. A kittiwake ringed here was recovered in Newfoundland, and a robin in Spain; conversely, a sparrowhawk, ringed in Iceland was caught on the May, as was a goldcrest only 27 days after it was ringed in Finland. Several thousand pairs of puffins are the most popular of the resident species.

David I gave the island to the Benedictine Monastery of Reading in Berkshire. They held it for many stormy years until it came under the see of St Andrews following the Battle of Bannockburn. The monks soon transferred to Pittenweem and the island's importance as a holy site declined.

In 1815 the island was purchased by the Northern Lighthouse Commissioners who then replaced the old beacon with the present handsome lighthouse in the centre of the island (Robert Stevenson, 1816). It flashes one long every 20 seconds. Next to it is the lower part of the original light which was set up in the seventeenth century. This was once higher and there was a grate on top where a coal fire was set. It could consume a ton of coal in a single night and needed constant attention. Dues were levied on shipping to pay for this service, the first light anywhere on the Scottish coast. Just over a century ago the May became the first light to use electricity.

The Low Light was built in 1843,

and with the main light, allowed a fix to be made on the treacherous Carr Rocks off Fife Ness. Despite the lights, the last century has seen 39 ships wrecked on the May. The hulks of the Latvian *Mars* on the North Ness and the Danish *Island* by Colmshole can still be seen.

The island is probably best walked in a clockwise circuit. From the landing, head up to the chapel ruins and down to the South Ness. The Priors Walk leads up the west side, crossing the Mill Door and the loch to reach the main light. At the north end is the Altarstanes (an alternative landing place) and an iron footbridge leads to Rona, with the foghorn and the North Ness. Holyman's Road leads back by the Low Light. Note the 'Heligoland Traps' used for capturing migrant birds. These are basically large funnel-shaped traps which become narrower and narrower to lead the birds on to a final catching box. The birds then have their vital statistics taken, are ringed, and released.

My first visit to May was with a school-party and on the boat back I noticed one boy's donkey-jacket sleeve seemed a bit bulgy. On demand he reluctantly shook out a rather ruffled puffin which went whirring off homewards, 'hell for feather'.

TO CRAIL

When we set off from the Fisheries Museum and cross an invisible burn, the Caddy, we are entering Cellardyke, yet another of the old royal burghs incorporated in 1929 as Anstruther (Ainster Wester, Ainster Easter, Kilrenny and Cellardyke). Cellardyke is a Lego-built lang toon which is rather sidelined by its big brother.

Keep along the shore road by the Sun Tavern, passing the harbour's two green leading lights and then swinging right. There are new houses, left, called Harbour Lea, highly praised for their sympathetic design. The road then swings inland, but we keep along the road parallel with the shore all the way through Cellardyke. This is James Street (not named initially) which leads along to Tolbooth Wynd. An 1883 municipal building (with clock) replaced the original tolbooth. The shaft of the 1642 mercat cross is pre-served against the wall. The shore road now becomes John Street. A new Boat Tavern sign is pleasant and two recently restored cottages with fore-stairs have pal stones protecting the stairs from traffic such as this street was not designed for. Double doors are another East Neuk feature to look out for. John Street changes to George Street. A house, left, has a plaque to 'Poetry Peter' (Smith), a Victorian local rhymester. On the street above (not visible from here) stood a rather decayed arch made from the bones of a whale. Captain William Smith erected it in 1830 as the beast was then the longest ever caught in the Arctic. (The arch was moved to the Fisheries Museum for safer keeping.)

The open space of the quiet harbour is something of a relief after Cellardyke's canyon street. There's a restaurant and a village shop. The harbour has no commercial use now, and little enough in the way of pleasure use either. The earlier name was Skinfast Haven. A reef, offshore, is Cuttyskelly.

It is a very old harbour but was rebuilt by Joseph Mitchell, Telford's fellow engineer.

In the mid-nineteenth century a small Greenland whale fishing company operated here for a while but could not compete with larger boats based at Dundee. A cod-liver oil factory has also long gone. Just past the end of the harbour, left, is a plaque to Captain Alexander Rodger (1802–77), a local fisherman who ended as master and then owner of several tea-clippers. The cottage, calling itself Taeping, commemorates the most famous of these, but he also owned *Min* and *Lahloo*. (His father, also a fisherman, died at the Burntisland drave in 1814.)

A contemporary of Rodger was Walter Hughes who roamed many seas, ran opium from China to Thailand till too dangerous, started a sheep-run the size of Fife in Australia, found copper there and became the richest man in Australia, buying respectability thereafter and even retiring with a knighthood.

The Braes and Town Green now lie on the left, while on the right there is a row of tidily restored houses, The Cooperage. Barrelmaking was once a big trade, employing 70 coopers in 1833, for example. Salted herring and beer filled the barrels. Cellardyke once had something like 24 breweries. This was not because the people were especially drouthy but simply that beer was our everyday beverage in those days. Tea was a luxury drink then – a strange role-reversal. Note the stone on the corner showing the tools of the trade. The Town Green was a gift from Captain Alexander Rodger.

After this, Cellardyke rather peters out. There's a children's play area, a war memorial up on the Braes and

The weathered sandstone pillars of the Caiplie Coves

another abandoned tidal pool before the final carpark. The rocks beyond the pool are the Cardinal's Steps, where the newly appointed prelate, Cardinal Beaton, embarked on his state barge to travel to St Andrews in style.

There's a caravan park now swamping the red pantiled roofs of the old Kilrenny Mill which used the burn for providing power. Kilrenny hamlet lies up beyond the A917 and from along the bay a bit you may glimpse its church spire, looking a bit like St Monans, and likewise used as a seamark by fishermen, many of whom lived in Kilrenny. To them it was St Irnie. Cellardyke was often called Nether Kilrenny.

We follow a track right on the shore. There's a bridge over the Kilrenny Burn. The shoreline track thereafter has been used for dumping and burning rubbish, so is a bit of an eyesore. The field before Caiplie Farm contained pigs last time I passed and there is quite a bit of pig farming in the East Neuk which has never gone in for a rash monoculture. Caiplie is unusual in being right down on the shore, rather than on raised-beach level. A decade ago the farm was derelict, showing just how quickly building (and land) use can change – for better, or worse. There's a walled garden and the farm buildings have an octagonal pantiled wheelhouse, a feature common on the east coast, south and north of the Forth. On the shore here there are several fossil tree remains, such as we'll see again at Crail.

The May Island is now at its nearest point to land and shows the steepest cliff profile, while several of the build-ings can clearly be seen. The Bass Rock and Berwick Law are clear, too.

At a wall, take the seaward of two stone stiles. A burn beyond has a foot-bridge, part of the work done in the early 1980s by a Manpower Services team, all the way round to St Andrews. Unfortunately, the follow-up has been less well organised and parts of the route have deteriorated; the sea has battered others and vandals have added their quota of destruction.

A few fields on we come on the notable feature of the Coves, a jutting prow of multi-hued sandstone on the 8m raised beach, carved by ancient seas into a whole web of caves, holes, passages and arches. In the main cave (with its carpet of sheep droppings) there is a series of small incised crosses (about head height) which probably date back to early Christian times when missionaries such as Adrian and Ethernan may have lived here. This is still known as Chapel Cave. The Covenanter Peden sought refuge here, and early this century the cave was occupied by a man called Covey Jimmy. Jimmy Gilligan hailed from Aberdeen, served in the army (Boer War, Afghanistan, etc.), spoke Latin and French but did not like city life; he came here in 1910, soon becoming a local character of note.

The coast becomes rougher; tucked in a bay, we come on a white cottage (once a salmon-fisherman's bothy) and a ruin, all that remains of saltworks that date back to about 1700. The Pans on the map remind us of this. A spring beyond makes for a marshy area (which can be turned either above or below) and then we are on the last wee bay before Crail. Note the strata laid

A fossil tree stump on the shore near Crail

bare at the far end. You can pick out the sea-rounded pebbles of a raised beach lying on the sandstone. Steps lead us up to a wired-off enclosure on top of the Braes where we pick up a farm road. Don't drop down (even at low tide) to the old coastguard hut and the fight round by the rocky shore: the cliffs are disintegrating and the rocks are viciously slippery. The best view of Crail Harbour is from higher up, anyway.

The farm road leads along to a gate and a row of Victorian terraced houses (Osborne Terrace) then bears right past some lopsided houses before turning sharp left up to the main road. At this bend, turn off right on the signposted footpath. Beyond the pantiled roofs, right, you have an open space for the classic view down to Crail Harbour, which some consider to be the best single view of the walk.

Turn right when the main road is reached. The red leading lights for Crail Harbour are passed, one being

Crail Harbour, the gem of the East Neuk

across the road by Temple Crescent, the other on our right. Just one building past the phone box (nearly opposite the Catholic church), turn right to pick up a stepped path down to the harbour. This tiny, picturesque harbour still has a few boats which go out after partans (edible crabs) and lobsters, but it is hard to envisage Crail ever being the most important port in the East Neuk, as it was early on.

Most of the buildings round the harbour date from the seventeenth century. The largest was once a customs house and bears the painted town arms on a plaque. Left of it is an attractive corner. The harbour office noticeboard is worth studying. As in every port, there are warnings about rabies, one of the most horrific dangers which Britain, being an island, has so far escaped – but just one pet smuggled in from abroad could change that. The comment on the lifebelt suggests we're quite capable of such monstrous stupidities. The fossil tree is a unique feature and worth seeing, but walk round the far harbour wall first, to see the harbour from all angles and, from the end, to pinpoint the site of the fossil tree. The gasworks, an ugly intrusion, was removed in 1960 so now only St Andrews (of all places) has a gasometer decorating its harbour. Gasworks were always near the harbours so coal could be taken there easily once landed – probably brought from the Castles Coast ports.

Coal used to be mined at Crail but only by open workings, not pits. At the end of the eighteenth century some poor folk were working a seam on the shore and found a coin dating to Queen Mary's reign which had been lost in workings of that period. Crail once had a tidal mill, a useful alternative in an area where big streams for power simply did not exist. (Industry never came to Crail because of lack of water for power, a blessing with hindsight.) The opening of the Forth and Clyde Canal proved a boon to Crail, giving a new, growing market for its surplus grain and farm produce.

From the pier end by the crane you'll see there is a small sandy bay, ending at a long seaward-running reef, then a short reach of sand and boulders before another reef, beyond which there is an obvious angled slab at the foot of the shaly cliff. The fossil tree is just before this slab, lying on the edge of a little sand that accumulates there. Once there, how do you spot it? Imagine a big tree sawn off a metre from the ground, leaving a stump more or less round on top, and widening out to spreading roots. This stump is what you find – but in stone! About 8m closer to the cliff is a section of trunk, which fits on the stump, and tight against the cliff is a further rather broken section of trunk. The shale yields other less dramatic fossils. (One sits in the case of the harbour noticeboard.)

Head up Shoregate. The 'Peppers' name for the first house harks back to my youth when our neighbours, the 'Pepper' Watsons lived there. Lots of the fishermen had nicknames, especially when a family, like the Watsons, had several fishermen in it. No. 28 is our old home, just two rooms, a loft and a large cellar where fishermen stored nets and gear over centuries, I reckon. On damp days the big beams would exude crystals of salt. We built a toilet in a corner of the cellar and I don't know how often one would be enthroned down there when the whistling kettle would let rip upstairs. A neighbour quite often nipped in and turned off the gas before the culprit could make it out the cellar, round the street and in the front door! We put in a companionway eventually. I made pocket-money by doing small paintings of the harbour and selling them on the front step.

Continuing up the steep Shoregate, St Adrian's, with the half-figure over the door and blue shutters, is a beautiful old house, named after the early missionary. Go up the steps (as the road bends) to follow Castle Walk, which gives a view down onto St Adrian's Garden and Maggie Inglis' Hole as the sea below is called. There's a panoramic view indicator and an old sundial on the corner. There once was a castle, the East Neuk being favoured by early kings, but the wall on our left now simply encloses a private house. The building at the end of the Castle Walk is the watch house.

Turn left there up a short road with garages on the left (the Big Trons) to come out onto Rumford, facing a row of old restored houses with all the classic East Neuk features. No. 5 and no. 6 were once the town's poorhouse and in 1961 gave the National Trust for Scotland its first project in its admirable Little Houses Improvement Scheme. Walk along by these houses (NTS plaques) to the gap at the end where the last house is built outwards on the second storey, and continue in the same direction (turning sharp left leads to the Crail Pottery) past the Coastguard post (left) and the Legion Hall (right). This is the

Nethergate (several accommodation options) and we turn up left, on the first street, Tolbooth Wynd, which leads up to the crossroads of High Street, St Andrews Road and the Marketgate, on which most of the other B&Bs are situated. Marketgate, eastwards, becomes Balcomie Road; West Green lies just behind the High Street. A map and accommodation list is on the tolbooth wall itself and the museum is in behind this fine building.

Parts of the tolbooth date from the early sixteenth century. The tower is eighteenth century. We've now seen several tolbooths (Inverkeithing, Dysart, West Wemyss, Pittenweem), one result of having such a concentration of old royal burghs along this coast. There are not many more in the whole of the rest of the country. Crail's church shows strong Dutch influence and has a Dutch bell of 1520, which still rings a curfew at 10 p.m. The weather-vane is a Crail 'capon'. The museum is operated by the Crail Preservation Trust and tells the story of the area. Open: June–August 10 a.m.–12.30 p.m., 2.30–5 p.m., Sun 2.30–5 p.m.; April, May, September, weekends, bank holidays 2.30-5 p.m. Tel: (0333) 50869. The library in the tolbooth sells postcards of old scenes in the East Neuk.

Along Marketgate from the tolbooth is a granite fountain commemorating Victoria's 1897 Diamond Jubilee, and the mercat cross, erected in 1887 using a seventeenth-century shaft and a modern unicorn in the style of such crosses. The original site and cross have been lost but the wide Market Street and tolbooth were once the heart of thriving markets. These were

Reflections, Crail Harbour

held on Sundays before the Reformation. There are many fine seventeenth- and eighteenth-century town houses as we walk eastwards, some with marriage lintels, including one dated 1619.

At the corner for the church gates there is an erratic boulder, the Blue Stone, which has many odd tales attached to it. Traditionally, the devil, on the Isle of May, took a scunner to the kirk folk of Crail and chucked a big stone at them. It split in the air, one piece landing close to the mark (this stone), and one piece ending on the shore at Balcomie (another Blue Stone, which we'll pass tomorrow).

A church has stood here from the earliest times. Dedicated to St

Maelrubha of Applecross in 1243, it later became St Mary's and also a collegiate church. Knox preached here and James Sharp (later archbishop) was one of its ministers. Being so near to St Andrews, it could hardly avoid being involved in affairs of Church and state. There were big alterations to the building in 1796, 1815 and 1963. The tower is thirteenth century. Inside, there are several items of interest including several early carved oak panels, a painted panel from the Sailors' Loft (all the guild lofts went in 1815), and a restored lancet window from the thirteenth century with lovely modern glass, more modern glass in the tower and a rather worn Pictish stone which originally stood near Fife Ness. The walls are covered in well-disciplined ivy.

The kirkyard has an unusual number of early memorials (some from the sixteenth century) round its wall, including those of Lumsden of Airdrie, dated 1598, and William Bruce of Symbister, his effigy in full armour. Behind the church is a mort-house where bodies were stored for weeks or months (depending on the season) before burial, thus foiling the resurrectionists. A tablet bears the cheery message 'Erected for securing the dead' and the date 1826. On a pleasanter note, in early spring the east side of the graveyard is a mass of snowdrops. There are various books on this important graveyard as the casual visitor will find many stones too weathered to read, never mind deciphering the Latin and old English spellings. Many stones are of important town families, indicating the prosperity of Crail in the past. One large piece of stonework now completely gone is the town walls with its various ports. The church tower has deep grooves where medieval archers sharpened their arrow tips.

Leave the churchyard near the mort-house and, once out, turn right to pick up a path down through the Denburn Wood, also a mass of snowdrops in season. The Rude Well is passed. Coming out onto the road, turn right then left down Kirk Wynd which leads to the Nethergate. A path, straight on, leads down to the sea at Roome Bay and passes a tubby sixteenth-century doocot, well restored, harled and whitewashed to act as a seamark. The rocks on the shore show fossil ripple marks. Follow the path round by a tidal pool. Gardens lie up the slope on the right and seaward is the rock of the Mermaid's Cradle. The path turns right to climb up the slope back to the Castle Walk and the Nethergate.

I've seen Crail spelt Carell on an old map, and the name really defies any sure derivation. Running back on our route, that same map showed Anstruther, Sandness (Pittenweem), Leauins mouth, Reuins heuch (Ravensheuch/craig), Kirk Caldey, Pretticur, Kinghorne and Brunt Iland. Crail was once *the* major port of Fife, trading with the continent; now it just ticks over with a little local fishing. A Crail lad (Lord Barham) was First Lord of the Admiralty at the time of Trafalgar, an appointment he received (Dundas influence?) at the age of 80. The town has been very much a backwater since, though the railway coming in 1886 opened it up for tourism. (A Glaswegian last century, asked if he'd been to America, replied, 'No, but I've a brother who's been to Crail.') Bathing was a serious business. An old guide admonishes: 'It is one of Crail's recreative laws which, it is hoped, will be honourably observed, that Roome Bay is available for gentlemen only up till eight o'clock in the morning.' Under 'Useful Hints for the Seaside' are notes on 'Swimming, Sailing and Drowning'.

You can test your landlady by asking for a Crail 'capon' for breakfast. This is a haddock treated in local fashion, once popular throughout the east of Scotland.

PRACTICAL INFORMATION / ACCOMMODATION

Telephone code: (0333)

Tourist Information Office   50869
(seasonal)

Crail has a variety of accommodation and
the hotels are reasonably priced, unlike
St Andrews.

16 Nethergate	50652
Croma Hotel, 33 Nethergate	50239
Selcraig House, 47 Nethergate	50697
Marine Hotel, 54 Nethergate	50207
Hazelton Guest House, 29 Marketgate	50250
Golf Hotel, 4 High Street (old coaching inn)	50206
Honeypot Guest House, 6 High Street	50935
Caiplie Guest House, 53 High Street (superb cuisine)	50564
East Neuk Hotel, 67 High Street	50225
21 West Green	50329
Woodlands Guest House,	
Balcomie Road	50147
Balcomie Links Hotel, Balcomie Road	50237

Kingsbarns, on the road to St Andrews, has
one B&B (3 Main Street, 0334 88 234) and
you could also go on to St Andrews or back
to Anstruther by bus. About 18 buses a day
operate on the service 95 route:
Leven–Anstruther–Crail–St Andrews–
Dundee. (Timetable on display at bus stop
opposite post office.)
Several cafés in Crail and hotels, pubs can
provide evening meals.

Camping: Sauchope Links Caravan Park
(50460) lies just east of Crail on tomorrow's
route. There is a shop and a small outdoor
swimming pool and the setting is superb.

Taxi: 50363 (garage opposite Golf Hotel) or
see under St Andrews or Anstruther.

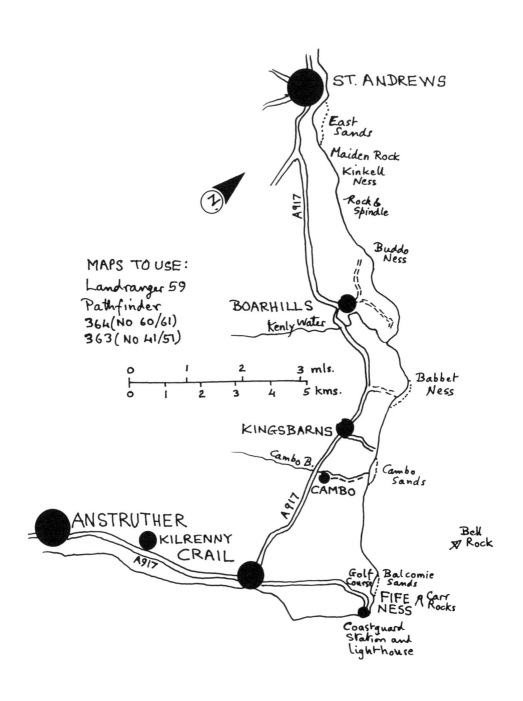

ST. ANDREWS

East Sands

Maiden Rock

Kinkell Ness

Rock & Spindle

Buddo Ness

BOARHILLS

Kenly Water

Babbet Ness

MAPS TO USE:
Landranger 59
Pathfinder
364(NO 60/61)
363(NO 41/51)

0   1   2   3 mls.
0   1   2   3   4   5 kms.

KINGSBARNS

Cambo B.

Cambo Sands

CAMBO

ANSTRUTHER

KILRENNY

CRAIL

A917

Bell Rock

Golf Course

Balcomie Sands

FIFE NESS

Carr Rocks

Coastguard Station and lighthouse

DAY 9 *The Cauld Coast*

Fife Ness–St Andrews

Maps to use: Bart 49, OSLR 59, OSPF 364 (NO 60/61)/363 (NO 41/51)
Walking distance: 19 km (110) km

Today's route produces the longest, hardest and most lonely walking of the whole trip, so expect it to be tougher and set off early and don't waste precious time along the way. Most people will be happy to take eight hours.

A decade ago a Manpower Services team made a coast walk, with sleeper-built bridges over the streams, markers and various signposts. While the bridges largely survive the path itself has been eroded in places by the sea, and a full tide will force a few diversions up onto cliff-tops where the going may not be so easy. The Kenley Water can necessitate the only fording paddle of the walk. All in all, today's demands are several grades higher than anything faced so far – but tomorrow is a lazy day! There are plans to upgrade or renew the path, so if this has occurred then there is no need to take diversions mentioned.

Carry food with you for the day and also plenty of liquid. By the time St Andrews is reached you may be gey drouthy. I neglected this one winter and was very dehydrated, but then I was carrying two cameras and had picked up fossils, skeletal cuttlefish for the parrot and driftwood for the fire. Cambo is the only place where refreshments will be available. Stream water should *not* be drunk.

OUT TO FIFE NESS

Start by walking out along the Nethergate, passing an 1878 Victorian terrace, right, and the Croma Hotel, left, and going along by some cottages. Looking across the Nethergate the tower of the priory shows; this is a modern building built to blend in with the architecture of the East Neuk, and does so very well. The site is old and once had a nunnery centuries ago but it, like the castle, has disappeared.

At the end of the Nethergate turn

right down the footpath past the doocot. Follow the path down and round (right) as far as the green hut at the bottom of the doocot field. From there you'll be able to see the entrance for the pigeons on top of the doocot and understand why it's called the Pepperpot. The priory perches up on the skyline and, below the path, is another rock bathing pool, now much silted up. A burn comes out as we turn back to head east again round the sweep of Roome Bay, with its pale and rufous sandstones. Just follow the path along above the sand, passing a children's play area.

As a lad living in Crail I was told a yarn about a doctor who retired and built one of the bungalows above Roome Bay. He called it Kilmeny. A second doctor shortly followed suit and (not to be outdone) named his house Kilmore.

The red cliff at the far end of the bay is obviously biting back into the slope and the original coastal path is now cut, so angle up the grass to the higher path for the continuation. Several types of trees have been planted (the first seven tubes I peered into all held

different species). From the top corner our diversionary path is followed. Looking ahead, the skyline holds obviously military buildings of the now long-abandoned RAF base. Nissen huts and hangars have all disappeared. We join a driveway which leads us down to the well-appointed Sauchope Links caravan park, once the site of Crail's original golf course, predating Balcomie. There is a small shop and camping is possible.

We walk right through the site, which has a strange urban feel which I suppose comforts those who live in crowded suburbia. A track leads on beyond the site, with a wartime pillbox on the brae and a view to the pinnacled point of Kilminning Castle at the end of the bay. Keep to the path nearest the shore but, about 75m before the knobbly 'castle' rock, turn up by a fence to the top of the brae and walk along the raised beach on what looks like a golf course without any greens. This is the Kilminning Coast Reserve (Scottish Wildlife Trust) and the carpark over on the left is sited on the foundations of an old hangar. You can still see the rusted channels for the sliding doors. The aerodrome attracted the attention of German bombers during the war and Crail was also hit. Twelve people were killed in St Andrews.

This is a good place to have a last look at Forth Estuary landmarks like the May, the Bass and Berwick Law and the now satisfyingly distant Pentlands. Drop down to rejoin the coast path which is always clear.

The *Wildfugle*, wrecked on Fife Ness in 1951 (© St Andrews University (Cowie) Photography Collection)

Channels from the frequent springs are bridged with sleepers. In places there's clawing brambles, gorse and thorn, about all that can grow on this exposed coast. A dyke is crossed and shortly the path heads up to a big farm shed (SWT board). The Dane's Dyke is an old puzzle for it seems that a man-made wall cuts off the end corner of Fife and was, romantically rather than accurately, given that name.

Suddenly we are at the coastguard station and the lighthouse. The houses are now privately owned though originally built as part of the station, which keeps an eye on shipping traffic operating up and down the coast and from the Forth and Tay estuaries (from Carnoustie to Berwick-upon-Tweed). All commercial shipping crossing a line from the North Carr, offshore here, and the South Carr, off the Lothian shore, comes under control of the Forth Ports Authority and will be met by a pilot boat off Inchkeith. There are about 21,000 'traffic movements' a year on the Forth, both in and out and including warships.

The light replaces the North Carr Lightship which we saw back at Ainster (the only one ever operated (1933–75) by the Northern Lighthouse Commissioners) and, out to sea ahead, we can see a beacon on the North Carr Rocks where the lightship was stationed for over 40 years up till 1975. In summer you may see Edinburgh's sludge boat, *Gardyloo*, passing. It deposits its cargo out by the Bell Rock. In 1915 HMS *Ariel* rammed and sank a German U-boat off Fife Ness.

We walk round the tip of Fife (Foreland Head) between the light and an old pillbox. The rock forma-tions are interesting with the hard grey rock full of pools. There is a gap with a strip of sand, then an upthrust of basalt pillars, square in section, and with a lit-ter of broken pieces beyond.

Fulmars have been squawking on every cliff or flying, stiff-winged and unblinking, along the thermals. They come in early in the year and disappear at summer's end, staying out at sea for autumn and winter. They are long-lived, start breeding at seven years old and lay but a single egg each year. Last century they only nested in the isles of the far north-west but they have now spread right round the coast of Britain, an unexplained explosion. Here we may be lucky and see the Concorde of seabirds, the gannets, as they fly round the coast. Many thousands breed on the Bass Rock which was such an historic gannetry that it gave its name to the bird, *Sula bassana*. The birds dive spectacularly into the sea after fish both in the Forth and off the coast – a memorable sight.

We join the small tarred road leading up to the coastguard station and, while not generally open to the public, if anyone is really keen to see inside, this would be possible (10 a.m.–3 p.m.) but ring the day before to arrange the time, (0333) 50666. I find the whole back-ground story and present-day working of the coastguards fascinating, but I'm biased – I live on this coast and several friends are auxiliaries.

The operations room looks like something out of *Star Wars*, with banks of consoles and modern computer machinery. One console is manned round the clock, watching on the emer-gency VHF Channel 16 and another is operating on their own communications channel. Everything is logged and recorded on computer, while a tape records every verbal message. When a 999 call comes in they can mobilise helicopters, lifeboats, cliff rescue teams, shipping, medical back-up and so on. There are 21 centres like this round the British coast with, of course, hundreds of local facilities as well. The service also does a great deal of advisory work, gives local information and publishes safety literature – which is why they are happy to talk to visitors.

The origins of the service were very different, being set up in 1822 to crack down on smuggling. (Fishing boats could have false compartments, trail brandy kegs from their keels or even weave tobacco into hawsers.) The saving of life was incidental to saving money for the Revenue. Initially, there was not much anyone could do for ships in distress, and spectators watched many a tragedy from close quarters. A friend of Nelson, George Manby, perfected a mortar which could carry a 500-yard line to a ship, a big breakthrough, and the 1865 Boxer rocket was so efficient it was used till after the Second World War. As smuggling died out, the coastguard became a recruitment pool for the Royal Navy but this was stopped after the First World War as the service suffered catastrophic losses. The modern life-saving role came then, but for a century volunteers (auxiliaries) have reinforced the regular officers. If today we think of inshore inflatables, radios and high technology, it is not so long ago that it was hand-carts and hard rowing. In the 50 years up to 1909 nearly 20,000 lives were saved.

BALCOMIE–CAMBO–KENLEY BURN

Heading off again, the tarred road curves round past several caravans on a green area which was once a village (one cottage alone survives) and the many walls are all from the old buildings. If the tide is out you'll see the sweep of what was Fife Ness harbour, mostly natural, and occupying a remarkably exposed spot with such a maze of reefs offshore. Yet it was here that Mary of Guise landed before going on to St Andrews and her marriage to James V. James V died just after the birth of their child, Mary commenting, 'It came wi' a lass and it will gang wi' a lass', but the Stewarts were to run on beyond Mary Queen of Scots . . .

If you look carefully down the edge of rocks on the north side, about 20m distance from the road, you'll see a stone circle in the rocks. Curiosity over these marks led me to much reading to find the answer: they were a capstan base, one authority stated; they were part of sluice gates for the old harbour, said another; or a well, or a wartime gun-site. So I was delighted to read the real story in a recent *Scots Magazine*. It concerned the Carr Rock again. Robert Stevenson's success with the Bell Rock lighthouse (where 70 ships had been wrecked in 1799 alone) led the Commissioners to tackle the Carr Rock.

The work was done from this spot, the old harbour restored for landing the stone to be cut carefully before shipping out to the reef. The plan was for a stone tower or beacon, with a bell (rung by tidal flow) and these marks were the template on which the masons cut the dovetailed stones. Coffer dams had to be created on every visit to the reef and in the first year (1813) only 41 hours of work was possible, in 1814 only 53 and in 1815 most of the work was swept away. By the next year the beacon stood 20ft (halfway), the following year it stood full height, only to be utterly smashed by a storm. They then rebuilt the base and erected cast-iron legs to support the round, cage-like marker. When these rusted away they were easily replaced. Now a single pole carries a radar reflector.

Once you wander past the large sandstone block to the start of Balcomie golf course, there is another well left of the road – a good old village pump. At the start of the golf course notices point out the coastal walk line which simply follows the line of white posts marking the bounds of the golf course. On the right is a tidal pool which was created for operating a tidal mill, now no longer visible.

Beside the path you may spot an odd shelter made out of a mine sunk into the grass (a change from collection boxes!) and a bit further on we come close to one of the greens where you can see the fine crested markers used by the club which, founded in 1786, is the seventh oldest in the world. On the crest the Crail 'ship' is topped by crossed golf sticks of the period. The course was originally designed by Old Tom Morris. If golfers are putting or driving off from here, do stand and watch rather than risk your movement being a distraction.

There's a section of gritty track leading past the next landmark, Constantine's Cave. Tradition has it that this king was killed here, c.874, at the hands of raiding Danes. The walls bear crosses similar to those at the Caiplie Coves.

Sandy Balcomie Bay now sweeps ahead with the Tullybothy Craigs and the Kneestone offshore and the Carr Brigs beyond leading to the beacon. Walk along to the obvious building on the edge of the dunes, a greenkeeper's store now, but the walled-up seaward end topped by two rondels shows its origins as a lifeboat station. (Anstruther and Broughty Ferry are now the two nearest sea-going lifeboat stations.) A crown over the date 1884 marks the right plaque, the other has a lifeboat above the letters RNLBI. At the end of the sand is the Blue Stone, the other erratic which is paired in legend with the one at Crail church. I've never found out where they came from originally but there are many erratics along our walk, transported here by a glacier during one of the ice ages and left behind when the ice disappeared. Inland we can see Balcomie Castle, now part of the farm, where Mary of Guise had B&B in 1538. The castle was built early that century by Lear-mouth of Dairsie.

Along on the point there is a shelter with a bench, a small burn, another buried mine and the notice indicating the 5th Hell Hole. Below this is Fluke Dub (flounder pool) and the last sweep of golf course, beyond which we will see very little of human activity. The links are being extended. A burn comes down, as many, many do before we reach St Andrews, so I'll not mention them again, unless there is some special reason. At the end of the shallow bay the crags run down into the sea at high tide and there are unhelpful fences right down to tide-level. Keep below the cliffs if the tide permits, or try a route up on the grass. At high tide one is forced to climb up and along the cliff edge. This jut is the site of Randerston Castle but there is nothing to see on the ground.

Descend into the next cove, which is backed by a small fall and a cave. (The prow gives some demanding rock-climbs for those willing to walk to their crag.) If the other side of the bay is not feasible because of the tide, there is a path contouring at mid-height so you don't have to climb all the way up again. After that, a flat grassy stretch leads on to the woods of the Erskines' Cambo estate. The made path keeps between fence and shore or on the shore and there are steps at one stage. The beach is littered with fossil-rock, a sort of compacted mass of oyster-like creatures. Bramble, briar and elder grow on the approach to the wood and the Cambo Burn has a substantial footbridge.

In early spring the woods are carpeted with snowdrops and I even saw some poking up through the tidal seaweed below the bridge. Later there are daffodils and wild hyacinths. Cambo is now a Country Park and well worth a quick diversion. Walk up the path beside the burn, passing the graceful curve of one of the old cast-iron footbridges and then crossing at a second. Nature Trail notices point out items of interest. The path follows outside the walled garden and through fenced areas with rare breeds of sheep. There are other animals at the farm and old machinery is on display. The octagonal horse mill is now a tea-room where a quick cuppa may be very welcome. We had ours at the picnic tables outside. Open: spring weekends, then May–Sept, 10 a.m.–2 p.m. Telephone: (0333) 50810. On the way back down it is possible to visit the walled garden by taking a path down from a gate on the seaward side of the wall to reach the entrance. (Honesty box on the door.) If you walk out onto the parkland beyond you can see Cambo House, below right, and beyond the grass, over to the left, is a very fine architectural doocot (a tower with finials). Wander back again to pick up the route back to the coast.

The Cambo name dates back to William the Lion who granted lands to the de Cambhou family. Sir Charles Erskine bought the estate in 1668 and it has remained in that family ever since. The original mansion was gutted in 1887 but soon replaced. The lush setting is quite a contrast to the wild, treeless coastline we have been walking.

Picking up the shore path again we wend through the coppiced wood, then past a spruce shelter belt to reach the warm, crisp Cambo Sands. You can walk on the sand or alongside the field fence. A red post on the rocks is a warning marker against swimming in that area. The bay ends at a carpark/picnic area, a brief intrusion on our solitude. The road leads up to the A917 at Kingsbarns, an old hamlet where the king did once have barns in which grain was collected and stored for use at Crail or Falkland. There was also a small port, and immediately beyond the toilet block we can turn off to see the remains of the harbour arms, the

On the coastal path to St Andrews, the loneliest miles of the coastal walk

dry-stane work now steadily decaying. Odd mooring posts still stick up.

Continuing our walk, we pass a sewage pipe running seawards then an oddly grand gateway with spur stones which seems to lead nowhere in particular, but Kingsbarns Castle stood just inland until it was demolished 200 years ago. The shore is littered with sandstone blocks. There's a broken sewage pipe, too, then the path wanders gently along a stretch of dunes. Every stone sticking up seems to be used as an anvil by thrushes and the colourful striped shells of land snails lie scattered about.

This pleasant area ends at Boghall Farm's dump. You can tell when there are farms inland: they all dump rubbish on the shore, some of it rubble to fight erosion but most of it just rubbish. There's a coastal path sign on Babbet Ness and the coast beyond is much wilder, a jagged chaos. The solitary cottage merely emphasises the wildness. Our general direction is now nearly *west* so the Angus coast, rather than open sea, fills our offshore view.

The underlying sandstone is overlaid by a jagged, harder sandstone. The latter was laid down in moving river water rather than as lake bottom sediment, which accounts for its appearance – a petrified torrent. This pockmarked stone was the envy of the alpine gardeners in our party. Note a stile into the field made of the ubiquitous fishboxes. If you have not already been given heart-failure by partridges, you may well meet them along here. We come on several areas where solid walling has been built against erosion, the first bit of wall at the end of a small bay sitting on dark bands of coal and shale. On top of the rocks there are the imprints (*stigmaria*) of prehistoric roots of *Lepidodendron* or *Sigillaria*. The old salmon bothy with its red pantiles has been allowed to fall into decay. There's a farm track on from it. Keep to the branch along outside the walled field. The swirling strata of the sandstone to seawards is marked.

We now come to the day's main obstacle, the Kenley Water (*cean liath*, grey head). Where the track turns up the den a slip angles back down to the shore and here, where the river is wider and flows slowly over kindly gravel, is the best place to paddle across. On a midwinter crossing I found it barely knee-high. If the tide is fully out you may be able to cross further out, and when the water is low in hot summer days it is also possible to cross from stone to stone – but beware, the stones can be slippery. At mid-tide, paddle rather than attempt the provocative rocks. At full tide crossing may be impractical. The nearest footbridge is well up, at Burnside Farm, which is hardly helpful, a long way up just to come down again. You may see a dipper rocketing up the burn or swans cruising by the sea. Once across walk along the bouldery beach to a stone slip where the path is clear again.

ON TO ST ANDREWS

Beyond is an area of thorn and elder scrub, with some marshy bits, a landscape much loved by passerines: wren, greenfinch, robin, whinchat and willow warbler. Tracks can confuse so don't be led off inland into the fields. Keep to the coast. A stile leads on to an artificial lochan which is rather hidden behind reeds above the shore. Its outflow creates a boggy area and you can either keep on, below the tideline, or turn up to walk along the embankment of the lochan which may have swans, ducks and other birds on it. I've always found it a bleak spot, with little life.

The large field beyond has a high wall (why is this one field so carefully walled?) and the walk along outside this is rough and not helped by the many boulders tipped onto it over the wall. There is scarcely room between wall and full tide line now so walking on the beach for once is the easy option, even if the shore stones are a bit knobbly. The going is easier once past the walled field and we catch a first view of St Andrews in the distance, as spired as Oxford.

Another old lifeboat shed sits amid Chesterhill Farm's rubbish. We are into sandstone country again, greys and reds, and round the bay we come on the notable sandstone 'castle' of the Buddo Rock. On the seaward side (only seen at the last minute) there is a natural arch, looking like a pillar with a large capping stone. The rock is split and there are steps up the passage and then hand- and footholds carved on the walls so it is possible to scramble onto the top. Our school-parties used to enjoy this array of natural climbing walls.

There are some shallow caves in the cliff beyond. Follow the path through the wall to angle up to the top of the bank where a wall is followed to the prow of Buddo Ness, marked by a trig point and with two well-concealed

The odd sandstone sculpture of the Buddo Rock

pillboxes below. We drop down again and then traverse the wildest single bit of coastal path. It switchbacks along through scrub and rocks giving conditions much more like those of the west coast.

Kittock's Den only has a small stream so does not present problems. (A 'kittock' is a giddy lassie!) The prow beyond is the site of a prehistoric fort. Except at full tide you can walk along the shore to cross a short, low wall; if the tide prohibits passage then you'll have to traverse higher up. There's a path notice beyond the wall (all the signs and notices are designed for people walking *from* St Andrews).

Kittock's Den (and the Kenley Water) both lead inland to Boarhills. Time rather rules out a visit to the village, which has two doocots, one a rectangular model, the other a sturdy cottage-like building, which is well seen from the A917. The scrub-covered den, and the jungly slopes we've just crossed, are a haven for winter migrants blown in off the North Sea. In November I've seen fieldfare and redwings passing like blowing leaves. Once in a blue moon you may see an eruption of waxwings. Wrens are common and these quiet strands are loved by waders, summer or winter.

The next rocky feature ('almost a pinnacle') marks a sudden change to volcanic rock. In early spring this richer basalt had this rock looking like a planted alpine trough. Beyond, we traverse a bluff where the ground is slowly giving way. Be careful. A tunnel through thorns leads over a burn and on to easier walking along the shore

The Rock and Spindle

edge to the Rock and Spindle, the phallic-like pinnacle ahead.

From this angle the rock presents a ray of basaltic columns, 'like petals on a daisy' (the spinning-wheel), while the slender pinnacle behind is a much easier, though exposed, climb than one would expect. (But leave climbs for the climbers!) This is a volcanic plug where lava has burst through the sandstone, which has weathered away, leaving this core. The Pathfinder map shows a whole series of them in their inter-tidal representation. Kinkell Harbour beside the Rock and Spindle has vanished, but the cart track from the hinterland hints at the one-time passage point. Various tracks also come down so carts could collect the seaweed for spreading on the fields – a ridiculously wasted natural asset today.

Kinkell Ness looms ahead and walkers can either keep along by the shore for a bit before climbing up obvious steps to the cliff-top or can head up directly and wander along the edge of the fields. The former is pleasanter but, even at low tide, head up at the steps when you come to them. (The coast beyond is a steeplechase of rock 'walls' – unpleasant going.) From above, St Andrews is clearer and nearer (note the gasometer). This area is known as the Kinkell Braes, and as we near the caravan park, take the path which descends (some steps) to run along above the Maiden Rock, another isolated sandstone feature, a marooned sea stack. Harold Raeburn was the first person to write about climbing on the Maiden Rock (1902) and he found the 'complete traverse of the arête a nice little climb'. No marks were observed of previous climbs. A path wends down

to the pinnacle but the easiest continuation is to keep along the braes. The rocks east of the Maiden are full of encrinites, the fossilised remains of ancient cylinder-like sea creatures which show clearly as white circles in the darker matrix.

There has been a big subsidence just before the start of Kinkell Braes caravan park, the only site offering camping at St Andrews. (Kinkell is *ceann coille*, head of the wood.) The path runs along the edge of the site and then drops down to the East Sands where there is a big leisure centre, with swimming pool, jacuzzi, squash courts, snooker and a café. Beware though, you can only reach a cup of tea by paying an entrance fee! Telephone (0334) 76506.

Along the East Bents we pass a coastguard building, the Gatty Marine Laboratory, a carpark, slipway and play area, and so reach the harbour with its classic skyline of St Rule's Tower and Cathedral ruins – and the gasometer! A retractable footbridge takes us across the harbour onto the Shorehead, dominated by a restoration that has the main block with flat roofs, completely out of keeping with East Neuk architecture. A pitched roof with pantiles, even now, would transform the harbour. Go round behind this ugly building and up a footpath which runs between the old walls and the sea. The foundations of an ancient Culdee church are passed, right, the ruins only coming to light last century when a gun battery was being installed.

The path forks: the right fork leads along the cliffs, past the Castle, to The Scores where Murray Park (left, near the far end) has many hotels and

B&Bs, convenient for our activities; the left fork comes out to the end of North Street and this, if followed in front of the cathedral, swings round and becomes South Street. The layout has not altered since medieval times. North Street has most of the old uni- versity buildings, South Street is more commercial, as is Market Street, which lies between the two. Other B&Bs tend to be on the outskirts or in the hollow south of the town. The Tourist Information Office is at 70 Market Street (halfway along).

PRACTICAL INFORMATION / ACCOMMODATION

Telephone code: (0334)

Tourist Information Office, 70 Market
Street, KY16 9NU   72021

St Andrews has several hundreds of places where one can stay, ranging from luxury hotels to cosy B&Bs. Even to list a selection would be unrealistic. Either take your chance on arrival, or telephone the Tourist Office the day before or visit it when you get there, or (best of all) send for their Accommodation List before setting off.

(Also available at Tourist Offices earlier in the walk.)

Camping: Kinkell Braes caravan park   74250
Taxis: St Andrews: 76787, 75150, 74
77788, 76622
Leuchars: 837279, 76787
Bus Station: 74238. Open office hours,
not Sunday. Timetables on display outside.
Byre Theatre: 76288
Cinema: 73509
Crawford Arts Centre: 74610

DAY 10 *Saints, Sinners and Golfers*

Exploring St Andrews

Maps to use: Bart 49, OSLR 59, OSPF 363 (NO 41/51)
Walking distance: 4 km (115 km)

This is an urban day but most people find the walking about and absorbing all the sites of interest every bit as tiring as 'just walking'. For convenience, I describe a walkabout route which will take in most of the attractions but there is no need to follow this slavishly. Early on we pass the Tourist Information Office so you can pick up a *What's On* if your landlady doesn't have one handy. Ask to be directed to the West Port, our starting point, at the west end of South Street. Unlike Kirkcaldy, the folk of St Andrews have their directions given accurately despite the positioning of the bay.

EXPLORING ST ANDREWS

St Andrews was originally called Kilrymont. One story explains the town's name by saying that the apostle's relics were carried here by St Rule (St Regulus) – but St Rule was a known Celtic missionary from an earlier period and his name may simply have been added to improve the story. A link with Northumbria may be nearer the truth. It was known that Hexham housed relics of the saint and the abbot may have brought or sold these to St Andrews. The town's royal charter was granted by David I *c.*1144.

The gateway at the West Port was reconstructed in 1589, based on Edinburgh's Netherbow Port. The plaque on the west side shows David I on horseback, a Victorian replacement of an older panel with the royal arms. The arms on the east side are those of St Andrews. In 1650 Charles II was presented with the keys of the city here. From the gateway head off eastwards on South Street. The Gifford tome has notes on almost every house on South Street but we'd need a day

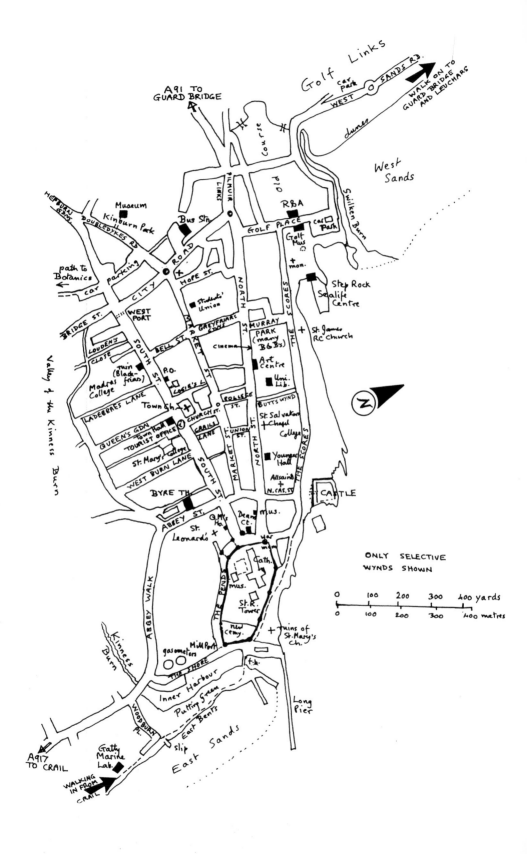

for each street if we looked at everything. On the right there's an older house with a forestair, and you'll see the oval logo of the St Andrews Preservation Trust which was founded in 1937 to rescue older buildings, a role taken on more generally by the National Trust for Scotland with its Little Houses Scheme – which we have seen all along our route.

St Andrews was fortunate that in the 1840s a retired military type from India became provost and set about rebuilding both the city's civic pride and something of its monuments and buildings. Sir Hugh Playfair has a mural tomb in the cathedral graveyard and the Town Kirk has a Playfair aisle. The minister was another Playfair and is commemorated by an elaborate marble pulpit. The initials of previous moderators who were ministers of the Town Kirk are shown on this, including Playfair's own, but no room was left for any further initials and, strangely, the kirk has not produced a moderator since.

Turn right through a pend into Louden's Close, just one of many alleys leading off South Street and such a feature of the city. The close is hemmed in by high walls and runs down to the Ladebraes Walk where we turn left to follow this serpentine alley which runs between town (Madras College) and the Kinness Burn. The burn was once an important source of power but no mills survive. The burn's long wide mouth forms the harbour. We turn back up to South Street by Ladebraes Lane, equally enclosed by dykes. Turn left, and on the left is the isolated ruin of Blackfriars Chapel with the lawns and buildings of Madras College behind.

Blackfriars Monastery has gone, having suffered initially in a riot following John Knox's St Andrews sermon in 1559. The chapel had been added in 1525 but only the apse survives. A crucifixion scene can be made out on the underside of the vaulted roof. As with most sites, there are explanatory notices. Behind the ruin is one about Dr Andrew Bell, founder of Madras College, 'a suave Jacobean manor' built by William Burn and opened in 1834. Bell was the son of a local hairdresser (and town bailie) who graduated at St Andrews, worked in the USA, was ordained and went as a missionary to India where he evolved his Madras monitorial system. The school was co-educational but few poor girls attended in its early years. The fine façade hid somewhat spartan realities. One rector wrote of putting on two sets of woollen underwear in October and keeping them on till April. Classes could start at 6 a.m.

Cross the street and go through a pend into the cobbled Burgher Close courtyard, so called from one of the many church splinter groups who moved here in the eighteenth century. The Preservation Trust restoration work makes this a quiet, attractive corner. Up the stairs in Hansa House is the studio of Jurek Pütter who has spent his lifetime researching into St Andrews' medieval past and turning his knowledge into vast, figure-crowded prints, quite unique. Do have a look.

Out again, turn past the post office, which has a plaque to John Adamson, a pioneer photographer who took the first calotype picture in 1841. We then come on the Town Kirk, but before considering it, we can make a circuit of the town hall and the old offices of the *St Andrews Citizen*. The Tourist Information Office can supply a town map, *What's On* booklet, and any other information. The town hall, near the kirk, on the left-hand side of Queen's Gardens, is a baronial pile with rather a surfeit of fiddly features and small additions. It dates to 1858, replacing the old tolbooth in Market Street, a stone from which, dated 1565, is built into the lobby. Other town souvenirs are arms dated 1115, Malcolm IV's charter, the executioner's axe, the silver keys of Charles II, a set of brass measures, the city seals, and the provost's chain of office – a roll lists the provosts back to the twelfth century. Royal burghs lost their special character with dull local government reorganisation in 1975. The provost's lamps stand in Queen's Gardens and there is also a mural mosaic commemorating the strong link with wartime Polish forces. The town hall clock is not on the tower but hanging over South Street.

Across South Street is a bookshop, J & G Innes Ltd, in a rather Tudor-style building which might be happier in Chester. The *St Andrews Citizen* was first published here in 1870 and is still going strong. Wheels within wheels: the site was earlier the home of Bailie Bell (father of the Madras College founder) who had a flair for things mechanical and worked with Alexander Wilson on perfecting a system of type founding that made Wilson's name. He was also associated with the foundry at Philadelphia which first cast the $ sign (1797). Another

local Wilson (James) emigrated to the USA after graduation to become a professor of literature and was directly involved in preparing the Declaration of Independence (1776). There's a turret on the corner, above a lantern, and a figure of St Andrew facing Church Street. Church Street was originally Kirk Wynd but, like far too many of the town's streets, has been changed or anglicised, a trend that should obviously be reversed.

Holy Trinity, the town church, was originally nearer the cathedral but moved here centuries ago. Only the *c.*1410 tower is of that period, the church being rebuilt early this century by MacGregor Chalmers. Entering the north door, the many-pillared arches reminded me of the great mosque at Cordoba. The tower was often used for locking up women who had strayed from the path of righteousness. There was also the branks, an iron frame which was placed over the victim's head with a bar which went into the mouth to render speech impossible. Three cutty stools (repentance seats) are another relic of those fanatical years. Archbishop Sharp had the branks put on one Isobel Lindsay to stop her heckling during sermons, so his assassination on Magus Muir could hardly have been surprising. Hackston of Rathillet, one of the ringleaders of this deed, was butchered (judicially) a year after and parts of his body hung up in various towns as a warning. A huge contemporary marble monument shows the hated archbishop's end (1679). In 1849 when his tomb was opened there was only a broken coffin inside – and no sign of human remains! John Knox preached his rabble-

The view from St Rule's Tower, looking along North Street to St Salvator's and the West Sands

rousing sermon here in 1559 which led to the direct destruction of church buildings throughout Scotland, a sad loss. A more pacific memorial honours Old Tom Morris, the Royal and Ancient's first golf professional. Gifford calls the church 'a dictionary of architectural quotations'. The chancel floor is of Iona marble. There's a blaze of stained glass. The roof was covered in Caithness slabs which gave a mammoth restoration job recently.

Behind the church take Logie's Lane beside the town library through a pend onto Market Street and turn right. This was the heart of the town at one time, where the tolbooth and mercat cross were to be found. The latter was removed in 1768 and its site, like the tolbooth's, is marked by a cobbled cross in the middle of the road. The hapless Chastelard, as mentioned in Day 3, was executed here in 1563. So was the Bohemian reformer, Paul Craw, who was slowly burned to death in 1433, a brass ball forced into his mouth to prevent him speaking to the crowd. The fountain is a memorial to the novelist, George Whyte-Melville, who died in a hunting accident. A street market is held here on Saturdays, and at the beginning of August there is the Lammas Fair, the oldest surviving medieval fair in Scotland. Trading fairs date back to 1153 and at one time there were five each year, attracting people from all over Europe in a combination of pilgrimage and business. In the end the Lammas Fair was largely a feeing fair (when workers signed on to work on local farms) and now it is simply a fun-fair.

St Salvator's Chapel, one of the finest buildings in St Andrews

Turn left along College Street (no. 24 noteworthy) to reach North Street. St Salvator's Church tower dominates the scene and the frontage is a superb medieval survival. (Pity about the cars!) North Street, and between it and the sea, is almost entirely taken up by university buildings. The Culdees on Kirkhill and then the Augustinians of the priory had organised educational work but it was Bishop Wardlaw who provided the spur for founding a school for higher studies, based on that of Orleans, in 1410. Two years later a papal bull confirmed what was Scotland's first university. Various colleges were founded over the years. St Salvator's ('Sallie's' in student parlance) was founded by Bishop Kennedy in 1450. Some of the history of this time is paraded in the Kate Kennedy Procession each year. Kate's part in the pageant is always played by a 'beardless bejant', the name given to first-year male students (pronounced 'bee-jant').

Originally the tower had no steeple, and in 1546 the Protestants who had seized the castle were bombarded by French cannon from the top of the tower. The spire was added four years later. If you cross towards the pend through the bottom of the tower, you will see initials PH on the cobbles. Patrick Hamilton, a well-connected and likeable student, was burned here in 1528, the first martyr of the Reformation. Not yet practised, they took several hours over the deed. Walk through into the largely Jacobean-style quadrangle and the entrance to the church is on the right, its gloriously rich interior mostly modern or, at least, Victorian. In the late nineteenth cen-

tury the vaulted medieval roof had become dangerous, so was unceremoniously demolished. The falling roof damaged several priceless features, including Bishop Kennedy's tomb which is still impressive, however. John Knox's pulpit is also in the church and in the vestry are several medieval maces. The restoration work is colourful and, walking out, the row of gilded coats-of-arms along the organ loft is eye-catching. Left of the door is a monument to the Borders poet, historian and folklorist, Andrew Lang, who studied at St Andrews, as did many men famous in different spheres. The Marquess of Montrose was a student here. I wonder if, as he drove golf balls along the links, he could have foreseen how his life would run.

The university has had a very chequered history and several times nearly ceased to function; several decades ago, however, a huge expansion was started, both within the town and on peripheral green sites – seldom, alas, built with any architectural flair, being of the utility concrete box era.

Return to Market Street and cross it, leftwards, to walk through Crail's Lane to South Street and over to the archway entrance to St Mary's College, a quadrangle in which buildings and trees set each other off. The huge holm oak was planted in 1728 but has centuries to go to match the propped-up thorn, right, by the bell tower, which is of the time of Mary Queen of Scots, and was reputedly planted by her. The college was founded by Archbishop Beaton in 1539, on the site of older schools, and some of his buildings still stand. Walk down the length of the garden, passing a 1664 sundial on a column. There's a secret garden through a gate, right, and at the end of the walk a rather overgrown doocot which would rather like to come up for air. The buildings on the east include the library, founded by James VI in 1612. In 1645 a meeting of the Scottish Estates was held here and the room has been called Parliament Hall ever since.

Continue east along South Street, lined with sturdy old town houses, many showing coats-of-arms on the walls, as at the house by the South Court pend where the Byre Theatre sign hangs. Walk through here, pass the theatre and turn first left to come out onto Abbey Street. The pend leads into South Court, lit in season by a flowering cherry tree. There is a plaque on the wall to Professor J.D. Forbes, one of the early Alpinists (Forbes Arête, etc.), and the man who first showed an astonished world that glaciers were moving 'rivers of ice'.

Byre is Scots for cowshed and the original tiny theatre was created in a byre in 1933. This friendly, cramped, characterful set-up lasted till 1967, when the 73-seat byre was demolished. The present building opened in 1970. Check what's on: you could return in the evening if there is a performance. Note the three-hole doocot entrance stone built into the Abbey Street frontage, part of the original byre.

Follow Abbey Street along to attractive South Street and turn right. The cathedral ruins are framed at the end of the street with, left, the leaning tower of the Roundel on the corner, and Queen Mary's House opposite it, where the queen stayed when visiting the city. The gateway beyond

is the Pends, the fourteenth-century entrance to the priory. The road through it comes out through the Mill Port/Sea Yett to the harbour. Walk down for 100m and on the right is the entrance to St Leonard's School and chapel. A hospice for pilgrims in the twelfth century and later one of the university college, the site is now a girls' school. The somewhat byre-like but attractive chapel is on the right and can be visited. There are imposing Renaissance mural monuments in the choir.

Returning, The Pends' arch frames Deans Court, now a students' residence, once the home of the archdeacon. The cobbled circle/cross before the gateway marks where 80-year-old Walter Myln, apprehended at Dysart, was burned at the stake in 1558 on the orders of Archbishop Hamilton, himself to be executed in 1571 for his involvement in Darnley's murder. Henry Forrest, another student, also suffered here in 1533. After looking in to the peaceful courtyard, cross towards the cathedral grounds. The town war memorial (undistinguished Sir Robert Lorimer) is seen set in the wall over to the left. Enter the extensive graveyard.

The cathedral is a 'rent skeleton' (Ruskin) but enough is left to impress with what it once must have been – the second largest in Britain (over 100m long). The site is well marked with noticeboards so I'll not try and describe it here. The museum in the old restored priory building is a good first port of call. There is a large collection of early sculptured stones (50 were dug up when excavating St Mary of the Rock, the old Culdee church above the harbour) and many show a Northumbrian influence. The panel of a sarcophagus dating from the eighth to the tenth century must be one of the most beautiful ancient relics in the country, a moving flow of animals, a huntsman with hawk on wrist and a large figure (David?) being attacked by a lion. There are some startling skeletons on grave-slabs, one (on a window-sill) shows death as a skeleton stabbing his victim in the back. There are several 'green men' stones. The enthusiastic keeper will be glad to show you round.

After that, the climb up the haunted St Rule's Tower is recommended, giving a bird's-eye view of the cathedral/priory area within its huge wall and also a view down to the harbour and the coast we've walked and over the town to the West Sands of tomorrow's route. The tower is 33m high, so the view is extensive. Both west and east sides of the tower are grooved, indicating where roofs joined the tower, and showing how these buildings changed over the centuries, as did the arches and doorways. Within the choir on the east side there is a mural slab with another startling skeleton, this one lying in a hammock. It looks across to a monument to Dr Thomas Chalmers, who was Professor of Divinity here among all his other activities. A walk round the wall to look at the mural gravestones will produce everything from full-rigged ships to golfers (Tom Morris, father and son, and Willie Auchterlonie – the last local to have the won the Open, in 1893!). Tom Morris senior won the second-

St Rule's (or St Regulus') Tower, St Andrews

ever Open in 1861 and then again in 1862, 1864 and 1867. His 17-year-old son won it in 1868 and then in 1869, 1870 and 1872. There was no championship in 1871, so his remains the first four-in-a-row success. Young Tom died at the age of 24. James Anderson, of a golf ball making family in St Andrews, won the Open three years in a row, from 1877 to 1879.

The cathedral was founded in 1160/61 and in the next century the great west front was wrecked in a storm. The cathedral was consecrated by Bishop Lamberton in 1318, with his staunch ally, King Robert the Bruce, present. Earlier, the bishop had been in chains as Edward I's prisoner for having crowned the Bruce at Scone. Edward stripped the lead off the roof to help in his siege of Stirling. Fifty years on a great fire gutted the cathedral and it took seven years to restore. One of its bishops, captured by English pirates, refused to be ransomed in order not to sidetrack vital funds. In 1409, at the time of Bishop Wardlaw (founder of the university two years later), the south transept gable was blown down. In 1472 it became the metropolitan see and had a century when nothing seems to have fallen down or burnt up. At the Reformation (1559) it suffered the 'burning of images and mass-books and breaking of altars' and simply became an easy quarry for building stone for the town. The more portable treasures simply disappeared. We do well to remember the burnings and the battles of our

own bloody history before we make comments on those of other nations.

From the cathedral walk along North Street. The Preservation Trust's friendly museum is on the left. (Open daily, mid-June–mid-September, 2–4.30 p.m.) Displays of town life (grocers and chemist shops) help balance the surfeit of history we're having.

Turn right into North Castle Street (ex Castle Wynd or Fishergate), lined on the right by older houses and on the left by Castle Wynd House and All Saints Episcopal church which, though not old, is worth a quick look as it is richly adorned. The foretower of the castle lies at the end of the street. Cobbled initials point this time to where George Wishart was burned in 1546 while Cardinal Beaton watched from a castle window. Not long after, a small gang of Protestants gained entry to the castle by mingling with the working masons and, catching the defence by surprise, quickly won the castle. The cardinal's body was hung out the same window where he had gloated over Wishart's agony. Henry VIII backed the Protestants who held the castle for a year but French bom-

A detail from the hunting scene on the unique sarcophagus in the cathedral museum, St Andrews

bardment, by land and sea, brought its surrender and the occupants (including the then little-known John Knox) were led off to the galleys. The castle had had various hammerings before that, of course, particularly during the Wars of Independence when it was 'dang doon' or rebuilt several times.

The first castle building went up *c.*1200 to be a more up-market home for Bishop Roger than he could find in the priory, and throughout its history it was the episcopal palace, town fortress and state prison. Ecclesiastics, for centuries, were much in the power game. When Archbishop Stewart died at Flodden in 1513, there was a squabble over the see. Gavin Douglas simply took possession of the castle. Prior Hepburn then drove him out and manned both castle and cathedral. James Beaton was also contending and eventually triumphed over Andrew Forman, Bishop of Moray, who had been elected. Douglas was imprisoned in the castle later on. No wonder John Knox wanted to sweep away the whole corrupt edifice, something often forgotten in the glib dismissal of Knox. For instance, he envisaged a school in every parish, something that only came to pass centuries later. Unfortunately, the reforming nobles were as set on power and possessions as their predecessors.

Little of the castle structure survives, but two special features do, and make a visit a must. In the Sea Tower is the notorious Bottle Dungeon. Carved out of solid rock, bottle-shaped, the only entrance was down the narrow 'neck', which lay higher

than could be reached. No one ever escaped its dark and dank depths and those who died there were easily thrown over into the sea. The sea in turn has completely removed the east range with its great hall (the whole cliff base of the site is now defended by concrete), yet below is sand. Every trace has been removed by the sea.

In 1546 the Earl of Arran was besieging the castle and started a mine (tunnel) to reach under the defences. The tunnel was 1.8m (6ft) wide and 2.1m (7ft) high, so that ponies could take away the stone. It sloped down to pass below the level of the defence ditch. A chamber was then made preparatory to undermining the walls, but at this stage a counter mine dug by the defenders broke through into their minehead. The counter mine is a much smaller tunnel which had a couple of trial starts and one false passage before worming into the enemy passage. The mines can be visited, and climbing through their passages gives a memorable experience.

Cardinal David Beaton was the nephew of Archbishop James Beaton and an ambitious Catholic climber. He rejected Henry VIII's idea of marrying

In the counter-mine tunnel leading out from St Andrews Castle

his son (later Edward VI) to the Scots heir, Mary (Mary Queen of Scots), and it was while fortifying the castle against Henry that Beaton was surprised by the Reformers and killed. He was succeeded by Archbishop Hamilton and the frontage we see today dates to his period. (The jutting foretower was the original entrance.) Thereafter, the castle went into decline and in 1654 the harbour was repaired by using its stonework. It was taken into state care in 1911.

That is really the end of our historic walkabout but at the other end of The Scores (how much pleasanter is the old name, Swallowgait) are two new attractions: the Sea Life Centre and the British Golf Museum, both worth a visit now, or in the morning. The cliff-top beside the Catholic church on The Scores gives a view down onto the Sea Life Centre. Fulmars nest below the rim or fly past on stiff-winged, dead-eye flight. The largest 'pool' is the old Step Rock tidal swimming pool, once very popular (even in winter) but latterly largely unused. Witch Hill, into which the Golf Museum cuts, was where these unfortunates once suffered. Either that, or they were thrown into the sea to test their innocence. If they drowned, they were obviously innocent. If they floated or won ashore, they were obviously witches – so were burnt. St Andrews' last witch was killed in 1705.

This area, dominated by the obelisk of the Martyrs Monument, is also the Bow Butts, where archery once took place. In 1457 James II tried to ban golf and football as archery skills were being neglected. I rather think the golf won. (The great Marquess of Montrose

won a competition when a student.) It was the royal game too: James VI and his mother both played the 'gowf'. The Martyrs Monument bears the names of Hamilton (1528), Forrest (1533), Wishart (1546) and Myln (1558). (Paul Craw from Prague was burned a century before these Reformation martyrs, in 1432.)

The Sea Life Centre is a wonderful window into the world of the sea – quite literally, as visitors can peer and pry in an exciting way through the viewing windows of the many different displays. Weird and wonderful sums up the scene, but the resulting ecological understanding can only help in an environment we have largely treated as a dustbin. Behind the scenes are scientific studies, breeding programmes and rescue projects. After an hour 'at sea' it is pleasant to sit on the café balcony and just watch the sea. Open daily, Feb–Dec 10 a.m.–2 p.m. Telephone (0334) 74786.

Below the Martyrs Monument is a Victorian bandstand. Seaward of that is what looks like a viewing platform – which it is, but it is also the roof of the British Golf Museum which is (appropriately?) bunkered in the bank. Open daily, May–Oct 10 a.m.–5.30 p.m.; at other seasons closed Monday. Telephone (0334) 78880. This thoroughly high-tech museum will fascinate everyone with even a passing interest in the game. There are historic objects as one would expect, but the state-of-the-art audio-visual displays are unique. You can see great moments, brush up on history, follow the careers of the golfing greats, study the development of clubs and balls and a great deal more.

In 1991 the St Andrews Museum opened in a mansion in Kinburn Park. It tells the story of the town using modern techniques (you can see, hear and smell it!) and there is a relaxing café. A good place to end the day. The museum is on Doubledykes Road, the continuation westwards of Market Street. To reach it from Golf Place turn right at North Street then first left along City Road; Doubledykes Road is first right after the bus station. Open daily, April–Sept 11 a.m.–6 p.m.; Oct-March, Mon–Fri 11 a.m.–4 p.m., and Sat and Sun 2-5 p.m. Telephone (0334) 7706.

One last place that may have a special appeal is the 18-acre site of the Botanic Gardens which lies south-west of the West Port. If you go through the gateway from South Street and continue straight on (Argyle Street), there is a sign pointing the way to the Botanics, via a carpark. The entrance is reached by walking along a footpath (Viaduct Walk) and turning right for 50m when a road is reached (the Canongate) – a ten-minute walk from the West Port.

Not only is the Kinness Burn site attractive but there are large glasshouse collections and a lively programme of demonstrations, etc. The cacti house has over 250 species on show, an orchid house is being created, and there are collections of rare alpines, rhododendrons and primulas. The rich setting is a strange contrast to the gale-smitten rim we have walked. Open daily, May–Sept 10 a.m.–7 p.m.; Oct-April, Mon–Fri 10 a.m.–4 p.m. Glasshouses open 2–4 p.m., weekdays only.

Twice when walking parts of the East Neuk with friends, we have ended our day's tramping by dining at Baburs, 89 South Street (facing St Mary's College) an Indian restaurant with a justified reputation. Recommended. (0334) 77778. The Byre Theatre is just two minutes' walk away as well.

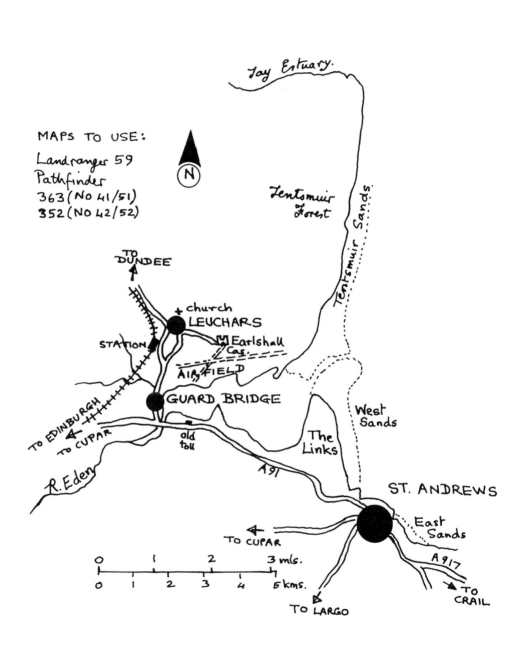

MAPS TO USE:

Landranger 59
Pathfinder
363 (NO 41/51)
352 (NO 42/52)

Tay Estuary.

N

Tentsmuir Forest

Tentsmuir Sands

TO DUNDEE

church
LEUCHARS

STATION

Earlshall Cas.

AIRFIELD

GUARD BRIDGE

TO EDINBURGH
TO CUPAR

old toll

R. Eden

A91

West Sands

The Links

ST. ANDREWS

East Sands

A917

TO CUPAR

TO CRAIL

TO LARGO

0   1   2   3 mls.

0   1   2   3   4   5 kms.

DAY 11 *Breezes and Bridges*

Guardbridge–Leuchars–Forth Bridge

Maps to use: Bart 49, OSLR 59, OSPF 352 (NO 42/52). For the Railway Bridge: Bart 46, OSLR 65, OSPF 394, 406
Walking distance: 16 km (131 km–82 miles)

This is an easy day but quite different from the olde-worlde feel of the East Neuk coast, being entirely on links and estuary before ending with two superb historical buildings, Leuchars Church and Earlshall Castle. This is followed by the rail journey through Fife to cross the Forth Bridge – as satisfying a rounding-off of our Fife coast walk as can be imagined.

SANDS AND ESTUARY

Wherever you have stayed the night, make for Golf Place, the road heading between the Royal and Ancient Golf Club and the Golf Museum; it passes a carpark and toilets (right) before swinging round the Bruce Embankment to the start of the huge West Sands. You can cut down at once but the Swilcan Burn edges the sands and may act as a deterrent, in which case just keep to the road for 60m until it swings over the burn, then cut down onto the sands. At the start of the links is the Ladies' Putting Green, known locally as the Himalayas. We've also

passed what many regard as golf's most historic corner. The Swilcan (Swilken) Burn with its humped footbridge and the huge sward up to the 18th hole of the Old Course is now instantly recognisable from TV coverage of the Open. The Society of St Andrews Golfers was formed in 1754 and became the game's regulatory body. The 'Royal' was added to the title when William IV became patron. The clubhouse was built in 1854.

The opening scene of *Chariots of Fire* with the athletes running along the margin of the sea, was filmed on the West Sands. Luckily the goose pimples didn't show, for this location

A golf-club factory in St Andrews at the turn of the century (© Andrews University (Cowie) Photography Collection)

was portraying the south coast of England. Hamilton Hall appeared as a hotel.

There isn't really much to say about the walk along the West Sands. You won't find many finer strands, and on a fresh morning it will breathe plenty of air into your lungs before the return home. 'Out of the world and into Fife' is another of the cynical traditional phrases about this area, but there have been serendipity moments and places enough for us, quite often, to feel that, on Fife's coastal walk, we have been both in Fife and out of this world.

When the mouth of the Eden Estuary is drawing near keep an eye open for Outhead, the fenced-off area at the end of the dunes (which is as far as motorists can travel); beyond is golf course and nature reserve. There is a noticeboard giving updated details of current wildlife interest, etc. Take the path from there but briefly turn off right to climb the prow of the dunes to see the estuary mouth. The sands are only briefly interrupted and run on for 12km by Tentsmuir Forest to Tayport at the mouth of the Tay Estuary.

A look at the map shows the great eastward-streaming sandbanks created by a mixture of Tay currents and the vast plantations of Tentsmuir, described a century ago as 'all but useful for agricultural purposes'. This is the sort of place massed conifers deserve to be planted, one feels. The Tay sands and dunes have long been studied, and, with the forest growing, their rate of growth increased as well. Seeds then blew onto the shore and baby conifers sprouted everywhere. The NCC debated this, one opinion saying the seedlings were an alien intrusion and should be removed, the other view being that since the trees were there, willy-nilly, the actual seeding was natural so the seedlings should be left. Good old compromise: they decided to clear half the area. Braehead School from Buckhaven was given the task of tree-pulling and we spent two visits camping at Morton and doing this work – plus exploring the dunes, swimming in the sea and birdwatching at Morton Loch where some of our trees were planted to screen the new hides.

The presence of RAF Leuchars may make itself known! The fighter base sprawls along the whole north side of the Eden Estuary. At the head of the estuary we can see the paper-mill buildings which we will be passing in an hour, pints permitting. Return to the path and follow it along, keeping as much to the edge of the golf course as possible. This is hallowed ground for the golfing fanatic. Nature does not treat it with any reverence, though, and defensive works against the persistent erosion of the sea here have been necessary to save the fragile, sandy edge of the golf courses. There are old groynes and recent gabions. Some of the tees perch right by the shore.

There are several courses on these links: the Old Course (so old it can't be dated), the New Course (1895), the Jubilee Course (Queen Victoria's, 1897), the Eden Course (1914) and,

probably complete by now, the Strathyrum (18-holes) and a new Balgrove beginners' course (9-holes). The Open comes here every few years. Winners, working backwards over the last few, have been Faldo (1990), Ballesteros (1984), Nicklaus (1978 and 1970), Lema (1964), Nagle (1960 – the Centenary Open) and Bobby Locke (1957).

Local people had a historical right to the links and when the burgh officials sold them in 1797 and rabbits were brought in, there was an outcry from the golfers. A legal ruling backed the golfers and said they had a right to kill the rabbits – which they did. The warren-owner then pled his case. It all went to the Lords but fizzled out eventually as there was no case – because there were no rabbits! Golf won. And won again when the railway planned to bash through everything.

Even a barren spot like this has a range of flowers in season; from the sealion grass to the lawns of the golf courses, clover, harestail, willowherb, yarrow, bluebell (the Scots bluebell, not the wild hyacinth), birdsfoot trefoil, purple milk vetch, yellow rattle and rest harrow were a few I recognised. Rest harrow is short for 'arresting-the-harrow' which is just what their tenacious spread was apt to do. Yellow rattle also had an old farming connection: when the pods were dry enough they rattled and that was an indication it was time for harvesting.

The Eden Estuary is a Nature Reserve and SSSI of international importance for its birdlife, the relatively pollution-free waters ensuring plenty of mussels, cockles, snails, worms and algae to feed the thousands of wildfowl and waders. Shelduck and red-breasted mergansers are common, and you could see long-tailed duck, eider, scaup, common and velvet scoter, oyster-catcher, ringed and grey plover, bar-tailed godwit, redshank, knot and sanderling, according to season.

Gabions run right along the back of the bay. Simply walk along beside the sea and avoid straying onto the links. Eventually we pick up the stone-built embankment which was built to protect the railway rather than golf courses. We come on a birdwatching hide and, looking back, can see the line of the railway swinging off through the golf courses as a rough track. The route of the line comes to an abrupt stop just west of a big water hazard as the fields have completely covered it. The embankment gives us a firm walkway and the farmers must be very grateful to the railway engineers for this sea defence.

The next landmark is a stone slipway where a small burn comes in. Not long after, the embankment stops and you can walk either on the grassy verge or on the shore, depending on the going. There are well-marked paths as horses exercise on this bit of bay. At one wet area, where a burn comes in, a diversion up the bank is advisable. The bay ends with the sandy stretch of Coble Shore to the Sand Ford Head, which suggests that, long ago, people crossed here at low tide. Opposite is Coble House Point but the far side of the Eden Estuary is now all RAF Leuchars.

Once round the point it is easiest to walk along the sandy shore (tide permitting) to a gate where a track leads on to another gate, at the now disappeared railway line. There's a small carpark for wildfowlers who come down in their camouflage gear to play one-sided war games with the wildlife. Walk out the now bigger track to the A91 and turn right, an unavoidable stretch of busy road.

GUARDBRIDGE

The first building on the right is an old toll house, then there is a snack bar at the Strathkinness road junction (left), then a bit of old road is seen isolated, on the right, with picnic tables and a Nature Reserve noticeboard. Take this. The noticeboard may have current notes on bird observations, etc. Carry on down this bit of old road past a police station and a garage to reach the butterfly-fronted Guardbridge Hotel. A pint or bar lunch at one of the outside tables might appeal. but do go inside as well to see the collection of old prints and paintings of Guardbridge that the enthusiastic owner has accumulated. A notice on a wall caught my fancy: 'Be warned that tickling and groping is an offence under section 27 of the Salmon and Freshwater Fisheries Act 1927'.

The Eden Estuary has now narrowed to a wide tidal river, 22 miles from its source in the Lomond Hills and its course through the rich farmland heart of Fife – which we'll see on the train later. This lowest bridging point has been well used over the centuries. No doubt, at times, it was well guarded. We walk across one of the most historic bridges in Scotland, for it dates back to 1419. Upstream, the

The old toll house on the St Andrews road just before Guardbridge

main road goes over a triple-arched concrete bridge, typical of its 1938 period, while downstream are the stumpy piers of the 1852 Fife Coast Railway (North British), which followed round from Leuchars Junction to St Andrews, Crail and the other East Neuk towns to Leven and Thornton Junction. The line was axed by Beeching in 1967. What a tourist lure it could have become with steam trains running on it now.

The old bridge was built by Bishop Wardlaw early in the fifteenth century, which makes it one of the oldest

bridges in Scotland as well as one of the most pleasing. In 1685 repairs were made from the revenues of vacant stipends and the bridge was referred to as Gair Bridge. Guard is just a corrup-

The last steam train crossing the Eden at Guardbridge in 1969 (© Guardbridge Hotel collection)

tion of this. There are bold cutwaters and six arches, the most easterly being smaller, and three refuges on each parapet, which may be of later date. Panels bear the arms and initials of Archbishop James Beaton.

Once over the bridge, turn right at a junction where there was once a toll house (telephone box) to walk through Guardbridge village, such as it is. On the left the open space is the site of the NB station, then there is the parish church, the only one we've encountered built in brick. A Victorian Co-op building is rather spoilt by additions along its front. There's a shop/post office (right) and, left, rows of sturdy houses (McGregor's Buildings, etc) and another church which has been converted into a house. This leads to the massive paper-works, with a street-side clock with 'G.B. Papers' on it.

The site was originally that of the Seggie Distillery (Haig family, 1810) and there was also a pulp-mill and brickworks. When these failed, the Guardbridge Paper Company was established in the distillery building in 1873, so there has been over a century of papermaking at Guardbridge – a famous name for this reason. Making paper I find fascinating, and these days quite a lot of waste products can be used and there's also recycling. Employing 300 people, this is a large concern by today's standards, and vital locally. Since 1984 G.B. Papers has been part of the US James River Corporation. Conducted tours can be laid on for small groups. Contact Human Resources Dept for details: (0334) 839551.

We then pass under another old bridge lying on the inland side of the A919. This was the Inner Bridge or Motray Bridge, only replaced by the new road in 1938. The Motray Water was essential for the paper-mill which, in 1967 for instance, used 20 million gallons a week (more than the town of St Andrews!). The estuary was necessary for exporting whisky, bone meal, wool, paper and agricultural produce, and three piers could cope with 32 vessels which seems incredible now. Something like 200 vessels came to grief on this part of the coast, so the coming of the railway was welcomed. The paper-mill was bombed on a sneak low-level raid during the last war, but no damage was done.

LEUCHARS AND EARLSHALL

There are playing-fields, houses and a junction, right, signposted for RAF Leuchars. We take this: the road crosses the end of the runway and then through a mix of the RAF station (right) and housing (left) so there's an odd feeling as women push prams along past high-security fences and guardrooms. The third weekend in September (Battle of Britain Day) sees an annual airshow which is very popular. If there is anything special on you will see the equivalent of twitchers along the roadside as you walk past. After almost 20 years of having Phantom squadrons the base now operates two squadrons of Tornadoes. A 'retired' Phantom is sited just inside the main gate. A Spitfire used to be there but they are so rare and valuable now that this one has been moved to a museum. You can gauge the popularity of the open day from the fact that the 1990 show raised £126,000 for charity. Mind you, you'd have to add a cluster of 0's to that figure to reach the price of just one Tornado. It's changed days since my National Service years in the RAF in the Canal Zone when the first jets (Meteors) were introduced.

Beyond the RAF station there is a bus turning loop on the left. The road swings left steadily but take the first road off, right, into a housing scheme. As you turn off look left for a sight of the magnificent church which will be our final point of interest, after we've visited Earlshall Castle.

Follow the road and after it swings left there is a crossroads. Turn right to pass a few houses and at the end of the straight bit of road ahead (a lime tree avenue) lie the policies of the castle, which soon becomes visible and is approached through a fine gateway, one of the Lorimer touches. The setting, with mature beechwoods, is a rich one for the windy east coast. The only snag is the close presence of RAF Leuchars and the air-crackling din of aircraft taking off and landing.

Earlshall is our last castle and is quite different from the stark castles we've seen earlier. Earlshall presents a cosy home atmosphere and, while full of interest, doesn't overwhelm the visitor. A hundred years ago the building was decaying but was then brilliantly restored by Sir Robert Lorimer. He is responsible for many of the intimate details but, so unlike his peers, he kept to the original plan so

The Lorimer-restored Earlshall Castle, to the east of Leuchars village

Earlshall is one of the best castles to show what such buildings really did look like several centuries ago. The garden includes a topiary (the trees look a bit like chessmen) and the potting-shed roof has finials of romping monkeys along its ridge.

The Bruce family of Earlshall probably built the castle in the days of James IV. The second laird lived through the reigns of James IV, James V, Mary and James VI. He fought at Flodden and died with James VI the acknowledged heir to the united kingdoms. His tombstone is in Leuchars Church, dated 1584, declaring Sir William had died in his 98th year. *Mors omnium est finis*. A later laird was an ardent ally of Claverhouse. He butchered Richard Cameron, the hardline Covenanter at Aird's Moss, and captured Hackston, one of the assassins of Archbishop Sharp, who was then barbarously executed in Edinburgh. After James VII went into exile he became a Whig. His son left only daughters and Earlshall went to the Hendersons of Fordell by marriage, after which it went through many owners.

Robert Mackenzie, a bleach merchant from Dundee, bought the castle in 1890. His peers thought him daft but he knew exactly what he wanted, and he engaged the young Lorimer to restore the building we have today. In 1926 he sold the estate to Sir Michael Nairn, the Kirkcaldy linoleum tycoon, who gave it to his daughter as a wedding present. Major Baxter, a descendant of the Bruces, is the present owner.

The Long Gallery has a rare painted ceiling and its walls are lined by ranks of Scottish basket-hilted swords. The Great Hall is richly panelled and furnished in oak and is separated from the Dining Room by a Lorimer screen based on the rood screen at Falkland Palace. The Drawing Room has a large collection of cat paintings by Lesley Ann Ivory and recent dog portraits are apt to romp next to a George Stubbs study. The laird's military background is seen in the items of war from centuries past, and his wife has collected a wide range of mugs from many periods, including the special 'rooks and rabbits' Wemyss Ware design. There are several Griselda Hill Wemyss-style cats to entertain the visitor, and it is this personal, lived-in, continuing atmosphere which makes a tour enjoyable – though there are also the expected secret stairs and a few friendly ghosts. (You can ask one of the ladies on duty to tell you about the little girl and her red shoes.) Mary Queen of Scots stayed at Earlshall, of course. (All monarchs in those days moved round their realms: which meant free D, B&B and allowed them to keep an eye on everyone.)

When you've exhausted both house and garden you can cross the castle yard with its well to have tea and cake in the Dummy Daws building. On leaving, note the old sundial and, along a bit, what looks like a small cottage, except it is windowless and has a projecting stone course round it (the telltale sign) indicating a rather superior doocot, dated 1599.

Leave the castle and backtrack towards Leuchars, keeping ahead at the crossroads and coming out to a junction at the church. Almost opposite, steps lead up into its grounds.

Leuchars church will at once remind us of Dalmeny Kirk – they are the two finest Romanesque churches in Scotland. Only the chancel and apse are twelfth century and the apse roof was replaced by the octagonal bell tower in the sixteenth century, with a lead weather-vane. Corbel heads above the upper arches are of animals, real or imagined, and human and grotesque faces. A papal bull mentions the church in 1187 but it was (re-)dedicated in 1244 with the name of St Athernase. One minister (a noted preacher), Alexander Henderson, was Moderator of the 1638 Assembly in Glasgow which abolished episcopacy.

Leave the churchyard at the far end. Steps lead down, left, to the Coach House Centre, run by the church, which includes a café. But first turn right for a moment to see one last example of the older East Neuk houses.

Take the steps down onto the main road through Leuchars. Turn right and walk through to a roundabout. There are shops, café, chip shop, Chinese carry-out, pubs, etc. We turn left at the roundabout (the A919 for St Andrews) and Leuchars Station signal-box can be seen ahead. St Bunyan's Place introduces further RAF housing which now runs out beyond a level-crossing to the station. Walk through the commuters' carpark and a footpath leads to the railway footbridge into the station which stands exposed to all the winds that blow. There are cosy waiting-rooms, toilets, ticket office and a small shop. Trains to Edinburgh run every half hour or so.

If coming by bus, the bus stop is by the station carpark just beyond the station, but ask the driver to let you know you've arrived. Buses leave from the St Andrews bus station: the infrequent no. 94, St Andrews–Cupar via Strathkinness; or, better, the regular no. 95, Leven–East Neuk–St Andrews–Dundee service.

FORTH RAILWAY BRIDGE

The train journey across Fife is pleasant, revealing first the rich agricultural Howe of Fife, then the more industrialised south, and ending with a glimpse of the towns of the Castles Coast. From Leuchars the line heads up the valley of the River Eden past Dairsie to Cupar, the historic market town for rural Fife.

Continuing along the Eden we have Springfield and then Ladybank Junction where a second line heads off to Perth. As a schoolboy I once set off from Crail for weeks of cycling in the north but had such a strong headwind that I gave up cycling and caught the train at Leuchars, destination Perth. I fell asleep, however, and only woke up at Kirkcaldy while, at Ladybank, my cycle was dutifully switched to the Perth train.

We cross the Eden, passing Freuchie, which hit the headlines some years ago by winning the British village cricket competition (at Lords), then pass through a gap under the Lomond Hills to the papermaking town of Markinch and the River Leven basin. Thornton Junction leads to Kirkcaldy, as unprepossessing as any big town when seen from a railway. From there on you'll be spotting familiar scenes. After Inverkeithing there is

a tunnel, a brief stop (some trains only) at North Queensferry Station, and then we are onto the high girders of the fretwork approach of the mighty Railway Bridge. It may be past its 100 years now but it is still one of the most memorable bridges in the world.

If the bridge still impresses us, what must it have been like to the public who saw it built? (Contemporary pictures show sailing ships in the background.) And what marvellous confidence the Victorian engineers enjoyed. Some of them. The work had actually started when the Tay Bridge blew down (with a train on it; 75 died) and the same engineer's design for the Forth Bridge was immediately cancelled by Parliament. Poor Sir Thomas Bouch. He retired to the country and was dead within a year, yet it was his 'floating railway' ferry that the bridge was to supersede, and his other successes are also forgotten. Earlier plans (*c.*1818) for a chain bridge had fallen through, which was fortunate (with hindsight) for it would not have survived either. Engineers had to learn the hard way. In 1808 plans had been made for a tunnel. Bouch's Forth Bridge, ironically, was a suspension bridge – or rather two suspension bridges, end to end, a bold concept.

Benjamin Baker designed the present masterpiece with its cantilever principle, and William Arrol was the contractor. Baker had started as an apprentice in a South Wales ironworks; he had then worked on building Victoria Station, and with his senior partner, John Fowler, they created the London underground system; he was consultant for the Aswan Dam and helped bring Cleopatra's Needle to London. Arrol, a workaholic, had built bridges over the Nile, the Thames in London and the Wear. John Fowler had designed the Pimlico Bridge, which carried the first railway over the Thames, built St Enoch's Station in Glasgow and pioneered the London Underground. Baker became first his assistant, then his partner, and was passed the Forth Bridge responsibility.

A workforce of up to 5,000 men took seven years to build the bridge, at the cost of 57 lives, a remarkably *good* safety record for the period. It was built throughout with steel, the first such bridge so built and the biggest man-made structure ever constructed at the time. Not everyone liked the bridge: John Ruskin loathed it and one book objected to its crude simplicity, wanting towers and finials and suggesting gilt paint would have been prettier!

The statistics alone are overwhelming: the bridge took 54,160 tons of steel, 740,000 cubic feet of granite, 48,400 of ordinary stone, 64,300 of concrete, 21,000 tons of cement and 6½ million rivets, weighing 4,200 tons. The surface area to be painted is 145 acres and a team of 20 painters covers this every four to six years, using 17 tons (7,000 gallons) of paint. The idea of starting at one end and working to the other in perpetuity is a myth but even today, for safety, no scaffolding is used over the track. (You daren't drop anything.) The men literally hang on with one hand and paint with the other. Baker, during construction, saw a hole pierced straight through a four-

St Athernase Church at Leuchars, with its magnificent Romanesque features

Back to the start – over the incomparable Forth Bridge, here viewed from the Fife shore

inch timber by a spanner which had dropped 300ft. One worker had a spanner enter down his waistcoat and out his trousers, ripping them asunder but leaving him uninjured. The dangers were real and horrific. The men in the caissons were especially vulnerable: 119 of 600 employed on the Brooklyn Bridge had the bends, 16 of whom died, and in St Petersburg a caisson sank on 28 men in the chamber. Baker lost no men under the sea. Familiarity

leading to risk-taking was the main cause of disaster, no doubt helped at times by the proximity of the Hawes Inn bar.

The three cantilever towers each stand on four platforms, most with undersea foundations, called caissons. These were 400-ton, 70ft diameter wrought-iron cylinders, constructed on the shore at Queensferry and towed out. On site, concrete was poured into them till they sank to the bottom. A 7ft space was left at the bottom, with a steel cutting edge all round, and this chamber was kept dry by compressed air and used by the workers who cut away the seabed below their feet until the required base was created. The working chamber was then filled with concrete too and steel bedplates attached to the top so the superstructure could be built. (On the Road Bridge the sheer weight of the south pier caisson sank it through the boulder clay of the river-bed.)

The three cantilever towers were then built and slowly their arms reached out sidewards till the ends all joined. The bridge was opened by the Prince of Wales (Edward VII to be) in 1890 and very little in the way of serious work has been needed since, despite the present 200 trains a day crossing at speeds up to 50mph. The bridge is 1⅜ miles long and soars 361ft above high-water mark. Two tracks cross it. The cost was £3 million.

The run in to Edinburgh leads us by Dalmeny Station, past Turnhouse Airport, South Gyle Station, Murrayfield Rugby Stadium, Haymarket Station, tunnels and gardens under the castle and so to Waverley. It is perhaps right that our walk reaches the buffers at Scotland's capital. Enjoy your time in what is a fine city, a bonus to the Castles Coast and the East Neuk of our Fife coast walk.

Following pages: How the Forth Bridge appeared from Queensferry in mid-1888 as it neared completion (© Queensferry Museum)

APPENDIX I *Updating of Information*

Practical details constantly change and guidebooks can go out of date quickly, so it is planned to produce a periodic update sheet listing things like alterations to the route, B&B news, opening hours, etc. The usefulness of this is obvious, but to be effective I need to receive information about changes. Would those who have walked the route please let me know of useful alterations so that this may be passed on?

To obtain a copy of these alterations, please enclose a stamped, self-addressed envelope and ten second-class postage stamps to: Scottish Mountain Holidays, FCW, 21 Carlin Craig, Kinghorn, Fife KY3 9RX.

APPENDIX 2 *Map List*

Bartholomew's 1:100,000 series covers the whole route in two sheets, 46 and 49, so these are worth having for the overall view. Estate Publications publish a simple leisure map at 1:100,000 which covers the route in one sheet: *Fife: Scotland's Holiday Kingdom.*

It would be perfectly feasible to walk the route using the Landranger 1:50,000 maps (sheets 65, 66, 59) but the Pathfinder 1:25,000 maps offer more details on coastal features – of some importance – and I'd recommend carrying these as the basic maps for the walk: 406 (NT 07/17), 394 (NT 08/18), 395 (NT 28), 385 (NT 29/39), 373 (NO 20/30) (only a tiny corner), 374 (NO 40/50), 364 (NO 60/61), 363 (NO 41/51), 352 (NO 42/52).

Also worth buying locally is the Smith street map of the *East Neuk and Largo* towns. This series covers everywhere except the Queensferry towns and would be rather a luxury in total, but for the East Neuk, with such a run of olde worlde villages, sometimes merging, the street maps would be useful. They are fairly widely stocked in the appropriate towns.

APPENDIX 3 *Fife Coast Architecture and a Scots Glossary*

Only when exploring some of the coast towns with an English friend did I realise how many of the architectural terms I used were, in fact, local or Scottish. Even some of the English terms can baffle so the following is a selective list of terms, many being Scottish variants, which may be of practical interest. The volumes of the 'Buildings of Scotland' series have big, illustrated glossaries. The Fife volume is indispensable for any study of buildings on our walk.

I've also listed some of the geographical or local words used in the text which may not be instantly recognised. Scots is *not* just a form of English and thus has a rich source of words which are no weel kent tae Sassenachs.

Abutment the support for a bridge, often all that remains if the arch or superstructure has disappeared.

Ashlar a building's masonry where the face is smoothed even and the edges squared (*see* Rubble).

Batter the inward lean of a wall.

Chimney pot features often overlooked and worth studying. See if you can work out Plain roll, two roll, ribbed, pocket roll, ornamental fluted, 'H', barrel-topped, cowl, octagonal, louvred or cap-top.

Close a passage giving access to a number of flats or houses. May be used just to mean a narrow lane.

Coping stone the top course of stones on a wall. (Coping is *lit.* capping.)

Corbel projecting stone (or stones) to support a structure.

Corbelling method of laying stones so the higher overlaps the lower, often forming 'beehive' roofs.

Course a continuous layer of stones in a wall's structure.

Crowstep Gable squared stones set like steps on the gable, forming a skew (q.v.). Often associated with pantiles, which could be easily laid from a beam resting on the gable 'steps'.

Den a glen, coombe, deep-cut valley, as in Kittock's Den.

Doocot dovecote. Early models were beehive-shaped, the commonest were lectern-shaped and, later, many became architecturally fanciful.

Doorway Features The following descriptions may be useful.

Fanlight small window above the door which gave illumination to the entrance/hallway.

Lintel the horizontal stone across the top of the door structure.

Jambs the vertical supports of the door structure (*lit.* legs).

Pediment a classical temple-style gable often set above a doorway.

Tympanum the area framed by the pediment.

Portico a porch, often pillared, in which the entrance is set.

Dutch gable a double-curving gable, often topped by an ornamental pediment, etc.

Dyke an intrusive band of rock within another. Often the dyke will be left standing, like a wall, after the rest has eroded away. Dyke is also the common Scots word for a wall.

Finial topmost decorative feature on a gable, spire, etc.

Forestairs external stairway leading to house entrance (the ground floor often being used for storage).

Gable the end wall, usually triangular at the top on houses with ordinary double-pitched roofs, often topped by a chimney.

Gait street, often prefixed with a descriptive word. e.g. *seagait, lowgait*.

Glebe the parish minister's land.

Granny the metal hood on a chimney pot, often turning in the wind.

Gulley Box the often richly ornamented cast-iron box at the top of a down-pipe, collecting water from the gutter. Not used now.

Harling *lit*. hurling; a roughcasting of aggregate and cement which is dashed on to rubble walls for weatherproofing.

Keystone the highest, central stone of an arch which, when inserted, locks the arch in place.

Kirk church.

Lade the leat/waterchannel bringing water to a mill.

Laird's Loft a balcony in a church reserved for the landowner's use.

Loupin-on stone mounting block for horsemen.

Manse the home of a Scottish minister (reverend).

Marriage Lintel one with dated initials of resident husband and wife, the date showing the work's completion rather than a marriage date.

Mercat cross market cross, focus of town life, often with symbols, arms on top; since Reformation, not a cross, though the name survives.

Ness headland, point, as Babbet Ness.

Pantiles roof tile, of continental origin, having a curved S-shaped section. From 'paans' (*Flem.*) meaning shingle. Often used as ballast by trading vessels so common along the Fife coast.

Pend a ground-level passage through a building.

Port/Porte Gate in walls of medieval towns (often royal burghs) frequently given a directional name, e.g. West Port.

Quoins dressed stones at the corner of a building. From 'coin' (*Fr*), meaning corner. When they are set alternatively long and short they are *rusticated*.

Refuges on a bridge, a small bay or niche where pedestrians could take shelter from passing traffic. Often the cut-water buttress would be extended upwards to incorporate a refuge bay.

Ridge tiles capping the apex of a roof, these are often ornamental.

Rubble masonry where the surface has been left rough (c.f. Ashlar). It may be *coursed* or *random* (the stones set randomly, not in courses).

Skew the stones, sloping or stepped, topping a gable, and standing higher than the roof.

Skewputt the bottom end of the skew (often ornamental).

Springer the lowest stones of an arch.

Spur stone (*Pal Stone*) stone set at base of a corner, tree, pavement, etc., to give protection from carriage wheels.

String course a course, often decorative, projecting from a wall.

Tolbooth medieval town offices, often with a prison and where tolls and export/import dues were levied.

Vennel narrow lane between houses.

Well covers every type of water source in Scotland: spring, fountain, even a tap. Ordinary wells (deep holes) are relatively uncommon.

Wynd a narrow lane, often twisting off from a village's main street.

APPENDIX 4 *Countryside Comfort and Behaviour*

BEFORE LEAVING HOME

• Ensure competence in basic navigational skills.

• Plan within your capabilities. Tired people are far more accident-prone.

• Learn something of elementary first-aid and prepare a small field kit.

• Acquire adequate waterproofs, comfy boots and emergency items.

• If going alone, organise some system of phoning home or to someone acting as base. If you break a leg by the Kenley Burn it is nice to know someone will be worried sooner rather than later and send out an SOS on your behalf. Know the distress signal.

• Read up about the areas being visited. The curious traveller is usually the happiest traveller. Buy all the maps you need and prepare by reading through this book *with* the maps.

ALONG THE WAY

• Close all gates. There is nothing calculated to annoy farmers more than having to round up strayed livestock. Don't go over walls or through fences or hedges – there are few places without gates or stiles on our route.

• Leave livestock, crops and machinery alone.

• Guard against all risk of fires. There is no need to light a fire of any kind. A lighter is safer than matches if you ever use a stove.

• Dump your litter in bins, not in the countryside. You'll see some bad sights, so don't add to them. Polythene bags can mean disaster to a grazing cow, broken glass is wicked for both man and beast, and drink cans are an insufferable eyesore.

• Leave wildlife alone. Collect memories not eggs or flowers. 'Lost' creatures are rare; parents will soon find their young unless some unhelpful person has carried them off.

• Walk quietly in the countryside. Nature goes unobtrusively and you'll see far more if you are not clad in garish colours and walking with a ghetto-blaster. (I joke not – I've met one on top of the Buddo Rock.) While most of this trip is on rights-of-way or other established walking routes, it is still running through a farmed and used landscape, so treat it with respect. Local people's livelihood depends on this countryside. There is no wilderness.

• Dogs are best left at home. In prime sheep/farming country they need strict control, so neither dog nor owner can relax much. In the lambing season (March–May) dogs are particularly unwelcome.

• Be extra careful when walking on roads, however quiet these appear. Maniac drivers are no respecters of pedestrians.

• Make local contacts. Rural people are still sociable and a 'crack' will often be welcomed. Use the tourist offices and bookshops along the way to widen knowledge and enrich your experience. Those met in bars, cafés or overnight stops are often a fund of information. They may even find *us* interesting.

• Keeping a record of some kind is usually rewarding – if not always at the time. I've seen some remarkable creations of notes, photos, postcards, drawings or, in the case of one girl, a bound collection of all her letters home to her absent husband. In later years these are great souvenirs.

AND AFTERWARDS?

• Start preparing for the next trip.

APPENDIX 5 *Bibliography*

The following is a selective bibliography for there is a huge literature about Fife and its coast, history, families, industry, wildlife, etc. Anyone wanting further research would find the libraries at Kirkcaldy, St Andrews and Dunfermline useful sources. There are many contemporary booklets and leaflets which I have not listed but which you could usefully buy *en route*. The date given is of a first edition. *Et seq.* indicates there were subsequent editions so the title is more likely to be available.

The Wemyss Environment Centre has produced a huge range of booklets on subjects and areas of interest to our route including several town descriptions, studies of wildlife, coal-mining, extracts from old school log-books, local architecture, etc. (Their coastal walk booklets were invaluable for my initial route-planning, but my descriptions in this guide are naturally more up to date.) It would be well worth while sending a S.A.E and asking for a price list of publications: Wemyss Environment Centre, East Wemyss, Kirkcaldy, Fife KY1 4RN. Local walkabout booklets may be found at Tourist Offices, the Kirkcaldy Museum bookshop, or The Book House, Tolbooth Street, Kirkcaldy. St Andrews has many bookshops both for new books and old and, of course, so too has Edinburgh.

Ballantyne, G.H. (ed.), *The Wildlife and Antiquities of Kirkcaldy District* (Kirkcaldy Naturalists' Society, 1982)

Ballantyne, G.H. (ed.), *The Wild Flowers of Kirkcaldy* (Kirkcaldy Naturalists' Society, 1970)

Ballingall, W., *The Shores of Fife* (Douglas, 1872; edited facsimile *The Kingdom of Fife in Bygone Days*, Lang Syne)

Barnes, R., *Coasts and Estuaries* (Hodder, 1979)

Bennett, G.P., *The Great Road Between Forth and Tay* (Markinch, 1989)

Beveridge, E., *The Church Memorials of Crail* (Constable, 1893)

Bingham, C., *The Stewart Kingdom of Scotland 1371–1603* (Weidenfeld & Nicholson, 1974)

Blythe, J.J., *Burntisland: Early History and People* (*Fifeshire Advertiser*, 1948)

Boucher, R., *The Kingdom of Fife: its Ballads and Legends* (Leng, 1899)

Brodie, I., *Historical Sketches of Pathhead and Vicinity 1863* (reprint, Kirkcaldy District Library, 1993)

Brodie, I. *Queensferry Passage* (West Lothian

History & Amenity Soc, 1976)

Brodie, I., *Steamers of the Forth* (David & Charles, 1976)

Brown, J., *Horae Subsecivae* (Black, 1908; Marjorie Fleming essay)

Brown, S.J., *Thomas Chalmers and the Godly Commonwealth in Scotland* (OUP, 1982)

Browning, R., *A History of Golf* (Dutton, New York, 1955)

Bruce, W.S., *The Railways of Fife* (Melven, 1980)

Buckner, J.C.R., *Rambles in and Around Aberdour and Burntisland* (Clark, 1898)

Burntisland, Portrait of a Town (Kirkcaldy District Museums, 1982)

Buxbaum, T., *Scottish Doocots* (Shire Publications, 1987)

Cadell, H.M., *The Story of the Forth* (Maclehose, 1913)

Cameron, M., *Methil: History and Trail* (Wemyss Centre, 1986)

Campbell, A.C., and Nicholls, J., *Hamlyn Guide to the Seashore and Shallow Seas of Britain and Europe* (Hamlyn, 1976)

Cant, R.G., *Old St Andrews* (1945)

Cant, R.G., *The East Neuk of Fife: Its Landscape and Architecture* (1968)

Cant, R.G., *The University of St Andrews: A Short History* (Scottish Academic Press, 1970)

Chapman, T., *Handbook to Elie and the East of Fife* (Purves, 1898)

Christie, G., *Harbours of the Forth* (Johnson, 1955)

Connolly, M.F., *Biographical Dictionary of Eminent Men of Fife* (Cupar, 1846)

Connolly, M.F., *Fifiana* (Glasgow, 1869)

Cowan, I.B., *The Scottish Covenanters* (Gollancz, 1976)

Cramp, S., Bourne, W.R.P., and Saunders, D., *The Seabirds of Britain and Northern Europe* (Collins, 1975)

Cruden, S., *The Scottish Castle* (Spurbooks, 1981)

Cunningham, A.S., *Lundin Links, Upper and Lower Largo and Leven* (Portobello, 1913)

Cunningham, A.S., *Rambles in the Parishes of Scoonie and Wemyss* (Leven, 1905)

Cunningham, A.S., *Inverkeithing, North Queensferry, Rosyth and the Naval Base* (Clark, 1903)

Cunningham, A.S., *Dysart, Past and Present* (Russell, 1912)

Darwin, B., *James Braid* (Batsford, 1992)

Dick, S., *The Pageant of the Forth* (Foulis, 1910)

Dickson, J., *Emeralds Chased in Gold: the Islands of the Forth* (Oliphant, 1899)

Donnachie, I., and Hewitt, G., *A Companion to Scottish History* (Batsford, 1989)

Douglas, H.., *Crossing the Forth* (Hale, 1964)

Eggeling, W.J., *The Isle of May* (Oliver & Boyd, 1960, *et seq.*)

Ellis, C., *The Pebbles on the Beach* (Faber, 1954)

Erskine, Ex-Bailie, *Glimpses of Modern Burntisland* (1920)

Fairley, A., *The Queensferry Companion* (Albyn Press, 1981)

Farrer, J.A., *Adam Smith* (Sampson Low, 1881; Stafford reprint, 1988)

Fawcett, R., and McRoberts, D., *Inchcolm Abbey and Island* (HMSO, 1990); official guide

Fife (RCAHMS); exhaustive

Fife Statistical Account, ed. John Sinclair, 1791-99, reprinted by EP Publishing, 1978

Fife's Early Archaeological Heritage – A Guide (Fife Regional Council, 1989)

Firth of Forth Wildlife, Teachers' Notes (Nature Conservancy Council, n.d.)

Fitter, R., Fitter A., and Blamey, M., *The Wild Flowers of Britain and Northern Europe* (Collins, 1974)

Fleming, M., *The Complete Marjorie Fleming*, edited by F. Sidgwick (Sidgwick, 1934)

Flemming, J., *Robert Adam and His Circle* (Murray, 1962, *et seq.*); standard biography

Forsyth, I.H., and Chisholm, J.I., *The Geology of East Fife* (HMSO, 1977)

Fraser, A., *Mary Queen of Scots* (Panther, 1970)

Fraser, D., *Historic Fife* (Melven, 1982)

Geddie, J., *The Fringes of Fife* (Chambers, n.d.)

Gifford, J., *Fife* (Penguin, 1988); from the 'Buildings of Scotland' series

Groome, F.H., *Ordnance Gazetteer of Scotland*, 5 vols. (1882–85)

Hammond, R., *The Forth Bridge and Its Builders* (Eyre & Spottiswoode, 1964)

Hendrie, W.F., *Forth to the Sea* (privately printed, 1980)

Hepburn, I., *Flowers of the Coast* (Collins New Naturalist, 1952)

House, J., *The Lang Toun* (Kirkcaldy Town Council, 1975)

Hume, J.R., *The Industrial Archaeology of Scotland 1: The Lowlands and Borders* (Batsford, 1976)

Inventory of Monuments and Construction of Fife, Kinross and Clackmannan (RCAHMS, 1933)

Jack, J., *The Key of the Forth* (Nimmo, 1858); May Island

Jack, J., *St Monance, An Historical Account* (1844)

Jackson, J., *Guide to Crail and Neighbourhood* (Cupar, 1896)

Jardine, I., *Seatoun of Largo* (Seatoun, 1982)

Kinghorn Historical Society *Historical Trail*, Booklets 1, 2, 3 (1984, *et seq.*); available from Kirkcaldy Museum bookshop or The Book House.

Kirkcaldy Burgh and Schyre (*Fifeshire Advertiser*, 1924)

Kirkcaldy Civic Society: *Kirkcaldy Walkabout* (KCS, 1982 *et seq*); series of six booklets, and other local interest publications. Available from Kirkcaldy Museum bookshop or The Book House.

Kirkcaldy District Council: *Dysart* (KDC, 1987)

Lamont-Brown, R., *Discovering Fife* (Donald, 1988)

Lamont-Brown, R., *The Life and Times of St Andrews* (Donald, 1989)

Lamont-Brown, R., and Adamson, P., *Victorian and Edwardian Fife from Old Photographs* (Ramsay Head, 1980)

Lang, T. (ed.), *The Kingdom of Fife and Kinross* (Hodder, 1951); from the 'King's Scotland' series

Largo 21. A compendium for the Largo Field Studies Society, 1967–1988 (Largo, 1988)

Leighton, J.M., *History of the County of Fife*, 2 vols (Swan, 1840)

Levenmouth Environmental Society, *Leven Walkabout* (LES, 1985)

Liddall, W.J.M., *Place-Names of Fife and Kinross* (Green, 1896)

Lindsay, M., *The Castles of Scotland* (Constable, 1986)

Lindsay, M., *The Lowlands of Scotland: Glasgow and the North* (Hale, 1953)

Livingstone, P.K., *A History of Kirkcaldy 1843–1949* (Allen Litho, 1955)

Love, D., *Scottish Kirkyards* (Hale, 1989)

Lyle, D.W., *Shadows of St Andrews Past* (Donald, 1989); mostly photographs

Macbean, L., *The Kirkcaldy Burgh Records* (*Fifeshire Advertiser*, 1908)

MacDonald, J.D., *Fife: from Kirkcaldy to Kincardine* (Albany Press, 1981)

MacDonald, N., *Fife: One Hundred and One Places to See or Visit* (n.d.)

MacDonald, N., *Aberdour: the Past Hundred Years* (privately printed, 1981)

MacGibbon, D., and Ross, T., *The Castellated and Domestic Architecture of Scotland*, 5 vols (reprinted J. Thin, 1990)

MacGibbon, D., *Ecclesiastical Architecture of Scotland*, 3 vols (1896–97) (reprinted, J. Thin)

MacGregor, A.R., *Fife and Angus Geology* (Scottish Academic Press, 1974)

MacGregor, F., *Salt-Sprayed Burgh (Anstruther)* (Pine Tree Press)

Mackay, A.J.G., *A History of Fife and Kinross* (Blackwood, 1896); from the 'County Histories' series

Mackay, S., *The Forth Bridge: a Pictorial History* (Moubray Press, 1990)

Maclean, C., *The Fringe of Gold* (Canongate, 1985); eastern fishing ports

Maclean, C., *Silver Highway: the Story of the Forth Road Bridge* (Moubray Press, 1988)

Mair, C., *Mercat Cross and Tolbooth* (Donald, 1988); Scotland's ancient burghs

Mair, C., *A Star for Seamen: The Stevenson Family of Engineers* (Murray, 1978)

Marshall, D.A., *Masons and Miracles* (privately printed booklet, 1986); Inchcolm history

Marshall, D.A., *Stepping Stone in the Forth* (privately printed booklet, 1984); Inchgarvie

Marshall, D.A., *The Little Jewels* (privately printed booklet, 1985); lesser islands

Marshall, D.A., *Bass Rock* (privately printed booklet, 1985)

Marshall, D.A., *The Black Stone* (privately printed booklet, 1986); Alexander III monument

Martin, P., *What to See in St Monans* (1991; booklet)

Martin, P., *What to See in Pittenweem* (1990; booklet)

Mason, J., *The Story of the Water Passage at Queensferry* (1964)

Millar, A.H., *Fife, Pictorial and Historical*, 2 vols (Westwood, 1895)

Millman, R.N., *The Making of the Scottish Landscape* (Batsford, 1975)

Mitchell, A., *A Field Guide to the Trees of Britain and Northern Europe* (Collins, 1974)

Mitchell, A.L., *A Beacon for the Carr* (*Scots Magazine*, April 1993)

Morris, R., and Morris, F., *Scottish Healing Wells* (Alethea Press, 1982)

Muir, A., *The Fife Coal Co Ltd: A Short History* (n.d.)

Munro, R.W., *Scottish Lighthouses* (Thule Press, 1979)

Murray, M., *In My Ain Words* (privately printed, 1982); East Neuk vocabulary

Nelson, J., *Highland Bridges* (AUP, 1990); interesting on bridges in general

New History of Scotland, 8 vols (Arnold, 1980s)

Nicholaisen, W.F.H., *Scottish Place-Names* (Batsford, 1976)

Pearson, J.M., *A Guided Walk Around St Andrews/Burntisland/Around North East Fife*; attractively drawn recent guide booklets

Peterkin, G.A.G., *Scottish Dovecotes* (Culross, 1980)

Pollock, D., *The Dictionary of the Forth* (Jack, n.d.)

Prebble, J., *The High Girders* (Secker, 1956, *et seq.*); Tay Bridge story

Pride, G., *The Kingdom of Fife* (RIAS, 1990); illustrated architectural guide

Proceedings of the Society of Antiquaries of Scotland. Annual, authoritative; articles on topics connected with our walk include 1957/58 (Vol. 91) Painted ceilings in Mary Somerville House, Burntisland and 1971/72 (Vol. 104) in Rossend Castle; 1874–76 (Vol. 11). Notes on the Wemyss Cave.

Queensferry: a Guided Walk (Queensferry Association, 1986)

Rankin, F., *Guide to the Wemyss Caves* (Save the Caves Society, 1989)

Rankin, F., *Auld Buckhyne* (Wemyss Centre, 1986)

Reid, A., *Inchcolm Abbey* (Romanes, 1901)

Reid, A., *Kinghorn* (1906)

Rendall, J., *A Light for the Carr* (*Scots Magazine*, May 1993)

Rintoul, L.J., and Baxter, E.V., *A Vertebrate Fauna of Forth* (Oliver & Boyd, 1935)

Rintoul, L.J., *Largo Village Book* (1932)

Ritchie, G., and Ritchie, A., *Scotland: Archaeology and Early History* (Thames & Hudson, 1981)

Ritchie, W., *Beaches of Fife* (Countryside Commission for Scotland and Geography Dept, University of Aberdeen, 1979)

Robertson, E.S., *Old St Andrews* (Dent, 1923)

Ross, W., *Aberdour and Inchcolm* (Douglas, 1885)

Royal Commission on the Ancient and Historical Monuments of Scotland, *West Lothian* (1929)

Royal Commission on the Ancient and Historical Monuments of Scotland, *Fife* (1933)

Rykwert, J., and Rykwert, A., *The Brothers Adam* (Collins, 1985); superbly illustrated

Saunders, L.J., *A Geographical Description of Fife, Kinross and Clackmannan* (*Scottish Geographical Magazine*, 1912)

Scott-Bruce, W., *The Railways of Fife* (Melven Press, 1980)

Scott-Moncrieff, L., *Scotland's Eastern Coast* (Oliver & Boyd, 1963)

Sibbold, R., *The History of Fife and Kinross*

(Cupar, 1803)

Silver, O., *The Roads of Fife* (Donald, 1987)

Simpkins, J.E., *County Folklore: Fife, Clackmannan and Kinross (Vol VII)* (Sidgwick, 1914)

Simpson, E., *Dalgety – the Story of a Parish* (Dalgety Bay Council, 1980)

Sissons, J.B., *The Evolution of Scotland's Scenery* (Oliver & Boyd, 1967)

Smith, A., *Fife* (Third Statistical Account of Scotland) (Oliver & Boyd, 1952)

Smith, J.A., *John Buchan* (Hart-Davis, 1965)

Smith, P., *The Lammas Drave and the Winter Herrin'* (Donald, 1985); fishing history

Smout, A.M., *The Birds of Fife* (Donald, 1986)

Snoddy, T.G., *Afoot in Fife* (Serif, 1950)

Statistical Account of Scotland (18th cent) and *New Statistical Account of Scotland* (19th cent) volumes on Fife and Linlithgowshire give interesting parish by parish descriptions of the times. (Also *Third Statistical Account* 1952)

Steers, J.A., *The Sea Coast* (Collins, New Naturalist, 1969)

Steers, J.A., *The Coastline of Scotland* (CUP, 1973)

Stephen, W., *History of Inverkeithing and Rosyth* (Fraser, 1921)

Stephen, W., *Story of Inverkeithing and Rosyth* (Moray Press, 1938)

Stephen, W.M., *The Binnend Oilworks and the Binn Village* (privately printed, 1968)

Stevenson, S., *Anstruther, A History* (Donald, 1989)

Taylor, S., *Mortimer's Deep* (Balmain, 1992); historical novel, much on Inchcolm

Thom, V.M., *Birds in Scotland* (Poyser, 1986)

Thomas, J., *Regional History of the Railways of Great Britain: Vol 6 Scotland: The Lowlands and Borders* (David & Charles, 1981)

Thomas, J., *Forgotten Railways of Scotland* (David & Charles, 1981)

Thomson, D., *Elie Kirk 1639–1989* (Elie, 1989)

Walker, B., and Ritchie, R., *Exploring Scotland's Heritage: Fife and Tayside* (HMSO, 1987)

Watters, A., *Graveyards* (Moray House College of Education, 1985)

Watson, H.D., *Kilrenny & Cellardyke* (Donald, 1986)

Watson, W.J., *The History of the Celtic Place-Names of Scotland* (Irish University Press, 1973)

Weir, M., *Ferries in Scotland* (Donald, 1988)

Wilkie, J., *Bygone Fife, from Culross to St Andrews* (Blackwood, 1931)

Wilkie, J., *A History of Fife* (Blackwood, 1924)

Willsher, B., *Understanding Scottish Graveyards* (Chalmers, 1985)

Willsher, B., and Hunter, D., *Stones* (Canongate, 1978); eighteenth-century gravestones

Wood, W., *The East Neuk of Fife* (Douglas, 1887)

Young, A., *History of Burntisland* (Fifeshire Advertiser, 1913)

Young, D., *St Andrews: Town and Gown, Royal and Ancient* (Cassell, 1969)

Wemyss Environmental Centre has produced a wide range of booklets over the years. The following are recommended: *Dysart, Village History and Walkabout*; *Look at Architecture in West Wemyss*; *West Wemyss Village Trail*; *East Wemyss Village Walkabout*; *From Macduff Castle to Wemyss Castle*; *Auld Buckhyne, Methil History and Trail*; *Leven Walkabout*.

INDEX

Italic page numbers refer to illustrations